FICTIONS OF THE FRENCH REVOLUTION

FICTIONS OF THE
FRENCH REVOLUTION

Edited by Bernadette Fort

NORTHWESTERN UNIVERSITY PRESS   EVANSTON, ILLINOIS

Northwestern University Press
Evanston, Illinois 60201

First printing, 1991

ISBN: 0-8101-0972-7 (cloth)
 0-8101-0986-7(paper)

Library of Congress Cataloging-in-Publication Data

Fictions of the French Revolution / edited by Bernadette Fort.
 p. cm.
 Essays originally read at a Colloquium on Fictions of the
Revolution, held Nov. 10–12, 1989 and sponsored by the Dept. of
French and Italian of Northwestern University.
 Includes bibliographical references.
 ISBN 0-8101-0972-7. — ISBN 0-8101-0986-7 (pr)
 1. France—History—Revolution, 1789–1799—Historiography-
-Congresses. 2. France—History—Revolution, 1789–1799—Literature
and the revolution—Congresses. 3. France—History—Revolution,
1789–1799—Art and the revolution—Congresses. 4. Political
culture—France—Historiography—Congresses. 5. History in
literaure—Congresses. 6. History in art—Congresses.
 7. Historicism—Congresses. I. Colloquium on Fictions of the
Revolution (1989: Northwestern University)
 DC147.8.F54 1991
 944.04—dc20   91-8228
                                                       CIP

Contents

Acknowledgments

THE ESSAYS GATHERED IN THIS VOLUME WERE ORIGINALLY READ AT A Bicentennial Colloquium which took place 10–12 November 1989 at Northwestern University and was sponsored by the Department of French and Italian. I am grateful to the Georges Lurcy Charitable and Educational Trust, the Alumnae of Northwestern, the Northwestern Center for Interdisciplinary Research in the Arts, and the French Cultural Services for their generous support of this event. In the French Department, I would like to thank Tilde Sankovitch, then Chair, for vigorously backing this project in all its phases, Gwenan Wilbur for dealing efficiently and graciously with all technicalities, and the students of my graduate seminar on the Revolution for providing an invaluable sounding board both before and after the conference. I am grateful to Sarah Maza, of the History Department, for expert and friendly advice, and to Christopher Herbert, of the English Department, for far more than consultation on the niceties of the English language. Special thanks go to Russell Maylone, Curator of Special Collections, Northwestern University Library, for organizing a superb exhibition of the French Revolution Pamphlet Collection, and to Joseph Roach, Professor of Theatre and English, for acting as liaison with the Theatre Department toward the production of Stanisława Przybyszewska's *The Danton Case*. The participation of Carol Blum, Lynn Hunt, and W. J. T. Mitchell, who also read papers at the colloquium, was greatly appreciated. Finally, I am grateful to Jonathan Brent, director of Northwestern University Press, for his enthusiasm for this publication project from the start, and to Susan Harris, who proved the most diligent and gracious managing editor one could possibly imagine.

I. INTRODUCTION

Bernadette Fort

The French Revolution and the Making of Fictions

I am well aware that I have never written anything but fictions.
—— Michel Foucault, *Power/Knowledge*

WHAT COULD BE LESS FICTIONAL THAN SOME OF THE "HARD FACTS" of the history of the French Revolution: the abolition of privileges, the seventeen articles of the Declaration of the Rights of Man, the execution of Louis XVI, the Jacobin dictatorship, the excesses of the Terror? All of these episodes have been the focus of meticulous investigations that retrospectively endow them with the objective status of scientific data. And yet there is not one of these events that we can possibly apprehend today, especially after the thousand commemorative manifestations of the Bicentennial, other than through the prism of fiction. As members of the general public, we have become used to consuming the French Revolution as a pleasurable spectacle, in the guise of literary and visual fictions extending from Dickens's *Tale of Two Cities* to Jean Renoir's *La Marseillaise* or the French TV soap operas on Marie-Antoinette and Axel von Fersen, which thrive on fictional license while catering to the public's unabating taste for the documentary and "the real." Indeed, one of the traits of the pervasive fictionalization of the Revolution in recent years has been the intricate embedding or superposition of a variety of fictional genres, elements, spaces, and times within the same artifact. One thinks here of Peter Weiss's play-within-a-play, the performance of the assassination of Marat by the inmates of Charenton under the direction of the Marquis de Sade, of Andrzej Wajda's 1982 cinematographic version of his 1975 theater production of Stanisława Przybyszewska's play, *The Danton Case,* of Ettore Scola's postmodern telescopages in the film *La Nuit de Varennes,* or—the

apotheosis of fictionality—of the heterogeneous mix of marching
Russian guards, revolving Chinese dolls, and singing black American jazz musicians incarnating the universalizing spirit of the
Revolution in the state-financed gigantic Bicentennial Champs-
Elysées parade on 14 July 1989. For the average French citizen,
the Revolution has become a hopelessly fictionalized and mediated
event.

The academic community has fared no better in this respect
than the general public. The production of explanatory models
and interpretations of the French Revolution has grown steadily,
especially in the decade preceding the Bicentennial. But we are
not any closer to a consensus on the meaning of the event than
in 1968, when Frank A. Kafker and James M. Laux published
their collection of "conflicting interpretations" of the Revolution.[1]
The first chapter of William Doyle's now-classic work on the
Origins of the French Revolution leaves one with a sense that all
these carefully worked out interpretive models, which periodically
eliminate their predecessors before being themselves discounted
or replaced, are so many fictional variations on a given theme.
Truth, that will-o'-the-wisp of historical writing, seems to recede
mischievously on the historiographical horizon the more one chases
it. On the other hand, polemics focused precisely on the issue of
the validity or fictionality of some of the dominant theories of
interpretation have proved very productive for the advancement
of the field. It is, for example, Alfred Cobban's plucky debunking
of the Marxist "myth" of the Revolution that ushered in the
revisionist movement in the Anglo-American historiography of the
Revolution.[2] Similarly, in France, François Furet's attack on the
proto-Marxist "Revolutionary catechism" of Albert Soboul and
Claude Mazauric and his reconceptualization of the issues gave
the impulse to an even more powerful revisionist movement, whose
triumph was celebrated in the many academic conferences and
colloquiums held for the Bicentennial in France and the United
States.[3] Significantly, the creation of a vast field of research on
the political culture of the Revolution rallying around Furet has
proved, as we shall see, extremely receptive and hospitable to the
study of "fictions" in a larger sense.

These might be reasons enough for inviting a reflection on
the "Fictions of the French Revolution." But there are other com-

pelling ones. Some have to do with the present state of critical inquiry in the academic community. As David Simpson remarks in this volume: "Our conference title is brilliantly apt for a critical and historiographic community living through poststructuralism, with its corrosive effects on the notions of essence, substance, and reference, and through postmodernism, with its reiterated distrust of totalities and overconfident explanatory models." Another reason for exploring the fictions of the French Revolution lies in the object of inquiry itself. Unlike any other period in French history, the Revolution was extensively narrated, fictionalized, and mythified by its own actors while it was still in the making, and this imposes an incontrovertible fictional paradigm for any subsequent study.

HISTORIOGRAPHY AS A POETIC ACT

Although quite a few academics still hold on to Aristotle's traditional distinction that the historian deals with "what happened" and the poet with "what could happen," the exploration of the "open boundary" between the real and the imaginary has proved very productive in recent years.[4] There are many areas, particularly in the constitution, interpretation, and writing of history, where historians constantly overlap with writers of fiction. To begin with, the pieces of the puzzle called history never lie in readiness for the historian's organizing hand. They present an impenetrable jumble, out of which it is his or her task to create order and form. The very choice of the significant event or chain of events in the anarchic chaos that makes up the raw material of history is a poetic act. But there is more. As they select, eliminate, connect, subordinate, or oppose the diverse and disconnected elements of historical reality, historians proceed very much as novelists do with their fictional objects. They impose their stamp on the historical material, shape and fashion it to their will. Trying, for example, to reconstitute, let alone to understand and interpret, the historical complexity of an event frozen in Revolutionary chronology such as the "March of the Parisian Women to Versailles, 5–6 October 1789" amounts to making a series of interpretations involving the motivations of its participants, their behavior on the road and at Versailles, their attitudes to their leaders, their king, and so on, that entail a lot of guesswork and of imaginative resourcefulness. The fact that historical events are psychologically motivated challenges the historians' speculative faculties at the same time as it conjures up the nightmare of seeing "reality" recede before them to the vanishing point. Locating the origin or cause for an event in human psychology is like trying to square the circle. Objecting to the *givenness* of such historical facts, Claude Lévi-Strauss asks:

> For, *ex hypothesi*, a historical fact is what really took place, but where did anything take place? Each episode in a revolution or a war resolves itself into a multitude of individual psychic movements. Each of these movements is the translation of unconscious development, and these resolve themselves into cerebral, hormonal or nervous phenomena, which themselves have reference to the physical or the chemical order. Consequently, historical facts are no more *given* than any other. It is the historian, or the agent of history, who constitutes them by abstraction and as though under the threat of infinite regress.[5]

If the historical facts are not given, but constituted, how do historians construct them? A standard procedure is to formulate a hypothesis, which undergoes a variety of changes and metamorphoses, until, having been tested enough and satisfactorily matched against the original data, whatever these are, the hypothesis is retained and given the stamp of "truth" or, at least, of veracity. In this process, again, imagination is of the essence, and constructive fantasy overrides the putative objectivity that resides in "facts." Expanding on Northrop Frye's theory of myths, metahistorian Hayden White has argued that both the construction and interpretation of a historical problem or sequence conform to a relatively small number of plot structures embedded in the cultural tradition of historians and their audiences:

> A historical interpretation, like a poetic fiction, can be said to appeal to its readers as a plausible representation of the world by virtue of its implicit appeal to those "pre-generic plot structures" or archetypal story-forms that define the modalities of a given culture's literary endowment.[6]

For Frye, the themes of Western fictions as well as the forms of their emplotment consist of a reworking of archetypal *mythoi* derived from classical and Judeo-Christian literature and fall into one of four basic categories: comedy, romance, tragedy, satire.[7] These archetypal structures are themselves grounded in linguistic paradigms, the four basic tropes: metaphor, metonymy, synechdoche, and irony. White in turn views these tropes as supplying the basic "modes of emplotment" of historical studies (comic, romantic, tragic, satirical), modes that he correlates with two sets of corresponding categories, modes of argument or explanation (formist, mechanicist, organicist, contextualist), and modes of ideological implication (anarchist, radical, conservative, liberal).[8] The historian's job, according to him, consists in matching up the set of historical events that he wishes to endow with meaning with a specific plot structure. This, White says, "is essentially a literary act, that is to say, a fiction-making operation."[9] The "fictions" of the French Revolution that can thus be generated are, if we accept White's formulation, although quite varied, finite in number: they are "limited to the modes of emplotment which the myths of the Western literary tradition sanction as endowing human processes with meanings."[10] White's chapter on Michelet's famous *History of the French Revolution,* for example, attempts to demonstrate how this historian combined "a Romantic emplotment and a Formist argument with an ideology that is explicitly Liberal."[11] Tocqueville, on the contrary, "emplots the fall of the Old Regime as a tragic descent," while Marx contrasts it "with the 'comic' efforts to maintain feudalism by artificial means in the Germany of his own time." White remarks: "It is as if Homer, Sophocles, Aristophanes, and Menander had all taken the same set of events and made out of them the kind of story that each preferred as the image of the way that human life, in its historicity, 'really was.'"[12]

White was right in anticipating that "this insistence on the fictive element in all historical narratives is certain to arouse the ire of historians who believe that they are doing something fundamentally different from the novelist."[13] And yet, even if one rejects White's metahistorical models as too rigid or too reductive, one has to admit that the sheer act of *writing* history, because it organizes elements of discourse in a temporal axis, puts the historian in the same discursive situation as the novelist. François Furet has insisted that the temporal character of historical writing is not so much a function of the chronology of historical time as of the sequential nature of narrative discourse: "History is the daughter of narrative. It is not defined by an object of study, but by a type of discourse. To say that it studies time has no other meaning than to say that it arranges all the objects it studies in a time sequence: to do history is to tell a story."[14]

Historical narrative shares with fiction more than its sequential organization, it also shares a need to engage an audience in make-believe. Just as novels have their implied or inscribed readers as well as their real ones, and program the first in function of the second, so do historical narratives court their readers with a hundred narrative enticements. Apprentice historians early on learn that, to be read at all, they have to adopt the fiction writer's complete bag of tricks. The choice of authorial voice, time frame, narrative pace, the management of episodes in relation to the main plot, the selection of main and secondary characters, the poetic use of descriptive passages or dialogue, all these basic strategies from the novelist's store are still freely used by today's historians. The most popular histories, as the recent best-seller success of Simon Schama's *Citizens* can attest, are those that give themselves out as *stories,* that thrive on those "thousand little details" in which Richardson and Diderot discovered the secret of realism. Whether these stories are told from an omniscient, godlike perspective or from a deeply individualistic, empathetic one, they all share the desire, to use Michelet's term, to "resurrect" the past in graphic and vivid terms.[15]

Attacks on narrative history have come in recent years from a variety of fronts. Narrative history, one argument goes, fosters political and intellectual passivity. Concluding a rich essay on Michelet's virtuoso play with all the expressive registers of Christian religion and Christian poetics, Lionel Gossman wonders whether that approach "does not encourage, on the one hand, a vicarious participation in revolution as a literary experience that can be comfortably enjoyed in the drawing room, a kind of political pornography, which is equally compatible with political quietism and with radical negation or nihilism, and, on the other, a potentially dangerous inclination to play out personal, probably erotic fantasies on the stage of politics, using other people as props."[16] Other critics worry that narrative history may drive out the need for conceptualization and argumentation in historiographic work. Writing in *The New York Review of Books* (13 April 1989), Norman Hampson criticized Schama's use of "merely picturesque" description and narrative, "a journalistic device for seizing the attention of the reader . . . but not the best way of conducting an argument."

In the past thirty years or so, efforts have been made to counter the dependence of historiography on fictionality. "Scientific" methodologies have been invented, or, rather, borrowed from "hard" sciences, such as mathematics, in order to minimize, if not eradicate, the historian's presence in the text of history. This was the case, for example, with one direction of the *Annales* school in the 1970s, whose analyses of virtually any subject from contraceptive practices to the circulation of pornographic literature submitted to the statistical imperative and bristled with graphs, charts, and curves. But there are also problems with this kind of "scientific" approach. For example, quantitative historical analysis could be regarded as an inadvertent fall into one of the numerous traps of fictionality, as it thrives on the illusion of having reached objectivity when in fact it has merely objectified the modern dream of scientificity.[17]

By far the most corrosive attack against the conception and practice of history as narrative came as a carryover from assaults on the notion of reality and truth by structuralist and poststructuralist critics reflecting on the object of literature. For critics from Roland Barthes to Jacques Derrida, the idea that there is a tangible reality outside the signifying processes of the written text is a residue from our misapprehensions about the function and nature of writing, and one of the tenacious illusions of realism. While there is a *signifié* called the French Revolution which forms the subject of the book that takes this period as object, this does not mean that it is transparent to the thing itself, nor that the *référent* is still accessible to us through the mediation of writing. Roland Barthes has warned against the dangerous collapsing of the signified and referent that characterizes all pretendingly "objective" narrative history and shown the danger of thus erasing "the fundamental term of imaginary structures, which is the *signified.*"[18] Recently, historical theorists like Roger Chartier and Dominick LaCapra have concentrated on the implications that history, like

literature, is a discursively constructed subject.[19] LaCapra, in particular, has differentiated between the productive and unproductive use of fiction in historical analysis: "Indeed, a belief that
historiography is a purely documentary or descriptive reconstitu-
tion of the past may be prone to blind fictionalizing because it
does not explicitly and critically raise the problem of the role of
fictions (for example, in the form of models, analytic types, and
heuristic fictions) in the attempt to represent reality."[20] Such theories have shifted the historical problematic from its Aristotelian
position to a poetic or rhetorical one where the emphasis is on
codes of representation. Fiction, instead of being the bête noire
of historiography, has become, at least in some circles, its bread
and butter.

THE FRENCH REVOLUTION AND ITS FICTIONS

For historians of the French Revolution, fictionality is not just
a condition of historiographical writing (presiding over almost
every operation, from assembling data to arranging them in a
meaningful whole and presenting them for readers), it is also a
central dimension of the material on which they work. Their
primary sources are texts of some kind or other, and, often, texts
that are explicitly fictions. Even the most "objective" of these
texts, the police records, the lists of suspects, the briefs to the
army, the committee memoranda, the minutes of sectional meet-
ings, the proceedings of the debates of the Convention published
in Le Moniteur make a return to "the real" problematic. These
texts suffer not only from the danger of human error and the
contamination of human intention but also from the bias of
generic convention: they select, omit, emphasize, minimize, hier-
archize, organize lived experience according to the poetics of the
genre they employ (the brief, the minute, the report, etc.). Furthermore, in the main texts of the Revolution, the author's desire
to establish the version of lived history worthy of being committed
to posterity significantly colors immediate experience.

This is nowhere clearer than when Robespierre, in the Report
of 18 Floréal an II, writes up his account of recent Revolutionary
history, and thus offers the first historical narrative "fiction" of
the overthrow of the monarchy and of the fight for power of

subsequent political factions: Girondins, Feuillants, Hébertistes, and Dantonistes. From the speeches of Robespierre to the *Père Duchesne*, self-reflexivity, dramatization, intentionality, and interpretation have already filtered and shaped "reality" so irreversibly that they have in fact displaced it. We can make little critical or interpretive sense of any of these texts except insofar as we read them as fictions. As fictions, they are echoes and extensions of previous fictions, they originate in and respond to paradigms and constraints that are proper to verbal art and not to historical occurrences. Carol Blum has shown what a powerful model Rousseau's heavily fictionalized self-image was for Revolutionaries who dramatized their life and ambitions in writing.[21] When, six months before her execution, Madame Roland sets about writing her memoirs in the prison of Ste. Pélagie, she models not only her autobiographical style but the larger plot of her life history, the management of secondary episodes, and the portrayal of characters, including her husband, on the two great monuments of French Enlightenment fiction, *La Nouvelle Héloïse* and the *Confessions*. The picture of Roland and of the Girondins that one glimpses in her narrative, therefore, has to be interpreted from within a poetics of autobiographical and, as feminist criticism has shown recently, of gendered writing before it can be pressed into service for historical documentation.[22] Similarly, the obscenities of the *Père Duchesne* must be accounted for first of all within a rhetoric of carnivalization whose precedents reach back beyond the *mazarinades* to the conventionalized low style of popular literature in the Middle Ages.[23] We know that the discourse of Revolutionary leaders and actors, both public and private, was deeply infused with the ideas and images of heroism, sacrifice, and patriotism that they found in Greek and Roman antiquity. The filiation from these distant models was a complex one, straddling, as Dorinda Outram has shown, many intermediary fictions (from Cato and Seneca to Voltaire's *Brutus,* or Rousseau's and Winckelmann's praise of Spartan restraint), so that they reached the men of 1789 with a weighty fictional ballast.[24] The broad availability to Revolutionary actors and the obsessive force of these fictions were such that they became conscious reference points and shaping paradigms for social and political practice. What this means for the historian is that approaches that tackle historical issues by looking in a sophisticated way at the textual and literary conventions of the documents in which they are embedded have more chance of turning up interesting information than those that take them at face value as direct emanations of reality.

The difficulty for the past historiography of the Revolution has been, not only to accept that no text is a transparent image of social reality, but to distance itself from the point of view of Revolutionary actors. François Furet has severely criticized the tendency of most subsequent historians to accept at face value the discourse of the Revolution about itself—a stance, he argued, that locked historiography in a strictly commemorative, that is, passive, unproductive, position.[25] In regard to the interpretation of the Terror, for example, an area of particularly intense controversy, writing "in the mode of identity" has meant accepting and sanctioning as historically valid explanations the rhetorical arguments and political ploys used by supporters of terror to validate their position and maintain their power. Thus, Furet argues, when twentieth-century French Marxist historians invoke the "circumstances," that is, the specter of civil and foreign war, as reasons for escalating repression in 1793 and 1794, they slavishly follow a fictional script written by Robespierre and his friends. They sweep aside massive evidence pointing to another view, for example the fact that mass executions did not start until *after* the threat of foreign invasion had been repelled and the revolt in the Vendée had been crushed.[26] In doing so, they pass on Revolutionary fictions for history and trade insight for blindness.

To counter this trend toward deceptive "commemorative" historiography, Furet has proposed a conceptualization of the Revolution that restores dignity and specificity to historiography by positioning it solidly on the territory of critical inquiry: it "must state the problem it seeks to analyse, the data it uses, its working hypotheses and the conclusions at which it arrives."[27] Furet's main contribution in this respect has been to shift the focus of research away from a Marxist analysis of social and economic factors as determinant agents in the revolutionary process—an analysis that tended to highlight the inaugural character of the French Revolution and thus the thesis of radical change held by its actors— to an inquiry into its political component, which stresses continuity with the centralizing efforts of the absolute monarchy. This historiographical move, which Furet attributes in its essence to Alexis de Tocqueville, is more than a shift from one form of emplotment to another. It has proved to be one of those Kuhnian paradigms that change the course of research for a whole field.

THE "POLITICAL CULTURE" APPROACH

Furet's historiographical revolution has not been achieved without a certain irony. For in the now-abandoned space of the long-dominant Marxist historiography of the French Revolution, revisionist historians have introduced in the last ten years a very fluid, expandable concept of "political culture." "If politics, broadly construed," one of the chief exponents of this concept writes, "is the activity through which individuals and groups in any society articulate, negotiate, implement, and enforce the competing claims they make one upon another, then political culture may be understood as the set of discourses and practices characterizing that activity in any given community."[28] Significantly, the introduction of the "political culture" concept has resulted in a radical revalorization of the fictional in its manifestation as symbolic field. Accepting the premise that a society largely estranged from political concerns and power during the Ancien Régime had to invent not only a new political language but also new forms of action and representation, scholars have directed their efforts to tracking the signs and manifestations of political consciousness in all nooks and crannies of symbolic practice. They have looked for them in political oratory, in icons and emblems, in songs and caricatures, in dress codes and modes of address, in rituals and civic ceremonies. In *Politics, Culture, and Class in the French Revolution*, a model for this kind of study, Lynn Hunt explains: "Although the subject of this book is politics, there is little in it about specific policies, politicians, partisan conflicts, formal institutions, or organizations . . . attention is drawn [instead] to the general principles of revolutionary language, to the operation of revolutionary symbols, and to the pervasive concern with ritual and gesture."[29] While ranging more broadly, the manifesto of the new historiography of the French Revolution, the three-volume international compendium *The French Revolution and the Creation of Modern Political Culture*, has the same underlying principle, as some of

the umbrella titles indicate: "Absolute Monarchy and Its Representations" (with an article on "The King Imagined"), "Forms
of Political Contestation," "The Evolution Concepts" (in vol. 1),
"The New Symbolism," or "Political Forms of Revolutionary Democracy" (vol. 2).[30]

In the new field of political culture, not only have fictions,
both collective and individual, taken pride of place, but methodologies and disciplines that are receptive to the study of fictions,
myths, and symbols have been called into service: discourse analysis and semiotics, psychoanalysis, sociology, anthropology. I shall
briefly discuss some of these, as they provide the interpretive
context of the essays collected in this volume.

A number of studies have focused on the Revolutionary fas-
cination with the word, on how both *les mots* and *la parole*
acquired new uses and new meaning. It is in nomenclative and
rhetorical activity that historians and literary critics have looked
for an understanding of political consciousness. For example, words
like *nation, citoyen, patriote* had acquired a subversive meaning
when used by contestatory *parlementaires* in the 1770s and 1780s.
Historians who take a performative view of language have argued
that when, after the summer 1789, such words became both rallying concepts and passwords, they helped constitute and shape
the new political community in crucial ways. According to Hunt,
"Revolutionary language did not simply reflect the realities of
revolutionary changes and conflicts, but rather was itself transformed into an instrument of political and social change."[31] Carol
Blum has shown the enormous mythical power invested in the
word *vertu* by Revolutionary politics. *Vertu* was at once the psychological characteristic and ethical marker of the Revolutionary,
the rhetorical weapon to be unleashed against enemies—who were
defined by its absence, or by its opposite—and the incarnation
of Republicanism. When Robespierre proclaimed in his *Rapport
sur les principes de morale politique* that "Terror is nothing other
than justice, prompt, severe, and inflexible; it is therefore an
emanation of virtue," his semantic radicalism (annulling previous
antinomies [terror vs. justice] and establishing new derivations
and new etymologies [terror = an emanation of virtue]) worked
symbolically to establish political radicalism and to enforce a new
political order. Revolutionary rhetoric, for theorists in political

culture, is no longer considered a mere tool of political propaganda, but the very motor of Revolutionary action.

Much thought has been given by scholars to the self-reflexivity present in Revolutionary linguistic fictions. Tracing the emergence and the changing signification of abstract words that reflect on the Revolutionary process has made it possible in some important instances to understand with more precision the workings and progress of political consciousness. Mona Ozouf, for example, has traced the evolution of the ubiquitous word *régénération* from a loose philosophical idea present in Enlightenment utopian fictions (from Voltaire's "Huron" to Diderot's Tahitian) to a central programmatic concept that energized all branches of Revolutionary activity.[32] Similarly, Keith M. Baker has followed the gradual elaboration of a political theory of *représentation* in the conflict over the signification of this concept from Hobbes to Rousseau and Siéyès.[33] Building on a study by Pierre Rétat, Baker has also identified the birth of the idea of *the* Revolution (with a definite article and capitalized, to signify its singular, unique, and inaugural character) in a prominent Parisian newspaper. In January 1790, responding to pressure from readers, the journal *Les Révolutions de Paris,* which ran articles on the current upheavals affecting the capital, published an overview of the events so far under the title "Clef de *la* Révolution."[34] This episode is significant in more than one respect. Not only was this foundational semantic move initiated under direct pressure from historical actors; it also consummated and gave as accomplished what was, historically speaking, still only an unfolding, incomplete process. Language thus anticipated history and directed it.

These efforts to understand the Revolutionaries' intense linguistic activity during the Revolution stem in great part from François Furet's reconceptualization of the field of political discourse in semiotic and symbolic terms in *Interpreting the French Revolution.* For Furet, "Revolutionary activity *par excellence* was the production of a maximalist language through the intermediary of unanimous assemblies mythically endowed with the general will" (p. 50). In harmony with poststructuralist theory, which denies the availability of empirical reality "behind" texts and proffers a conception of history-as-text, Furet moved the entire discussion of popular agency in the Revolution from the empirical domain of socially constituted events to that of the symbolic field: "The 'people' was not a datum or a concept that reflected existing society. Rather, it was the Revolution's claim to legitimacy, its very definition as it were; for henceforth all power, all political endeavour revolved around that founding principle, which it was nonetheless impossible to embody" (p. 51). The competition of discourses for control of the verbal symbols that legitimated the incarnation of the will of the people in this or that leader or faction thus created a "semiotic circuit" that Furet sees at the very center of politics during the Revolution.

Significantly, this semiotic approach has the advantage of drawing into the political orbit of the Revolution spontaneous collective fictions like the *Grande Peur* and the *complot,* or conspiracy, which were previously regarded as accessory epiphenomena accessible at best to the historian of *mentalités.* The notion of a ubiquitous, tentacular, and yet elusive aristocratic conspiracy that pervaded Revolutionary life and politics from the summer of 1789 to the Thermidorian reaction is given by Furet the status of a founding myth of the Revolution: "There are myths that make real History: the aristocratic plot was such a one."[35] While previous historians conscientiously sorted out the various empirical components that gave this myth its plausibility and its efficacy (e.g., the flight of the king to Varennes, the emigration of aristocrats, the secession of Catholic priests, counterrevolutionary uprisings, the war), Furet regards "the plot" as the other side of the will of the people. It is "its negative, its reverse, its anti-principle": "Like the people's will, the plot was the figment of a frenzied preoccupation with power; they were the two facets of what one might call the collectively held image of democratic power [l'imaginaire démocratique du pouvoir]" (p. 54). This is a full rehabilitation of the power of fiction in Revolutionary politics.

Equally crucial to the understanding of the field of political discourse during the Revolution has been the recognition of nonlinguistic fictions as crystallizers of political drive. Revolutionary festivals are an excellent case in point. In the work of historians from Albert Mathiez to Albert Soboul, the trend was to view the state-engineered festivals as tools of propaganda fulfilling specific political aims on the part of their instigators. The Festival of the Supreme Being, it was argued, was a means to reconcile Catholicism with the Revolution, to impose Jacobin rule, and to establish Robespierre's dictatorship. But this proved a rather narrow "instrumental" view of the political.[36] By observing from a broader sociological perspective the function of rituals and ceremonies, Mona Ozouf was able to show that Revolutionary festivals were a whole society's attempt to construct its identity on new foundations. Drawing her theoretical ammunition from the work of a sociologist who had himself incisively reflected on the Revolution, Emile Durkheim's *The Elementary Forms of Religious Life,* she argued that festivals allowed a fragmented French society not only to coalesce and find a new sense of solidarity and community but also to erect itself as god and to make its new order and new values sacred.[37] Individual festivals could now be reinterpreted in more interesting ways. For example, sociological and anthropological studies on the nature and function of sacrifice could be invoked in a close reading of the festival of the Supreme Being, stressing how each of its moments implies the sacrificial ritual (e.g., Robespierre setting the monster of atheism on fire in front of the assembled people) and showing the sacralization of the sacrificer in a ceremony whose aim is to invest the profane with sacred meaning.[38] From this broader perspective, it could be shown that the Revolutionaries' reliance on a variety of literary, religious, and mythological traditions and emblems, and their idiosyncratic transformations of such fictional material, contributed in fundamental ways to the new political culture of the Revolution.

Along with semiotics and sociology, psychoanalysis has proved a helpful interpretive tool in investigations of Revolutionary political culture. Because it gives the fictions engendered by the unconscious a prominent place in solving the mystery of neuroses, and because the Revolution can be construed as a state of acute crisis and trauma in the life of a nation, scholars have looked to psychoanalysis for a key to understanding the mechanics and the messages of the political unconscious in Revolutionary representations, particularly caricature. Thus Albert Boime interprets the scatology in anti-British caricatures commissioned to David by the Committee of Public Safety from the perspective of Freud's concept of anality. For Lynn Hunt, caricatures can function "as the equivalent of dreamwork in psychoanalysis." She focuses especially on Freud's scenario of the "family romance" to pry open a recurring obsession of the Revolutionary imagination as expressed in political caricature: the overthrow of the father-king and the establishment of a republican fraternity.[39] In the essays that follow, Peter Brooks shows that there is a remarkable convergence between the workings of Revolutionary melodrama (conceived both as a literary genre and as an ideological stance) and of psychoanalysis: "Melodrama constantly reminds us of the psychoanalytic concept of 'acting out': the use of the body itself, its actions, gestures, its sites of irritation and excitation, to represent meanings that might otherwise be unavailable to representation because they are somehow under the bar of repression." Similarly, Patrice Higonnet uses Freud's notion that suicide is inverted narcissism to reflect on the politicization of sentimental suicide in the Revolutionary years.

THE ESSAYS

It is within this very open and productive interpretive context that the following essays are situated. Disciplinary boundaries crumble as historians investigate pamphletary rhetoric (Jacques Revel), fictions of sentimental suicide (Patrice Higonnet), or the influence of Revolutionary memory on the nineteenth-century political imagination (François Furet), while scholars in literary criticism and art history search for the political meaning of melodrama (Peter Brooks) and the nude (Thomas Crow), or analyze the ideological interpretation of the Revolution abroad (David Simpson). Similary, boundaries between the historian's traditional territory, "the real," and the fictional dissolve in a consensus to approach history as a text as well as through textual representations. The category of "fictions" here encompasses a wide range of material: official documents such as Jacobin speeches, underground writings such as political pamphlets, and private accounts such as letters and memoirs, as well as artistic representations (novels, paintings, theatrical plays) and ideological constructs. In exploring the symbolic content of these fictions, the writers of the following essays make no distinction between canonical texts and marginal, or ephemeral, literature. Revel points out that his material is repetitive, boring, "second-rate literature," and Brooks admits that Sylvain Maréchal's carnivalesque play is "pretty silly stuff." But from the point of view of a fiction-based investigation of the political culture of the Revolution, pornographic pamphlets against Marie-Antoinette are considered as rich a source of information as Rousseau's *Social Contract*.

"Coverage" of a topic as vast as Revolutionary fictions is precluded by the deliberately modest dimension of this volume. But themes and interpretations echo from one essay to the next, highlighting the richness of the object of inquiry and the coherence of the methodology. Taken together, these essays offer a state-of-the-art approach to the political imaginary of the Revolution.

Reflections on the Body: Peter Brooks and Thomas Crow

In his essay "The Revolutionary Body," Peter Brooks focuses on a problem that has been at the heart of discussions by historians, political scientists, and art historians lately, namely, the centrality of the imagery of the human body and, correspondingly, of the symbolic of the body politic, for Revolutionary consciousness.[40] A change in attitudes and beliefs about the body, it has been argued, was precipitated by the execution of Louis XVI, which put an end to traditional representations of sovereignty. Sovereignty had been vested for centuries in the sacred, mystical body of the king as well as located in his physical, temporal being. After the eradication of divine right monarchy and the decapitation of the regal body, sovereignty was transferred to the nation.[41] Joan Landes has drawn attention to the iconic representations of this change. She has charted how the old Hobbesian image of the despotic and hierarchical Leviathan evolved into the Rousseauian figure of the sovereign body of the people united in the general will. She has also analyzed representations of the symbolic desacralization and dismemberment of the royal body and of the subsequent re-memberment of the new republican body.[42] Before Landes, Lynn Hunt's pioneering investigation of the seals and emblems of the Republic had centered on a major symbolic shift in the gendered representation of the Republic. The male Hercules, itself transformed from a symbol of power of individual kings into "the representation of a collective, popular power" by David at the height of Jacobin rule, gave way, according to Hunt, to the contemplative, distant, abstract, "arcanely allegorical" female figures of Marianne and Liberty in the post-Thermidorian

era.[43] In her recent book, *The Body and the French Revolution,*
Dorinda Outram makes much larger claims for the significance
of the body in the Revolution. She argues "firstly, that attitudes
towards the body actively created the new public world of the
Revolution, and hence influenced the sort of state it created; and
secondly, that the physical behaviour and public physical projection
of the participants in the French Revolution may well have paradigmatic lessons for patterns of political behaviour today."[44]

All these studies are informed, explicitly or implicitly, by Michel Foucault's major insight that the history of bodies is inextricably linked with the history of the state. The argument of
Discipline and Punish is well known: the body is "directly involved
in a political field: power relations have an immediate hold on
it; they invest it, mark it, train it, torture it, force it to carry out
tasks, to perform ceremonies, to emit signs."[45] Whereas Foucault
refuses to specify a precise moment for the emergence of the
profound epistemic change affecting the body, Brooks, who concentrates on literary constructions of this change, is more specific:
"One can see in the revolutionary moment the origins of what
we might call an aesthetics of embodiment, where the most important meanings have to be inscribed on and with the body."
Arguing that this revolution had its most important literary precedent in Rousseau's *Confessions* (the famous episode of the spank-
ing is glossed by Rousseau in Freudian terms that reveal the
centrality of sexual experience for the formation of the self), Brooks
investigates evidence of this new aesthetic in political, social, linguistic, and dramatic practice during the Revolution. He draws
parallels between the uses to which Jacobin rhetoric and politics
put the body—conceived as the ultimate signifier and bearer of
truth—and the function that devolved upon it in Revolutionary
melodrama, which was to explicate or indeed replace verbal language and to act out power relationships. What both discourses
(the political and the theatrical) share, according to Brooks, is the
polarization of categories, the exclusion of the in-between, and
the investment of the body with full responsibility for the individual's actions and thoughts: "Melodrama simply enacted on the
stage, in a heightened, excessive, Manichaean, hyperbolic drama,
the national drama being played out in the Convention, in the
sections, in the tribunals, and on the scaffold."[46] Brooks gives

striking examples of the Revolutionary obsession with bodily accountability and of the literalism with which both in real life and
on stage the extirpation of criminal ideas, like that of monarchy,
were enacted on the body: the eradication of the deposed kings
by a volcano in Sylvain Maréchal's *Last Judgment of the Kings*
thus mirrors in the carnivalesque mode, Brooks argues, the ghoul-
ish disinterment of the French kings at Saint-Denis in the same
month (October 1793). He also shows the perdurance of this
"aesthetics of embodiment" across centuries and literary genres,
taking Hugo's novel *Quatrevingt-treize* (written in the aftermath
of the Commune in 1871) and Peter Weiss's *Marat-Sade* as focal
points. Brooks's conclusion, however, in opposition to former studies, insists on the ultimate irreducibility of bodies to political
pressures: "the grand melodramatic gestures performed with and
on the body leave us with an unresolved problem of the body
and its desires."

The body and politics are also the focus of Thomas Crow's
essay. It centers on two of the most famous and mystifying representations of the male body in paint during the Revolution,
David's *Bara* and Girodet's *Endymion*, and addresses the important question of the nature and location of the political meaning
of paintings produced by Revolutionary artists.

A comprehensive political interpretation of the art of the Revolutionary period has yet to be written. Torn as it has been for
generations between traditional investigations of neoclassic style
largely divorced from its historical and political context, on the
one hand, and narrowly Marxist approaches that viewed Revolutionary art mainly in terms of propaganda, on the other, the field
of art history of the Revolutionary period is undergoing major
change under the impulse of Thomas Crow's groundbreaking
work, *Painters and Public Life in Eighteenth-Century Paris*.[47] In
the present essay, Crow pursues in relation to David's *Bara* the
paradigmatic investigation he initiated in this book regarding
David's *Oath of the Horatii:* individual stylistic choices and private
concerns, collective artistic practice and public career are shown
to intersect with political allegiances and historical context to shape
the artist's pictorial representation.

There is perhaps no better example of the Revolutionary imagination at work on itself than the manifold transfigurations of the
deaths of the martyrs of the Republic into eternal emblems of
patriotic sacrifice in popular and official culture at the height of
the Jacobin rule. We know, for instance, how David's brush met-
amorphosed the leprotic body of Marat into a secularized emblem
of radiant self-immolation in the painting that has been called a
"Jacobin pietà."[48] In the case of the thirteen-year-old victim of
the counter-Revolution, Joseph Bara, who died at the hand of the
Vendean *brigands,* we can even trace the process of mythification
in written documents. First came the naive panegyric by Bara's
commanding officer, Desmarres, which used conventional narrative style: "This courageous youth, surrounded by *brigands,* chose
to perish rather than surrender himself and a pair of horses."
Three weeks later, at a moment when the repression of the uprising
in the Vendée was being stepped up, Robespierre, requesting the
pantheonization of Bara, lifted the incident into a Manichean
allegory of good and evil: "Surrounded by *brigands,* who, on one
side, presented death to him, and on the other, were urging him
to cry 'Long live the King!,' he died shouting 'Long live the
Republic!'" In a third stage of mediation, Desmarres sent spec-
ifications for the picture that the Convention had commissioned
to David, this time casting the episode realistically. Bara was to
be represented as he died, "his two feet on the ground, holding
his horses by the bridle, surrounded by *brigands,*" and apostro-
phizing them defiantly in pungent (and somewhat obscene) patois.
David's picture came at the end of this long chain of fictional
reworkings. But significantly, David discarded both Robespierre's
noble allegory of self-sacrificial heroism and the general's anecdotal
genre scene, and selected a third option, that of painting the
young hero expiring away from the combat, his pubescent naked
body stretched in solitude on the ground, his hand pressing the
tricolor cockade to his heart.[49]

This puzzling artistic choice of David's is the point of departure for Crow's reflection: "Where," asks Crow, "might he
have gotten the idea that a vision so insubstantial and erotically
charged could be any kind of persuasive representation of Revolutionary virtue?" Instead of viewing, as has been done before,
the apparent discrepancy between artistic form and political intent

as a sign of failure, a failure that would possibly explain the "unfinished" state of the painting, Crow proposes a radical revision of what constitutes "political" meaning in a work of art and offers a rereading of the picture, and of Revolutionary art, on totally new premises. For one thing, he refuses to take depicted actions uncritically as primary signifiers and to locate political meaning strictly in external factors such as the circumstances or the explicit propagandistic purpose of the commission. Instead, he looks for cues in visual forms and in the meaning these forms acquire when discussed or handled by artists who take part in the political experience. In the 1780s and 1790s, the representation of the body in paint, Crow argues, was a site of acute contestation, not only of Old Regime academic aesthetics, but of the Old Regime itself: Winckelmann had established an important ideological connection between the canon of male beauty and the civic virtue of the ancient Greeks. On the other hand, the perception of the political engagement of an artist by his contemporaries could radically influence the way his paintings were read. Exciting detective and interpretive work enables Crow to propose that Girodet's hermaphroditic *Endymion,* illustrating Winckelmann's ideal of male perfection and exhibited at a moment when news of the painter's patriotic action in Rome reached the capital, was "political" in both these senses—a move which revolutionizes the traditional interpretation of this painting. Linking the pupil's work back to his master's, Crow is then able to demonstrate not only that the representation of a beautiful youth in repose could, in the turbulent Jacobin era, represent a political statement, but that this meaning was so understood and emblematized by the leader of Revolutionary artists in his picture of *Bara.*

The Public and the Private: Patrice Higonnet and Jacques Revel

Both Brooks and Crow view artistic representations in the Revolutionary period as indissociable from a powerful process of restructuration of the public sphere during the eighteenth century. In *The Melodramatic Imagination* Brooks argues that the Revolution is "the moment that symbolically, and really, marks the final liquidation of the traditional Sacred and its representative institutions (Church and Monarch), the shattering of the myth of

Christendom, the dissolution of an organic and hierarchically co-
hesive society." In the Revolution, melodrama constituted an attempt to resacralize life in personal terms.[50] Similarly, Crow has
shown that the Salons of the Academy of Painting and Sculpture
in the eighteenth century constituted a public arena in which a
fierce competition was waged for the control of opinion in a state
where royal authority was on the decline. Such views coincide with
the theory of the sociologist Jürgen Habermas, who argued that
in eighteenth-century France, private men speaking in their own
name from within loose cultural institutions such as the cafés,
the salons, and the press were able gradually to invest and thus
radically to transform the public sphere abandoned by royal representation.[51] Habermas's thesis has profoundly shaped the recent
historiography of the French Revolution, stimulating investigations
in the emergence of the concept of public opinion and inspiring
studies of the articulation of the private and the public during
the Revolution.[52] The latter direction is beautifully illustrated in
both Patrice Higonnet's essay on suicide and Jacques Revel's on
the pamphlet campaign against Marie-Antoinette.

Focusing on the theme of sentimental suicide, Higonnet investigates the enactment of literary fictions of self-chosen death
in real life. His analysis is set historically between two important
fictional paradigms, the discussion of suicide in Rousseau's *La
Nouvelle Héloïse* (1761) and its performance by two unhappy lovers
in Mme de Staël's *Delphine* (1802), which is set in 1790–92.
Between these two literary landmarks Higonnet parades before us
a series of real and attempted, potential and imagined suicides
by both obscure and prominent Revolutionary actors, thus highlighting the convergence of life and literature and looking for a
connection between sentimental and political suicide during the
Revolution. Higonnet draws attention to an especially interesting
case in this respect, that of Marat, who, having justified suicide
in his 1772 sentimental novel, *Les Aventures du Comte Potowski*,
and in his *Plan de législation criminelle* (1774, repr. 1790), nearly
acted out suicide on the floor of the Convention, and continually
courted death symbolically in his provocative journalism. Higonnet's interest is in charting the revolution of attitudes toward a
particular brand of suicide, which he calls "joint sentimental
suicide," under the pressure of politics during the Revolution. He
views 1789 as the turning point after which sentimental suicide,

tolerated before, becomes politically "incorrect" and is considered an "aristocratic residue," as emphasis is put more and more on civic values and a patriotic ethics. Over the next six years, however, Higonnet argues, under the increasing clash of political factions and the rise of extremist politics, not only did suicide become a more and more real option, but its nature changed as well: the urge to die with the beloved was transferred to the nation, and heroic political suicide became eroticized: "on his symbolic and self-immolated body the politicized lover of the Revolution allegorically inscribes the existence of the (failed and female) nation."

Like René Favre, John McManners, and recently Dorinda Outram, Higonnet looks at the roots of heroic suicide and inquires into the reasons for its valorization during the Revolution.[53] He identifies one in the reappropriation of the Christian value of suffering for patriotic ends manifested in Robespierre's well-known statement: "true heroes are not those who are triumphant, but those who are suffering." But, in his view, the major reason for the increase in politicized sentimental suicides in that period lies in the "pre-romantic quest for melancholic absolutes" that prevailed in the "absolutist" framework of the Jacobin republic. This, for example, is the root for the suicide pact of the most famous case of joint suicide during the Revolution, that of the so-called *martyrs de Prairial* in 1795. Political suicide, Higonnet concludes, instantiates one of the fundamental principles of Jacobinism, "the collapse into one another of the private and the public."

One of the most prominent issues in the investigation of the private-public dichotomy spawned by Habermas has been the role of women in the Revolutionary process. Whereas a number of feminist studies have stressed the involvement of women as political actors in popular uprisings, as activists in clubs and popular societies, and as theorists putting forth claims for equal political rights, recent research had concentrated on the fact that women became more and more perceived as a threat to republican virtue and on their increasing marginalization by Revolutionary politicians. In Joan Landes's words, "the Republic was constructed against women, not just without them."[54] Critics have investigated the discourse of misogyny in the politics, literature, and art of the Revolution and thus shed light on the symbolic eradication of women from the public sphere before the execution of their most prominent public representatives under the Jacobin Republic. Four of the essays in this volume touch on some of the symbolic constructions of gender during this period. Peter Brooks suggests that the anxiety of Jacobin leaders faced with the interference of women in the public realm finds an emblematic representation in David's *Marat,* where the sex of the murderess is symbolically inscribed in the mortal wound on Marat's chest. Interpreting the wave of executions of women who had held a public role (Marie-Antoinette, Mme du Barry, Mme Roland, Olympe de Gouges, Théroigne de Méricourt), Brooks comments: "In the general need to read crimes as bodily, where women were on trial there seemed to be a specific need to place criminality squarely on their sexuality." Much of Thomas Crow's engagement of the notoriously androgynous *Bara* and *Endymion* consists in exploring the deeper political meaning of the representation of gender instability and displacement. And Patrice Higonnet insists that political suicide, whether sentimental or heroic, was simply not an option open to women, whose place in life as in pictorial and literary representations was confined to the passive role of onlookers, sufferers, mourners, victims, but not actors. Transferring the Revolutionary martyr's eroticized death wish to an abstract, impersonal, female allegory of the nation did not convey respect for women but, on the contrary, sealed their exclusion from the public sphere. As Lynn Hunt has shown in her work on female Republican emblems, "Woman could be representative of abstract qualities and collective dreams because women were not about to vote or govern."[55]

A key figure of Revolutionary antifeminine discourse is, of course, Marie-Antoinette. Attention has been given lately not so much to her involvement in public scandals such as the notorious "Necklace Affair" or to her real or alleged counter-Revolutionary maneuvers, but to the symbolic construction of her persona in the flood of political pamphlets and caricatures that both registered and contributed to the desacralization of royalty in pre-Revolutionary decades.[56] This is exactly Jacques Revel's perspective in this volume.[57] But, rather than focusing on the symbolic aspects of this process, he scrutinizes the mechanics of producing beliefs about the queen in pamphlet literature: "How can one explain that these pamphlets could fuel so many beliefs, or better yet, form the basis of so many certainties?" Instead of working, as historians traditionally do, from empirical data to their encoding in fictions, he takes the reverse route and investigates the textual procedures through which the staging of a "paper queen" in pamphlet literature could for thousands of readers transform blatant fictions into credible reality, to the point of completely eclipsing the "real" queen from collective perception.

Revel brings to this investigation his expertise as a prominent member, along with other scholars such as Roger Chartier and Christian Jouhaud, of the team of print culture specialists at the Ecole des Hautes Etudes en Sciences Sociales.[58] For these scholars, the conditions of production, circulation, and reception of printed material, the sociology of authors and readers, difficult as they often are to establish, are at least as important as its message. Revel's main emphasis here, however, is on the poetics and rhetoric of the fictional representations of the queen, and he uses discourse analysis to try and lay bare the principles that govern them. In the way pamphleteers handle historical material, for example, Revel notes a double—and contradictory—procedure: "on the one hand, authors want to accredit what they insinuate; on the other, they seem to yield to verbal intoxication to a point that questions the possibility of such accreditation." The same principle of ambiguity is at work in the use of hyperbole—a characteristic that connects these pamphlets to melodrama, labeled by Brooks "the mode of excess." Revel's important insight is that, in pornographic narratives staging the queen as a Messalina, the number of partners, male and female, of postures, and of sexual acts works, not as *effets de réel*, but as the reverse, namely, as strategies of *déréalisation* that beget their own autonomous authority as referents: "Pamphletary fiction is to itself its own authority. It constructs its own reality, and each text refers not to facts outside itself, but to the collection of pamphlets taken as a whole." Revel's conclusion may displease die-hard believers in the possibility for historiography to recapture past reality through the texts it leaves behind, but it opens up the field of popular and satiric representations as an important quarry for those who hold that history constructs itself through its fictions.

Post-Revolutionary Fictions: David Simpson and François Furet

The essays noted so far are concerned with the engendering and use of fictions in social practice, political rhetoric, and literary and artistic representations during the French Revolution. The next two move to the complex issue of the reception of the Revolution and the debate over its significance outside its limited spatial and temporal boundaries, more specifically in the Britain of the 1790s (Simpson) and in nineteenth-century France (Furet). Both authors look at the Revolution as an issue that subsequently determined political and ideological divisions, and they investigate the fictions by which it could function within a larger discourse of self-legitimation for subsequent generations of political thinkers, writers, and critics.

We know how polarized the reception of the French Revolution was in England from the beginning. Edmund Burke and Thomas Paine have come to represent the extreme positions of a wide spectrum of response that went from scornful rejection to enthusiastic endorsement.[59] The first histories of the Revolution were told by British writers who cast them in the opposite modes of the dysphoric (Burke's picture of the Revolution as apocalyptic cataclysm) and the euphoric (Wordsworth's "Bliss was it in that dawn to be alive!").[60] Simpson's chief interest lies not in the poetic but in the political coding of these and other fictions and in their legacy for the contemporary political and academic establishment.

It is only fairly recently, with Daniel Mornet's *Intellectual Origins of the French Revolution,* that historians have come to dispute the first article of what Michelet called the "Revolutionary Catechism" ("Who brought on the Revolution?—Voltaire and Rousseau"). The major thrust of historiographical research in the last ten years has been to rearticulate the answer to this question, replacing the notion of a direct intervention of specific authors or texts with that of a more fluid agency, an increasingly vocal and powerful "public opinion." Simpson, however, draws our attention back to the significance of "la philosophie" in the interpretive scheme of the first British commentators of the Revolution, and he uncovers the subsequent ideological exploitation of this scheme. He concentrates in particular on the tendentious antinomy set up by Burke and other conservative British writers between theory, logic, and method, on the one hand, which are presented as the dangerous attributes and hallmarks of French Enlightenment philosophy, and, on the other, the values of practice, custom, and intuition, praised as those of British empiricism. Just as system, method, and reason are associated with political radicalism, so empiricism in this discourse is always aligned with and propounded by conservatism. Simpson stresses that this polarization, far from being a temporary one, belonging to a particular historical context, is in fact an enduring structure of modern Western thinking. He investigates its roots as far back as sixteenth-century Ramist educational theory and traces its resurgence in late twentieth-century academic debates on literature and critical theory.

With his title "The Revolution That Will Not Finish," which takes issue directly with François Furet's famous dictum "la Révolution est finie," Simpson seeks to challenge the cosy self-complacency that follows, according to him, from the revisionist historiography headed by Furet. The associations that Simpson thus weaves between late twentieth-century center-Right political positions and the denunciation of theory in the early reception of the Revolution by British conservatives will come as no surprise to those who have reflected on the implications of the widespread Tocquevillian revival initiated by Furet in *Interpreting the French Revolution*. In a brilliant chapter of *The Old Regime and the French Revolution* on "How Towards the Middle of the Eighteenth Century Men of Letters Took the Lead in Politics," Tocqueville argues that "new political theories, once they are generally accepted, inevitably rouse popular passions and bear fruit in deeds."[61] Like Burke, and for the same reasons, he highlights the French *philosophes'* taste for "abstract and general political theories," their "love" of "systems," their "trust" in "individual reason," their habit to "speculate without any restriction on the origin of society, on the nature of government, and the essential rights of man," their belief "that what was wanted was to replace the complex nature of traditional customs governing the social order of the day by simple, elementary rules deriving from the exercise of human reason and natural law."[62]

Significantly, this propensity for speculation is treated by Tocqueville with the same distrust and revulsion that attach to fictions in the Platonic tradition. Imaging abstract thought as a fiction that "haunted men's imagination off and on for three

millennia," Tocqueville shows it alighting on the *hommes de
lettres* in the Enlightenment and, by an infectious process, "de-
scending in the masses, there to take the consistency and heat of
a political passion, to such effect that general and abstract theories
on the nature of society became the daily talk of idle people, and
inflamed the imagination even of women and the peasants." (Note
Tocqueville's use of gender and class to disparage and condemn
theory.) Simpson insists on the perdurance of this alignment of
abstraction with radicalism and diagnoses its nefarious effects both
in the hostility toward intellectuals in Thatcherite England and
in the frequent antagonism toward "theory," particularly of the
French brand, in Anglo-American academic institutions. His insight that "we all live with the fictions of the Revolution" should
be taken seriously, to mean, for example, that in our current
debates over Marxism and theory we are in a way still repeating
well-rehearsed arguments and positions and should learn to eschew
the tendentious polarization of categories practiced by the first
commentators of the French Revolution.

"I dream of a much longer history of the French Revolution,
extending even farther downstream, and ending not before the
late nineteenth or early twentieth century," François Furet wrote
in *Interpreting the French Revolution.* Ten years later, Furet published his monumental *La Révolution française: de Turgot à Jules
Ferry: 1770-1880,* a work which traces the century-long struggle
of the French to secure in political institutions the principles of
1789.[63] In the present paper, Furet condenses into a strikingly
concise overview the six hundred pages of this book. His topic is
a particularly apt one for a reflection on historical fictions: the
"tyranny" which the memory of the Revolution exercised over
French political imagination to the Third Republic.

Implicit in the background of this essay is Marx's famous *The
Eighteenth Brumaire of Louis Bonaparte,* which provides both the
image and the metahistorical structure of an interpretation of the
Revolution as the "nightmare" that preys on all future generations.[64] In Furet's view, this nightmare consisted for the men of
the nineteenth century not only in the oppressive paradigm of
1789 but in the incapacity of either political camp created by the
Revolution, the Left or the Right, to project retrospectively a vision

of their past that would empower them to dominate it and thus to create a new present. Marx had presented the politics of his time as a reprise in the farcical mode of the tragic performance of 1789. Furet briefly uses the theatrical metaphor ("Bonaparte would close the theatre of the Revolution for some time," "he enriched the repertoire of those few years"), but prefers the textual one of the written script, which puts the emphasis on the creative reworking and rewriting of the Revolutionary master plot. In this perspective, Bonaparte "reinvents" monarchy and, after him, the Bourbons and France are seen as "an odd couple condemned to reinvent a history which would neither be that of the Ancien Régime nor that of the Révolution."

Furet's own metanarrative is, significantly, ripe with metaphors of the occult and the repressed: Bonaparte, for example, is said to have "relegated the gang of regicides to the shadows," or: "Like an evil spirit, the ghost of the 'tabula rasa' perpetuated itself." There is the recurrent notion of "exorcizing" the phantom of the Revolution, whose "irresistible force" no party and no politician can master. Because Furet sees the nineteenth-century imagination as "composed of transfigured memories and passions lived over and over again," his interpretive model moves at times close to psychoanalysis. For example, in its attempt both to eradicate the Revolution and to supplant it, nineteenth-century politics is shown as if laboring under a protracted oedipal complex. But this analogy is itself a fluid one. In final analysis, la Révolution, not only "the political matrix of all of France's political families" but the womb of modern French history, is, of course, a mother: it engenders nineteenth-century political divisiveness and social antagonisms, together with their temporary palliatives and remedies. In this metahistorical model as in psychoanalysis, repetition is viewed as a curse: each of the revolutions of the nineteenth century—1830, 1848, 1871—"would constantly renew the Revolutionary project under the pretext of ending it." In Furet's view, France rids itself of its nightmare only in the Third Republic, when it finally overcomes the parental model and does what 1789 was unable to achieve: establish a durable democracy on solid political foundations.

Undeniably, the French Revolution lives on as an empowering fiction for men and women caught in the political struggles of today's world. According to Furet, "one only has to see in it not a national institution but a matrix of universal history, in order to recapture its dynamic force and its fascinating appeal."[65] This is what is happening at the turn of this last decade of the twentieth century, as Eastern European countries reject one after the other authoritarian governments and elect to go the hard way of democracy. What we are witnessing as the Berlin wall is dismantled and democratic elections replace decades of police-enforced Communist one-party rule is in effect the creation of a new fictional paradigm for the interpretation of the French Revolution: instead of looking to Jacobinism as a retrospective model and justification to the Bolshevik revolution, as Albert Mathiez did, or to the Terror as a precedent for Auschwitz, as, implicitly or explicitly, Simon Schama does, the "happy year" of 1789, which proclaimed the principles of freedom, equality, and democracy, can now be invoked as a tutelary genius under which to carry out worldwide reform.[66] The Revolution continues in this guise to serve as mythical foundational event and principle of legitimation for present and future history—a testimony to the endless power of its fictional charge.

II. THE BODY AND
REVOLUTIONARY POLITICS

Peter Brooks

The Revolutionary Body

THE REVOLUTION, ACCORDING TO BAUDELAIRE, WAS MADE BY VOLUP-
tuaries: "La Révolution a été faite par des voluptueux."[1] The
remark occurs in his notes on *Les Liaisons dangereuses,* whose
sexual combat he apparently sees as preparatory of the Revolution.
The "voluptueux" he has in mind are of course Laclos and his
revolutionary protector, Philippe-Egalité, and no doubt such other
aristocrat revolutionaries as Mirabeau and Talleyrand. The characterization clearly does not extend to Robespierre the incorruptible, or to the Jacobin idea of the Republic of Virtue, which
increasingly revealed a puritanical aspect, a determination to put
an end to the libertine tradition, and created in the Fête de l'Etre
Suprême a symbolic return of the censorious name of the father.
But Baudelaire's remark may serve as a useful reminder of the
extent to which the body, its freedoms, capacities, pleasures, and
responsibilities, became a central concern of the Revolution and
the focal point of its expressionist aesthetics.

Consider, in this context, the performative quality of revolutionary oratory.[2] It is a language that claims to be doing things
with words—to be remaking reality by so ordering—and what it
is doing very often concerns the placement of bodies on one side
or the other of the line that separates virtue from terror. Jacobin
oratory is abstract, but it is also violent and excessive, and when
its abstractions are translated into actions, people are to live or
die as a consequence of rhetorical moves. Bodily punishment demonstrates that the discourse of Law is not merely abstract, but
reality itself: the idea embodied.[3] When Saint-Just, in his first

speech before the Convention, concerning the judgment of Louis
XVI, states: "Pour moi, je ne vois point de milieu: cet homme
doit régner ou mourir" (I can see no middle ground: this man
must either reign or die), he gives us the essence of Jacobin
rhetoric: the exclusion of the middle ground, the polarization of
categories, and the assignment of persons exclusively to one of the
categories in such a way that their bodies must bear witness to
the result.[4] The king's body is of course an absolutely key token
in this rhetoric. As Saint-Just well understands, in traditional
jurisprudence the body of the king is sacred, impersonal; its nature
is to reign. This is why he believes it would be a mistake to judge
Louis as a simple citizen. Saint-Just in fact restores the special
aura of the king's body, which is different from that of any other
citizen's—restores the Ancien Régime sense of kingship precisely
in order to extirpate it. Louis must be judged as an enemy, as
that very body that is contrary to the principle of popular sovereignty, and therefore must be expelled from the citizenry. If he
is not to reign, he must die.

The king's body is merely the initial and foundational instance
in a rhetoric of the demarcation of bodies. In his "Rapport" that
led to the declaration of Revolutionary Government until the time
of peace, Saint-Just states: "There is no prosperity to be hoped
for so long as the last enemy of liberty shall breathe. You have
to punish not only the traitors, but even those who are indifferent;
you have to punish whoever is passive within the Republic and
does nothing for her: for, from the time that the people manifested
its will, everything that is opposed to it is outside sovereignty;
everything that is outside sovereignty is enemy."[5] One notes, with
a certain chill, the process of differentiation under way here: the
rhetorical exclusion of any position in-between, the impossibility
of in-difference. If one does not accept the will of the people as
articulated by the Comité de Salut Public, one is outside the realm
of sovereignty, and therefore one is enemy—a status to be paid
for with one's body. The implacable logic continues in Saint-Just's
"Rapport sur les suspects incarcérés," where he states: "What
constitutes a Republic is the total destruction of everything opposed to it."[6] And in the same report, he makes the definitions
in terms of which this statement becomes a truism: "Monarchy
is not a king, it is crime; the republic is not a senate, it is virtue.

Whoever is soft on crime wants to reestablish the monarchy and immolate liberty" (pp. 196–97). These propositions claim the status of mere evidences. They allow of no argument, no compromise, no middle position. Bodies are on the line, on either side of it: in the camp of virtue or that of crime; and in the latter case, the guillotine awaits them. And the guillotine itself represents an abstract notion of judgment embodied in a machine for the exemplary punishment of bodies.

The rhetorical imperatives of the Terror are thus played out in *la prise de corps*, the seizing of bodies, and in their decapitation, in a grim realization of the traditional metaphor of amputation of the gangrened members of the social body. As Dorinda Outram has recently argued, the Revolution saw the development of a new controlled, autonomous, impermeable, stoic body, which was "of vital importance to its users and its audience at a time when the first use in French history of state terror on a mass scale was demonstrating how, on the contrary, in reality the body was frail, vulnerable, ultimately disposable."[7] More than in any prior political regime that I can think of, the individual must take responsibility for his body, account for it, which is in part a consequence of the new emphasis on the individual brought by the Enlightenment, and the "bodiliness" given to this emphasis by Rousseau, whose *Confessions* are in large part about the importance of bodily determinants in the formation of the individual. Saint-Just's "Rapport sur les suspects incarcérés" ends with a decree from the Committee that reads in part: "The Committee of General Security is invested with the power to liberate patriots in prison. Any person who asks to be freed will give an account of his conduct since May 1, 1789." This summons to individual responsibility for one's actions is the obverse of the accountability of individuals to the power of the state. Its outcome is very much what Simon Schama calls "the body count": failure to produce a correct accounting of one's actions holds one responsible, in one's own body.[8]

This insistence on "bodiliness" is strikingly in evidence in one of the more bizarre and macabre episodes of the Revolution, the disinterment of the bodies of the kings of France from the Abbey of Saint-Denis. In the process of extirpating the criminal idea of monarchy, the Revolution discovered that it needed to get rid of what *Les Révolutions de Paris* called the "impure remains" and the "vile bones" of past monarchs.[9] During October 1793, the desacralization of kings reached its apogee. The bodies of those mythic figures from the past, including the monarch dear to every French heart, Henri IV, and including the Sun King, Louis XIV, were exhumed and thrown into quicklime in the common pit— the fate also of Louis XVI after his execution in January of the same year. Even Saint Louis ended up in this grave of commoners. It may be a strange comment on the enduring charisma of the anointed body of the king that even inanimate it had to be destroyed, effaced, reduced to nothingness. Regicide was somehow incomplete until the substantial body left behind at the passing of kings was wholly eliminated from the new regime of virtue. The positive gesture complementary to this act of eradication was of course the transport to the Panthéon of the bodily remains of those intellectual precursors of Revolution: Voltaire in July 1791— shortly after the king's attempted flight ended at Varennes—and Rousseau, belatedly, in October 1794, following the demise of the Jacobin Republic for which later historians so often held him responsible.

October 1793 also saw the execution of Marie-Antoinette, following a trial in which her crimes against the Republic were made to appear inextricably linked to her sexual immorality. Accused of insatiable "uterine furors," of liaisons with both men and women, the *Autrichienne*'s alleged conspiracies with the enemy were matched by her supposed attempts to debauch and ruin the Bourbon males, not only her husband but also her son, the Dauphin. The *enragé* Hébert managed to introduce into the prosecution the claim that she initiated the Dauphin into incestuous games and masturbation, thus seriously damaging his health. In the generalized need to read crimes as bodily, where women were on trial there seemed to be a specific need to place criminality squarely on their sexuality. They were aristocrats, thus libertines— both Agrippina and Messalina, in the classic rhetorical accusation—thus lacking in the modesty and fidelity characteristic of good petite-bourgeoise sans-culotte wives, thus out of their place, thus driven by an ungoverned ambition finally attributable to an ungovernable sexuality.

Much excellent recent work on women in the Revolution—by
Lynn Hunt, Joan Landes, Sarah Maza, Dorinda Outram—has
made us aware of the peculiarly relentless exclusion of women
from the radical renovation that ought logically to have furthered
their liberation. The Republic of Virtue did not conceive that
woman should occupy public space; female virtue was domestic,
private, unassuming. As Dorinda Outram writes: "The same arena
which created public man made woman into *fille publique.*"[10] It
was October 1793 that also saw the defeat of revolutionary radical
feminism, as the feminists were beaten, literally, by the proletarian
poissardes, and the Convention went on, early in November, to
order the closure of the women's revolutionary clubs. Mme Roland
went to the guillotine, and shortly before her, Olympe de Gouges,
the author of *Les Droits de la femme et de la citoyenne* (1791)
as well as the anticonventual play *Le Couvent, ou les voeux forcés*
(1790). As Chantal Thomas has noted, Marie-Antoinette, Olympe
de Gouges, and Mme Roland were grouped together by the
Moniteur Universel as examples of unnatural women: "Marie-
Antoinette . . . was a bad mother, a debauched wife, and she died
under the curses of those she wanted to destroy. . . . Olympe de
Gouges, born with an exalted imagination, took her delirium for
an inspiration of nature. . . . The Roland woman, a fine mind for
great plans, a philosopher on note paper, the queen of a moment . . . was a monster however you look at her. . . . Even though
she was a mother, she had sacrificed nature by trying to raise
herself above it; the desire to be learned led her to forget the
virtues of her sex."[11] Political women, scribbling women, debauched women: they all come together as examples of "the sex"
out of control, needing the ultimate correction in order to conform
to what Saint-Just calls the "mâle énergie" of the Republic.

Even more than these three women, the danger of the sex in
politics was represented—as Chantal Thomas also has shown—by
Charlotte Corday. Stabbing Marat in his bathtub brought clearly
into the symbolic arena the hand-to-hand combat of denatured
female aristocrats—indulgents, federalists—and male friends of
the people. For her judges, she was simply a "monster" in female
guise, something like an example of demonic possession, to which
women traditionally were most prone. In the subsequent cult of
Marat, Charlotte Corday is present only in that gash in Marat's

breast, a kind of displaced representation of her woman's *sexe*: her sex as wound on the martyred man. David's painting says it all: the ecstatic face of the martyr, the drops of blood on the immaculate sheet, the quill pen still grasped next to the kitchen knife fallen on the floor, the bathwater become a pool of blood—all these elements suggest the intrusion of an ungoverned female sexuality on a life dedicated to the higher cause. The male body has been made to pay for the primal drives of the woman's body. At the same time, Marat's apotheosized body has gained a realm to which the woman's body has no access (see p. 60).

It is through David's painting that Charlotte Corday's letter, written in order to win an audience with the great man, has been immortalized. We can still decipher it today: "Il suffit que je sois bien malheureuse pour avoir droit à votre bienveillance" (The simple fact of my misfortune is my claim to your benevolence). The letter makes of the Friend of the People a victim of his very benevolence, here ignobly practiced upon by a consummate hypocrite. The letter is all the more perfidious in that its language of Rousseauian sensibility belongs to the repertoire of the good guys, not the villains. It is in fact a sentence typical of those spoken by the virtuous characters in melodrama—the genre that had not yet been so christened in 1793, but which had already seen its protoexamples on the stages of Paris: Boutet de Monvel's *Les Victimes cloîtrées* of 1791 is often considered the first melodrama.

October 1793 saw the staging of the representative melodrama of the Terror, Sylvain Maréchal's *Le Jugement dernier des rois,* which opened to great acclaim at the Théâtre de la République—formerly the Théâtre-Français—two days after the execution of Marie-Antoinette. "There is a fit spectacle for republican eyes," gloated Hébert in *Le Père Duchesne.*[12] The Comité de Salut Public ordered 3,000 copies of the printed text, and the Ministry of War then signed up for 6,000, to send to troops at the front in order to kindle their republican zeal. But the best measure of the success of the play may be the fact that the Comité de Salut Public—at a moment when gunpowder was one of the most precious commodities in France—granted the petition of the Théâtre de la République for "twenty pounds of saltpeter and twenty pounds of powder" needed to produce the volcanic eruption that ends the play and kills off all the monarchs of Europe—the "crowned villains"—that it has assembled on a desert island.

Le Jugement dernier des rois, a "Prophecy in One Act," envisions a Europe in which the sans-culottes of all the nations have risen up against their monarchs, deposed them, and brought them, under the watchful eye of an international sans-culotte police force, to a desert island, where they find a virtuous old Frenchman, who was cast away on the island because he dared to protest against the abduction of his virginal daughter by royal courtiers. He lives in a hut set against a boulder, on which he has inscribed the motto: "Better to have as neighbor / A volcano than a king. / Liberty . . . Equality." The castaway has made friends with the savages who paddle over in canoes from a neighboring island, who are naturally noble and, once instructed by the castaway—acting on the example of the *vicaire savoyard*—come to join him in worship of the sunrise. The sans-culottes lead in the deposed monarchs one by one: George III of England, Francis II of the Austro-Hungarian Empire, William of Prussia, Ferdinand of Naples, Vittorio-Amedeo of Savoia, Charles of Spain, Stanislas-Augustus of Poland, Catherine, Empress of All the Russias, plus the Pope. Predictably, they fall into monarchical—that is to say, the worst possible—behavior. George tries to beg off on grounds of his insanity; Charles of Spain implores the Pope to solve their difficulties by performing a miracle; Catherine tries to lure Stanislas into an amorous tryst in a cave. They fall to squabbling over a crust of bread, and the stage is littered with broken scepters and crushed crowns. Their dissension is ended by the eruption of the volcano, and they descend in flames into the open trap of the theater.

Maréchal's play, in any sober view, is pretty silly stuff, but it is animated by Jacobin rhetoric of both sensibility and ferocity, virtue and terror, in a theatrical form that demonstrates why melodrama was the artistic form created by the Revolution—perhaps its only enduring cultural creation. It indeed suggests that saying melodrama was the artistic genre of the Revolution is nearly a truism, since revolutionary public speech itself, as our examples from Saint-Just suggested, is already melodramatic. Charles Nodier would later claim that "melodrama was the morality of the Revolution," by which he meant that it is inherently a democratic

form, in which the humble of the earth stand up to overbearing
tyrants and express home truths, about the value of the good
heart, the sanctity of the domestic hearth, the essential moral
equality of all, and the fraternity of the virtuous, and win through
to see villainy punished and virtue rewarded, in spectacular fashion, in the last act.[13] Refining on Nodier's words, we might say
that melodrama is the genre, and the speech, of revolutionary
moralism: the way it states, enacts, and imposes its moral messages, in clear, unambiguous words and signs. It is a hyperbolic
mode, of course, and preeminently the mode of the excluded
middle, which one finds in Saint-Just's speeches and in all Jacobin
rhetoric: those who are not with us are against us, there is no
compromise possible between polarized moral positions, the world
is defined by a vast Manichaean struggle of light and darkness.
Saint-Just, in a famous line of his "Institutions républicaines,"
states "the republican government has virtue as its principle; if
not, terror. What do they want who want neither virtue nor
terror?"[14] The in-between of virtue and terror is simply unthink-
able. As in melodrama, there is no place for such moral indif-
ference or nuance, there are only pure, unadulterated moral
positions.

Subtlety is not the mode of *Le Jugement dernier des rois* or
of any other melodrama. Its world is the world-turned-upside-
down of carnival. The kings are in chains, the sans-culottes reign
supreme, handing down sentences both just and inflexible and
stated with all the high moral sententiousness of melodrama.
There are all the sonorous clichés of Jacobin rhetoric, both the
denunciations of Old Régime rulers for sexual immorality as well
as tyranny—"Was there ever a nation that at the same time had
a king and had decency?" asks the leader of the sans-culottes—
and the fulsome praise for the domestic as well as civic virtues of
the sans-culottes, "who earn their bread by the sweat of their
brow, who love work, who are good sons, good fathers, good
husbands, good friends, good neighbors, but who are jealous of
their rights as they are jealous of their duties."[15] As in all melodrama, people are characterized in unambiguous epithets: "ven-
erable old man!" "brave sans-culottes!" "crowned monsters!"
Home truths are emphatically announced: "these savages are our
elders in liberty: for they have never had a king. Born free, they
live and die as they were born." The presence of these somewhat

superfluous noble savages is interesting: their speech through gestures attaches this play firmly to the origins of melodrama in
pantomime. Gestural speech is a constant in melodrama because
it permits the creation of visual messages, pure signs that cannot
lie, the most undissimulated speech, that of the body.

The play also participates in what one might call the pathos
of Jacobin rhetoric, which is always trying to bring into being a
reality that does not yet exist. It is subtitled "a prophecy," since
it envisions the extension of revolutionary reversal to the whole
of Europe. It is the vision of the self-styled "Orator of the Human
Race," Anacharsis Cloots, who claimed that he would not rest
until there was a republic on the moon. Like the oratory of the
Convention, the rhetoric of the play—indeed, the play itself—is
performative, seeking by the power of an ever more violent word
to impose the Jacobin Republic on a recalcitrant world. *Le Jugement dernier des rois* in effect says: "Be it enacted that there are
no more kings." But between that rhetorical moment—the fictive
moment of the play itself—and its realization stand all the foreign
armies and the internal traitors, the hoarders, the federalists, the
indulgents, and so on.

As the rhetoric of denunciation at the revolutionary tribunals
needed not merely to inculpate but to destroy—to create the
rationale for elimination—so here, once all the monarchs have
been lined up on stage, the leader of the sans-culottes draws up
his bill of particulars:

> It's for the service of this handful of cowardly brigands, it's for
> the whim of these crowned villains, that the blood of a million,
> of two million men, the worst of whom was worth more than
> all of them, was spilled over every inch of the continent, and
> beyond the seas. It's in the name or by the order of this score
> of wild beasts that entire provinces have been devastated, pop-
> ulous cities changed into piles of ashes and corpses, innumerable
> families raped, stripped bare, reduced to famine. . . . Here they
> are, these butchers of men in time of war, these corruptors of
> the human species in time of peace. . . . Nature, hasten to finish
> the work of the sans-culottes, breathe your fire-breath on this
> refuse of society, and plunge kings forever into that nothingness
> from which they never should have emerged.

If in the world outside the stage, the performative is enacted by
the guillotine, the purgation of those who cannot understand that
there is no middle ground between virtue and terror, onstage
"Nature" is under the command of rhetoric, and the volcano
promptly erupts to destroy the kings, consuming their very bodies.
We are, I think, forcibly impressed again and again by the
"bodiliness" of revolutionary language and representation, the
need to conceive the revolutionary struggle in both a practice and
a language which hold the body ultimately responsible, its position
within the scheme of things the necessary measure of success or
failure. One can hence see in the revolutionary moment the origins
of what we might call an aesthetics of embodiment, where the
most important meanings have to be inscribed on and with the
body. This is, I would argue, a relatively new phenomenon in the
history of literature, one that in many ways finds its precursor in
the very man held responsible for the Revolution, Rousseau, who
in his *Confessions* gives a dramatically new role to the body—his
own body—as a prime determinant of his life's meanings, and
the way the narrative of that life has to be constructed: as, for
instance, in the marking of his body in his childhood punishment
at the hands of Mlle Lambercier, which, he tells us in a passage
which seemed particularly prescient to Freud, determined his sexual orientation and even his character for the rest of his days. This
is not to argue that the body is unimportant in literature before
the late eighteenth century: many examples start coming to mind,
from the Greeks onward. And certainly in Ancien Régime France
the body, be it the tortured body of the criminal or the sacred
body of the king, is very much a part of everyday life and symbolism. But the Old Régime body belongs to a traditional system,
a product of both Christian and popular cultures, that is taken
for granted. It is when this traditional system is evacuated of
meaning by the Revolution that a new aesthetics of embodiment
becomes necessary. The loss of a system of assigned meanings is
followed by one where meanings must be achieved, must be the
product of an active semiotic process in which the body is newly
emblematized with meaning. The body in early Romantic literature, and thereafter, assumes a new centrality as a site of meaning.
And during the Revolution, in the popular genre of melodrama,

we have a kind of literalistic realization of this new importance of the body as the site of signification.

The melodramatic body is a body seized by meaning. Since melodrama's simple, unadulterated messages must be made absolutely clear, visually present, to the audience, bodies of victims and villains must unambiguously signify their status. The bodies of the virtuous victims are typically subjected to physical restraint. Boutet de Monvel's *Les Victimes cloîtrées* (which, I noted, is often considered the first example of the new genre) offers a final act in which the heroine and the hero are confined in the deepest cells of a convent and a monastery, respectively, in representation of the evil power of the monks who act at the behest of the aristocrats. They will be liberated by a republican mayor, draped in his tricolor sash, in a clear dramatic gesture of freeing the body from oppression. One has a similar use of sequestration in the *in-pace* of a convent in the unfortunate Olympe de Gouges's drama, *Le Couvent, ou les voeux forcés,* and there are numerous other examples. The body sequestered, enchained, unable to assert its innocence and its right to freedom, becomes a dominant element of melodrama that endures long after the Revolution, that indeed appears consubstantial with the genre. Guilbert de Pixerécourt, the first undisputed master of the genre, returns again and again to the situation, in such plays as *Le Château des Appenins, Les Mines de Pologne, La Forteresse du Danube, Latude, ou trente-cinq ans de captivité:* the titles alone suggest the nightmarish Gothic spaces in which the virtuous are confined. And none of these melodramas can reach its denouement until the virtuous bodies have been freed and explicitly recognized as bearing the sign of innocence. This sign is often, notoriously, inscribed on the body itself, in the form of a birthmark or other stigmata, or an emblem worn on the body since childhood: marks and emblems that eventually permit the public recognition of the virtuous identity. *La croix de ma mère*—the token that eventually establishes identity—indeed has become proverbial as the sign of the melodramatic recognition scene. And very often the final act of melodrama will stage a trial scene—as in some revisionary version of the revolutionary tribunal—in which the character of innocence and virtue is publicly recognized through its signs, and publicly celebrated and rewarded, while the villain is bodily expelled from the social realm: driven out, branded as evil, relegated to a space offstage and outside the civilized world.

Melodrama constantly reminds us of the psychoanalytic concept of "acting out": the use of the body itself, its actions, gestures, its sites of irritation and excitation, to represent meanings that might otherwise be unavailable to representation because they are somehow under the bar of repression. Melodrama refuses repression, or rather, repeatedly strives toward moments where repression is broken through, to the physical and verbal staging of the essential: moments where repressed content returns as recognition, of the deepest relations of life, as in the celebrated *voix du sang* (You! my father!), and of moral identities (So you are the author of all my wrongs!). It is of course in the logic of melodramatic acting out that the body itself must pay the stakes of the drama: the body of the villain is publicly branded with its identity, exposed in a formal judgment scene, then, if not put to death in hand-to-hand combat, driven from the stage and banished from human society; while the body of persecuted virtue is rewarded, fêted, married, and emblazoned with all the signs of the public recognition of its nature.

It is in the context of melodrama's constant recourse to acting out, to the body as the most important signifier of meanings, that we can understand why nearly every melodrama has recourse to moments of pantomime, which are not simply decorative, which in fact often convey crucial messages. *Le Jugement dernier des rois,* for instance, has that group of noble savages with whom the Europeans can communicate only in gestures—but without misunderstandings, since "the heart's the heart in all countries." In an important moment of the play, these savages instinctively express their horror and loathing for the kings of Europe in bodily language, representing before our eyes the right, unprejudiced, nonverbal, visible reaction to the fact of tyranny. And as the genre develops, one finds many more highly elaborated examples of the mute role, which is often the bearer of the most sublime messages in the play. I have elsewhere discussed the instance of the mute Eloi, in Pixerécourt's *Le Chien de Montargis,* who faces the excruciating experience of standing trial for a crime he did not commit while unable to defend himself verbally. His gestures and bodily postures constantly evoke a realm of higher law and truer judgment in which he will be vindicated. Much late eighteenth-century reflection on the nature of language and its origins tends to the view that gesture is the first and ultimately the most passionate form of communication, that which comes to the fore when the code of verbal language lapses into inadequacy. As Marmontel put it, "It is especially for the most impassioned moments of the soul that pantomime is necessary."[16] Only the body can speak for the soul at those moments.

I have perhaps said enough to suggest, in a general way, the importance of an aesthetics of embodiment to melodrama, and of melodrama to the Revolutionary situation. I would not want to argue that the Revolution is the absolute cause and origin of the aesthetics of embodiment—for the Revolution was prepared, culturally as well as politically, in the writings of Rousseau, Diderot, and many others—but it does bring a first full realization of these aesthetics. Indeed, the connection between melodrama and the Revolution was, to the first writers on the subject, notably Charles Nodier, something self-evident. Melodrama simply enacted on the stage, in a heightened, excessive, Manichaean, hyperbolic drama, the national drama being played out in the Convention, in the sections, in the tribunals, and on the scaffold. It was a genre that had to be invented to do justice to—to match, as it were—the excessive rhetoric and action in the streets. And conversely, the aesthetic "system" of melodrama codified and legitimated the rhetorical drama of Revolutionary combat and the effects it played out on the body.

I have argued elsewhere that there is a convergence in the concerns of melodrama and of psychoanalysis—and indeed, that psychoanalysis is a kind of modern melodrama, conceiving psychic conflict in melodramatic terms and acting out the recognition of the repressed, often with and on the body. I am thus interested in the fact that the Revolution presides at the birth of modern psychiatry, notably in the work of Philippe Pinel, who was appointed chief physician for the insane at Bicêtre in 1793, then took over the hospital of the Salpêtrière in 1795, in both of which he developed what he called the *traitement moral* of insanity, attempting to work on the obsessive ideas (or "monomanias") that had inscribed themselves on patients' bodies in the form of symptoms. Let me pause over one suggestive case history reported by Pinel—brought to our attention by Jan Goldstein in her impressive recent work on nineteenth-century French psychiatry—that of one of the most famous clockmakers in Paris, who was obsessed by the idea of building a perpetual motion machine.[17] Overwork, combined with the constant terrors of the Revolution, finally led to insanity, in the form of the belief that he had been decapitated on the guillotine, and then, in a reversal of his sentence, given back a head—but the wrong one, not his own. To combat this obsession, Pinel enlisted the help of another inmate at Bicêtre, who opened a discussion with the clockmaker about the miracle of Saint Denis, who after decapitation is said to have walked with his head in his hands while covering it with kisses. The clockmaker argued that the legend was wholly plausible, citing his own case as proof. To which the other inmate queried, with mocking laughter, with what Saint Denis could in the situation have kissed his head—perhaps with his ass? Pinel tells us that this remark so shamed the clockmaker that he ceased to speak of his decapitation, returned to work and eventually to his family, and never had a relapse. This farcical recombination of the body, with its inversion of a kind of bodily pun on ass-kissing, looks forward to some of Freud's ingenious bodily hermeneutics, his readings of symptoms, where symptoms are conceived as what is written on the body by the conflicts of unconscious desire.

One could pursue this problematics of embodiment, including the relation of symptom and acting out to the melodrama of psychic life, in a number of post-Revolutionary texts: in Romantic drama, for instance, in the novels of Balzac, notably, and Eugène Sue, even, I think, in political thought, especially that of the utopian socialists. I cannot undertake so far-ranging a discussion here. Instead, I want in the pages remaining to evoke briefly two texts from the imaginative afterlife of the Revolution that both refer in self-conscious ways to the aesthetics of embodiment and the central role of the body in the enactment of meaning. The first of these is Victor Hugo's *Quatrevingt-treize,* his novel about the year of the Terror that was written during that later *année terrible,* 1871, in the wake of the Commune and its repression. Hugo wrote his novel in an attempted gesture of reconciliation between the deeply divided camps of his compatriots, by way of a kind of demonstration of the interdependence of revolution and counterrevolution, the old and the new eras, the values of feudal France and of republican France. In so doing, in *Quatrevingt-treize* perhaps even more than in his other works, Hugo makes clear the melodramatic premises of his own imagination. In returning to the thematics of Revolution, he dramatizes the consubstantiality of his own aesthetics with the revolutionary moment.

Quatrevingt-treize is a melodrama of history, a "legendary" history as Hugo put it, one that strives toward the sharp outlines, simple contours, and primary colors of the *image d'Epinal*. When he stages Marat, Danton, and Robespierre in conversation, they appear as popular images of themselves, three figures from a pageant of history. And the novel proceeds by a series of simple embodiments of the principles at war in 1793. First, there is the *ci-devant* Marquis de Lantenac, leader of the Vendéens, at war with his kinsman Gauvain, commander of the Army of the Republic. Within the Vendéen camp, the extremist politics and methods of Lantenac are set in opposition to the eternal, irreducible claims of the mother, Michelle Fléchard, whose three children become key tokens in the struggle for the future of France. On the republican side, the noble and generous Gauvain, whose flaw is his penchant toward indulgence, is set against the inflexible Cimourdain, former priest and fanatic of the new order. And there are further characters, derived and created by this same process of bipolar opposition, each the incarnation of some pure essence of the revolutionary-counterrevolutionary struggle. The ultimate confrontation between Lantenac and Gauvain comes in the siege of the medieval fortress of La Tourgue, symbol of Breton feudalism, whose very architecture offers a personification of the hierarchical social structure of the Old Régime, from its proud summits to the *cul de basse fosse,* the underground cell that denied a person's very right to exist.

The keep of La Tourgue is fissured at the base by a breach opened by a land mine, and it is through this fissure that the republican army makes its desperate assault on the band of seventeen under Lantenac's command, who are resolved to die fighting. As the assault proceeds, a stream of blood pours from the breach, forming a steaming pool at its base. "One would have said that the tower itself was bleeding, and that the giantess was wounded," comments the narrator.[18] The tower losing blood through its breach is exactly matched by the fearful l'Imânus, the nearly bestial Breton peasant loyal to his seigneur and his king, who at the last fights holding a pistol in one hand and with the other holding up his intestines, which are falling out through the wound he has received. In his final act of defiance, he sets down the pistol and, still holding in his guts, with his free hand sets fire to the fuse that will explode the powder in the library— setting fire to the inaccessible wing in which the three children are held hostage, avenging on the children "our child," the young Louis XVII imprisoned in the Temple.

The fire in the library, and Michelle Fléchard's great cry of anguish and despair as the flames sweep toward her children, will produce from Lantenac—who has escaped the siege of La Tourgue through a hidden staircase—a gesture of pure chivalric romance: a return to the tower with the key that unlocks the steel door into the library, and a daring rescue of the children. Gauvain must then match this gesture with his own, freeing the Lantenac whom he has pursued for so many months, dressing him in his own cloak so that he can pass the sentinels—a gesture he explicitly sees as a victory of the principles of 1789 over the horrors of 1793. As a result, Gauvain must suffer the fate of so many liberal aristocrats: Cimourdain, embodiment of the very highest of Republican principles, the Law, sentences him to the guillotine. And this moment opens up Hugo's final and most remarkable bipolar embodiment of opposed principles: on the one hand, the medieval fortress, La Tourgue, on the other, the modern agency of retribution, the guillotine. The guillotine erected on the plateau facing the castle walls looks like "a hebraic letter, or one of those Egyptian hieroglyphs that comprised the alphabet of the old enigma" (pp. 373-74). The narrator comments: "An edifice is a dogma, a machine is an idea." Hugo's prose begins to animate the edifice and the machine. La Tourgue appears to have eyes—"a tower watches, the façade of an edifice contemplates," the narrator comments— and it scrutinizes the guillotine. And from this scrutiny the embodiments of feudalism and revolution, of past and present, come alive as personifications of dogma and idea, enter into a dialogue, in which the guillotine says to the fortress: "I am your daughter" (p. 376). And the fortress takes fright at what it has engendered, the new ferocity that will destroy its long history of ferocity.

The final pages of *Quatrevingt-treize* would, of course, deserve much more detailed comment than I can give them here. They proceed through a remarkable series of postulations of embodiment, physical representations of all the positions under debate, in order to reach these animated objects that summarize and incorporate all the disputed terrain of the Revolution. When the blade of the guillotine falls on Gauvain's neck, Cimourdain takes a pistol and shoots himself, and the novel ends with this sentence: "And these two souls, tragic sisters, flew off together, the shadow of the one mingled with the light of the other." 1793 finally becomes a piece of chiaroscuro, one of Hugo's preferred aesthetic devices, which here becomes almost the yin and the yang, the principles of Manichaeistic struggle for man's fate. The novel earns the terms of this final cosmic melodrama by its constantly resourceful melodramatic rhetoric, its progressive dramatic analysis of the revolutionary struggle in terms of grandiose opposed embodiments of large principles and forces.

My other example is from what I consider the most remarkable attempt to redramatize the revolutionary oppositions in our own time, Peter Weiss's play, *The Persecution and Assassination of Jean-Paul Marat as Performed by the Inmates of the Asylum of Charenton under the Direction of the Marquis de Sade*. In the debates between the two protagonists, Marat keeps returning to the urgency of his writing, the need to compose his call to the people, whereas Sade opposes to this the irreducible claim of the body. As Charlotte Corday stands over the bathtub, Sade speaks:

> Marat
> forget the rest
> there's nothing else
> beyond the body
> Look
> She stands there
> her breast naked under the thin cloth
> And perhaps she carries a knife
> to intensify the love-play[19]

When Corday finally delivers her blow, the resulting tableau of Marat dead is designed to mimic David's painting, which Sade's speech has now explicitly invested with the sexuality we noted in

it. But this does not occur before Sade has continued his reflection
on the body:

> Marat
> as I sat there in the Bastille
> for thirteen long years
> I learned
> that this is a world of bodies
> each body pulsing with a terrible power
> each body alone and racked with its own unrest
> In that loneliness
> marooned in a stone sea
> I heard lips whispering continually
> and felt all the time
> in the palms of my hands and in my skin
> touching and stroking
> Shut behind thirteen bolted doors
> my feet fettered
> I dreamed only
> of the orifices of the body
> put there
> so one may hook and twine oneself in them [Pp. 130–31]

Weiss's Sade takes us back through revolutionary embodiment to
the body itself, no longer the bearer of messages, no longer the
token in political struggle, but the ultimate integer that politics
cannot touch, yet that infirms all politics because it demands a
deeper psychic revolution that political revolution ignores. Sade
ends his speech:

> Marat
> those cells of the inner self
> are worse than the deepest stone dungeon
> and as long as they are locked
> all your Revolution remains
> only a prison mutiny
> to be put down
> by corrupted fellow-prisoners [P. 131]

We are, of course, in the madhouse at Charenton, in a world of
bodies only barely held in control by the wardens and nurses.
What Weiss has done, I think, is to make us reflect on the history
of embodiment that seems so much a political and aesthetic legacy

of the Revolution, and to make us see that the grand melodramatic gestures performed with and on the body leave us with an unresolved problem of the body and its desires. We might finally ask: if the Revolution, to return to Baudelaire's phrase, was made by voluptuaries, seekers of pleasure, did they know what they wanted?

Thomas Crow

Revolutionary Activism and the Cult of Male Beauty in the Studio of David

FROM THE EARLIEST PHASE OF DAVID'S CAREER AS AN INDEPENDENT master, his studio was distinguished by an exceptionally close and cooperative interchange between students and teacher. The biographies of the pupils who joined him on his return from Rome in 1781 attest to the reciprocated personal and intellectual attachments in the community of the studio.[1] As to the practical manifestations of its egalitarian ethos, we have not had much more than scattered surviving reports, along with some suggestive attribution problems. There are accounts, for example, of the twenty-one-year-old Jean-Germain Drouais's substantial assistance on the *Oath of the Horatii* (Paris, Louvre), painted when both master and pupil were in Rome in 1784.[2] There has long been a dispute over the authorship of the masterful replica of the *Horatii* in the Toledo Museum of Art (Ohio), with one side suggesting Girodet—then nineteen—on the basis of stylistic differences in the details (fig. 1).[3] The abandoned studio copy of the *Death of Socrates* that has recently surfaced in the collection of the Princeton University Art Museum displays, in its finished section to the far left, a quality of paint handling that is thoroughly assured in technical terms, but distinctly different from David's—Girodet again being the prime available candidate (fig. 2).[4] In light of this pattern, I have long wondered about the abrupt shifts in quality of surface between different sections of the great *Brutus* of 1789 (Paris, Louvre) (fig. 3).

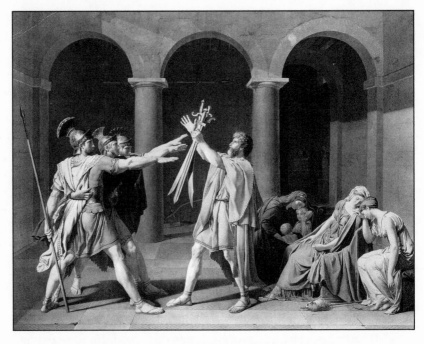

Fig. 1. Anne-Louis Girodet, after Jacques-Louis David, *The Oath of the Horatii,*
1786, oil on canvas, 127 × 162 cm., Toledo (Ohio) Museum of Art

There is a document that bears on the question of David's
elevation of very young students to close to the status of peers.
It was left by P. A. Coupin, a prominent critic of the Restoration
period and the editor of Girodet's papers.[5] It is in the form of
an addendum, attached to some copies of a commemorative pamphlet written after David's death.[6] Offered with apologies to his
lay readers, it is a systematic summary of the various contributions
of David's students to the paintings bearing his signature, which
Coupin feels he must set down for the sake of the future "history
of art."[7] One question it settles definitively is the authorship of
the Toledo *Horatii*—Girodet entirely and alone, except for a few
added accessories.[8] On the subject of the *Brutus,* it ties the surface
discontinuities of the painting directly to David's habit of be-
stowing startlingly mature responsibilities on his young appren-
tices. Coupin gives two pupils credit for crucial sections of the
finished painting. The nineteen-year-old François Gérard, we are
told, did the entire figure of the grieving nurse.[9] Girodet took

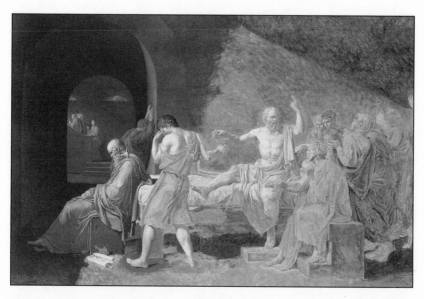

Fig. 2. Studio of Jacques-Louis David, after David, *Death of Socrates,* 1787–1790?, oil on canvas, 130 × 196 cm., The Art Museum, Princeton University. Museum purchase, gift of Carl D. Reimers.

over the finishing work on the face, left arm, and foot of Brutus's wife—and indeed these are among the sections of the painting brought up to a closed finish that is again more consistent with his way of working than with David's rougher treatment of glazes.[10] And he went on, we are told, to intervene in a passage of maximum subtlety and importance to the picture's narrative and emotional effect. Gérard having finished the shadowy background behind the head of Brutus, David found himself unable to adjust the treatment of the head in order to bring it sufficiently forward; so he called on his more experienced assistant to complete the work because "Girodet in truth understood chiaroscuro better than he did."[11]

Such a process of division and delegation of labor would doubtless have continued and expanded had the project of the *Tennis Court Oath* (Versailles), with its enormous cast of life-size figures, gone further than the preliminary stages. As it was, the much smaller-scaled public paintings that David did complete during the Revolutionary period continued to rely on his pupils' work both directly and indirectly.

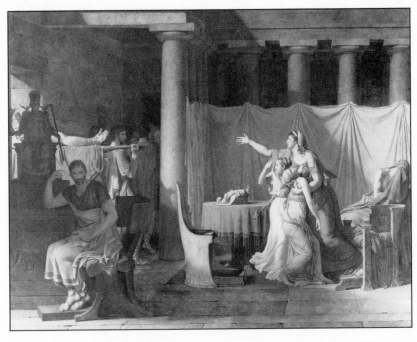

Fig. 3. Jacques-Louis David, *Lictors Returning to Brutus the Bodies of His Sons,*
1789, 323 × 422 cm., Paris, Louvre

Again according to Coupin, Gérard's assistance was crucial in
David's rapid completion of the now-lost martyr portrait of the
regicide deputy Le Peletier de Saint-Fargeau (fig. 4).[12] It is something which we can now never confirm from physical evidence,
but Coupin, inviting his readers to test his claim, states that it
was obvious from the appearance of the surface that Gérard had
completed the entire body of the murdered Republican aristocrat.
The famous portrait *Marat at His Last Breath* (Brussels, Musées
Royaux) was an assignment that put David's powers of invention
and rapid execution to an even more demanding test (fig. 5).
Here we know of no direct contribution by Gérard or any other
assistant, but David did manage to enlist the absent Girodet
through a painting his pupil had left behind. The last work done
by the younger artist before his departure for Rome had been an
enormous canvas depicting the Virgin and the dead Christ (Church
of Montesquieu-Volvestre), painted for an obscure provincial monastery (two of his aunts had retired to a neighboring convent and

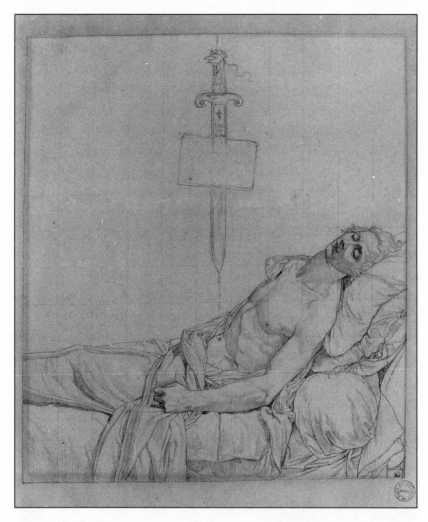

Fig. 4. Anatole Devosge, after Jacques-Louis David, *Michel Le Peletier de Saint-Fargeau on His Deathbed,* 1793, 46.7 × 40 cm., black chalk on paper, Dijon, Musée des Beaux-Arts

seem to have been the intermediaries for the commission) (fig. 6).[13] About three and a half meters high, it was precociously ambitious in scale and represented, in its bare simplicity and gloomy tenebrism, a new kind of picture for the Davidian group. David, we are told, registered his approval of the painting before Girodet left Paris with it, and the *Marat* reflects a very tangible memory of his pupil's work.[14]

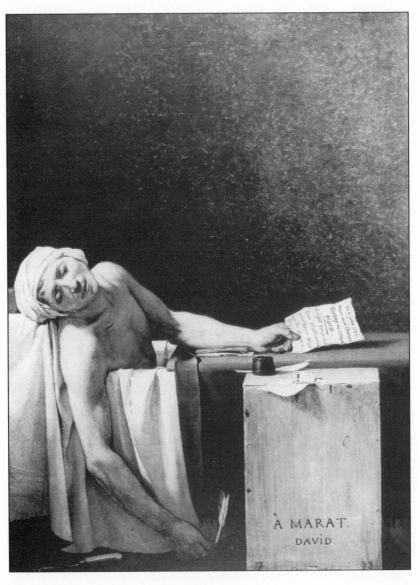

Fig. 5. Jacques-Louis David, *Marat at His Last Breath*, 1793, 165 × 128 cm.,
Brussels, Musées Royaux des Beaux-Arts

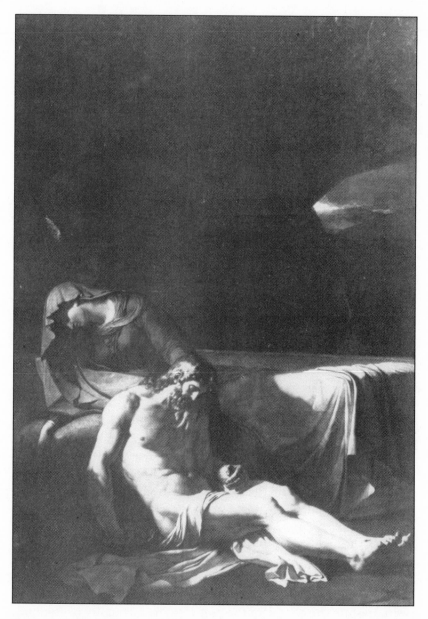

Fig. 6. Anne-Louis Girodet, *Pietà*, 1790, 335 × 235 cm., Church of Montesquieu-
Volvestre, Haute-Garonne

In general terms, the pose of Girodet's Christ, the drastic
reduction of accessories, the proportional division of the format
effected by the horizontal sarcophagus, the angle of the light,
and the obscure upper zone created by the shadowy wall of the
cave—all provided David with clear cues in his conception of
Marat's moment of martyrdom. Another feature the paintings have
in common is the use of a fictive inscription that enters the name
of the painter into the commemoration of grief. And the most
obvious sign of David's use of Girodet's *Pietà* is the tracing of
the contour along the head and shoulders of the Virgin into the
line of the sarcophagus; in a startling transposition, this has become almost precisely the line of Marat's head and body as it
emerges above the bath.

For the third of his Revolutionary martyr portraits (Avignon,
Musée Calvet), however, David imagined Joseph Bara, a boy-victim
of the counter-Revolution, as an umblemished, eerily beautiful
ephebe, suffering but without visible wounds, dreaming more
than dying, near to but not within the fury of combat (fig. 7).
The commission came at the end of 1793, shortly after the completion of the *Marat*. A terse report had come from the campaign
against the violent counter-Revolution in the Vendée region of
the west of France: a young aide to a Republican officer had been
murdered trying to protect the horses of his superior. Over the
next few weeks, the story expanded in the minds of Robespierre
and others in the Jacobin leadership: the boy had been cut down
because, when commanded to say "Long live the King," he had
instead defiantly shouted "Long live the Republic." A festival in
his honor was voted in the National Convention, and David was
once again called upon to immortalize a martyr in paint.[15]

Where, we can ask, might he have gotten the idea that a
vision so insubstantial and erotically charged could be any kind
of persuasive representation of Revolutionary virtue? The regard
of the artist, with which we are invited to identify, appears to
have scandalously little to do with civic virtue or battlefield heroism, despite the charge to the painter. The sensuality of the body
goes beyond a beauty appropriate to its age and innocence. Commentators have assumed with near-unanimity that the painting
suffers from an overbalancing from the public to the private: that
the nudity, especially this kind of nudity, could carry anything

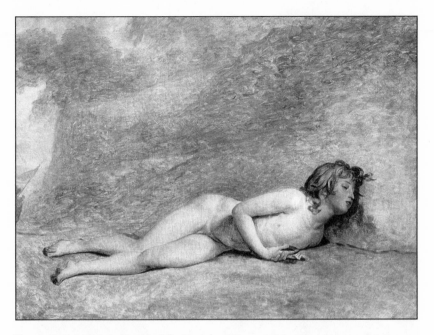

Fig. 7. Jacques-Louis David, *The Death of Bara,* 1794, 118 × 155 cm., Avignon, Musée Calvet

but an inappropriate or unseemly private significance has, until very recently, been close to an impossible thought.[16]

But this reasoning has gone on without considering David's well-established reliance on the work and example of his pupils when faced with a novel and difficult assignment. Girodet was, of course, absent from Paris in 1793—he would not return for two more years—but he was represented in Paris by the painting that made his reputation and that, in many ways, came to take over his identity: *The Sleep of Endymion* (Paris, Louvre) (fig. 8). In that picture, he had transformed the conventions of the nude *académie* into a floating vision of otherworldly beauty: the shepherd boy whom the smitten moon goddess has sent into perpetual sleep and who, as we see him, is illuminated by her nocturnal embrace.[17] It has been taken by modern commentators, particularly those on the Left, to have been the reversal of the politically engaged art of his master.[18] But the existence of the *Bara* is enough to suggest that this figure type at least, the languishing nude ephebe, was not so taken by David himself.[19]

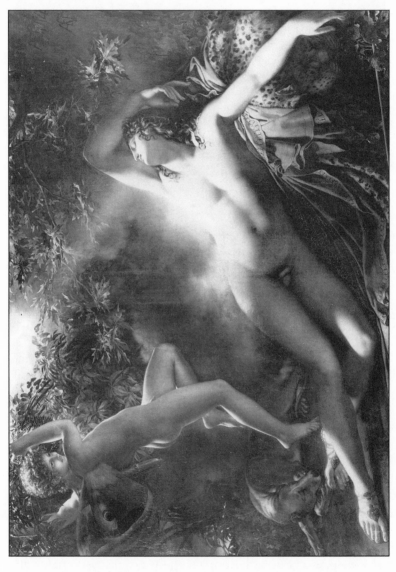

Fig. 8. Anne-Louis Girodet, *The Sleep of Endymion*, 1791, 198 × 261 cm., Paris, Louvre

The question that arises, then, is whether David's private fascinations with the subject, and perhaps with the *Endymion*, were simply leading him astray, or whether he had some cogent reasons for finding in Girodet's image an analogue to the state of sacrificial suffering he was required to envision in his *Bara*. Opting for the second, more positive alternative, we could see those reasons as being of two possible kinds: (1) the conspicuous originality of the image as an effort to express the supreme independence of the artist from any entrenched authority or hierarchy; and (2) a correlation of the image and Girodet's actual experience in Italy during 1792 and early 1793.

To begin with the first of these, what we might call the politicization of classical aesthetics, part of an explanation for David's response to the Bara commission may well lie in the pressure exerted on the genre of the nude academic study by his own followers—the late Drouais and Girodet in particular. In their hands, it had become a privileged emblem of virtue and self-sacrifice in youth. Just how this came about needs to be described.

*   *   *

The genre of the reclining male nude had been, since the mid-1780s, one of the principal instruments of the academy's authority. Since the reforms instituted by Vien on his assumption of the directorate in 1775, the satisfactory completion of such a study was one of the first requirements faced by the young prize-winners on their arrival in Rome, Drouais included.[20] At the same time, he was determined, as was David on his behalf, that he function as an independent creator obedient only to his own inner virtue, talent, and civic responsibility. The pupil outdid the master in refusing in every way open to him the hierarchy and control to which the pupils were required to submit.[21] Barred by entrenched authority from devoting his talents to the highest genre of narrative historical painting, he would do his utmost to elevate a demeaning obligation to the same exalted plane.

In his first effort, a work of 1785 conventionally titled *The Dying Athlete* (Paris, Louvre), he reached to invest a single body with complexity and inner differentiation characteristic of multi-figured narrative (fig. 9).[22] The work transforms the balanced studio pose on which it is based into a moment of tense concentration. The vacant upward stare of the model becomes a gaze of focused

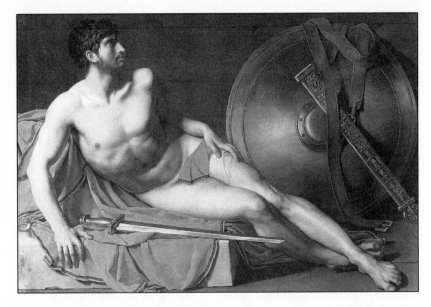

Fig. 9. Jean-Germain Drouais, *The Dying Athlete* (or *Wounded Soldier*), 1786, 125 × 183 cm., Paris, Louvre

inward and outward concentration. The effort it costs the warrior is registered in the contrast of the supporting right hand with the left. What had been no more than the model's fatiguing effort to maintain the pose becomes an inner determination to hold the body upright to the end, to refuse collapse into unconsciousness.

As depicted, the wound is all but invisible, but the entire body is organized to mark the spasm of pain that energizes the figure. Although the body as a whole seems fully drawn out along its continuous lower contour, it is in fact twisted unnaturally at the center along a harshly incised transition. Its languid extension is violated at the center of the torso in a contraction that reads as an involuntary spasm of pain. The raking light further throws that area into shadow so that the body is divided by zones of light and dark as well as by its disposition in space. The light is the zone of control; despite the wrenching pain, the warrior's reaction to it is limited to the dark zone; he resists and contains it so thoroughly that the overall beauty of his figure is undisturbed. In keeping with Winckelmann's notion of the beautiful style, the legs and the relaxed left hand of the *Athlete* express an unconscious grace we take to be innate in a noble character. That Praxitelian elegance, when maintained in the face of mortal suffering, is the source of the painting's drama and pathos—the pain alone would not suffice.

Drouais's nuanced command of the classical canon of male beauty as codified by Winckelmann is bound up with his anti-authoritarian stance as an artist. Thirty years or so after their first publication, the German antiquarian's ethical readings of ancient Greek sculpture had been taken up in pre-Revolutionary France and transformed into terms of open social critique: a corrupt state, it was said, produced corrupted bodies, imperfect flesh. An artist who could offer even a glimpse of physical perfection would, in the process, indict the corrupt state in which he lived.[23]

What is intriguing about the biographies of Winckelmann that appear in the 1780s is their ambition to make the antiquarian more than a mere guide to the heroic; he was to be a hero in his own right, a lonely, courageous figure who had struggled against adversity, prejudice, and entrenched privilege in order to reveal the true sources of a corrupted tradition.[24] Winckelmann the man was reconstructed as an analogue to the artistic persona prized in the studio of David: an artist equipped through a scholar's knowledge of antiquity to live out—against the odds—the devotion to civic virtue exemplified by his Greek forebears. This meant being responsible for one's own classical learning, and one was required to master Latin, if one did not know it already. At least two knew Greek.[25] In his characterization of grand and beautiful moments in Greek sculpture, Winckelmann had relied explicitly on rhetorical points of reference: the reader is to think of the angular, broken quality in the oratory of Demosthenes in order to comprehend the grand style in sculpture, the polished literary execution in Cicero to grasp the essence of the beautiful.[26] Drouais belonged to an emerging generation of artists who possessed independent access to these literary models and who were both motivated and equipped to follow and complicate this reasoning for themselves.

As they would have known, Winckelmann was far from the first to see the difference between rhetorical styles as figured in differences between male bodies—living bodies whose shape, musculature, fat, and skin are described with strong erotic overtones. In classical Greece, the grand style had been compared to the body of the ephebe, the young trained athlete: fleshy, amply developed, harmoniously proportioned; in contrast, the lower forensic style came to be compared to the body of the veteran soldier with its taut and lean muscularity. By the third century B.C., values had shifted to the point that soldierly strength and power began to seem as "grand" in their own way as full-fleshed, conspicuous symmetry and pleasing roundness. The agonistic strength of Demosthenes' manner was seen to embody the kind of elevation proper to impassioned public speech, the trained but untested body of the athlete belonged to the shaded grove of philosophical retreat.[27]

This figural transformation of rhetorical decorum into the imagination of male bodies to be contemplated and admired by male students of oratory was one means by which erotic charge was lent to the activity of verbal persuasion. For classicizing painters in early modern Europe, it provided a means by which the inherently erotic male nude could be invested with an articulateness appropriate for a broad range of messages. No one, before David's pupils, had mapped this continuum with greater effect than Poussin, principally in his early series of male nudes taken from Ovid and from Tasso's epic *Jerusalem Delivered*. In *Tancred and Erminia* (Birmingham, Barber Institute of Fine Arts), Tasso's great Christian warrior, after his fearful, bloody defeat of the pagan Argantes (canto 19), collapses and takes on the pose and beauty of that mythological paragon of beauty in death, Adonis, as seen in Poussin's nearly contemporaneous painting of the subject (Caen, Musée des Beaux-Arts). The body of a yet more imposing Crusader, Rinaldo, who stands in the allegory of the epic for the irascible and fierce, radiates an erotic desirability when surprised in sleep by the witch Armida (Dulwich Picture Gallery) (fig. 10).[28] His beauty is such that her intent to murder him is replaced by love: another form of triumph which ensures his ability to prevail on the battlefield in the future (canto 14:66).

The distinction between athlete and soldier can be resolved by creating a body that contains both—and here Drouais may have gone a step further than his great forebear. It is striking in this regard that Drouais's nude has been given two different titles. When it was sent back to Paris for judgment by the senior academicians in 1785, they called it *The Dying Athlete;* when it was

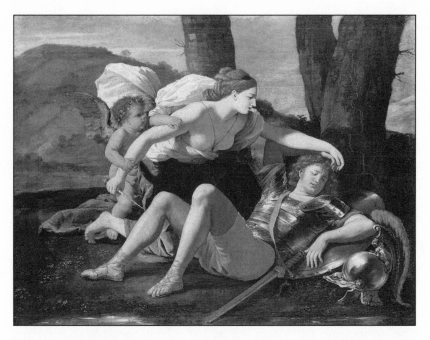

Fig. 10. Nicolas Poussin, *Rinaldo and Armida,* 82 × 109 cm., Dulwich Picture Gallery

engraved by Monsaldy, it was captioned *The Wounded Soldier.*[29] This divergence captures the complex double nature of the figure, and, in the two adjectives chosen, confirms this code of the hero's body. Only wounded, still capable of resistance, it is the taut soldier's body; finally surrendered to death, it becomes the unmarked, flawless body of the athlete. The body of the hero is one that can pass from one state to another, depending on circumstance. The grandeur and terror-inducing quality of the body in battle has as its counterpart a nautral beauty that his body assumes—as the preeminent sign of his heroic essence—when retired from field, either voluntarily or through injury and unconsciousness.

*   *   *

Drouais would never have the opportunity to finish another canvas on the theme of the heroic body.[30] In 1788, while still in Rome, Drouais died suddenly from smallpox. First place among the students now fell to Girodet, but it was to be no easy substitution. David, who had gone to Rome to paint the *Oath of the Horatii* in order not to be separated from his pupil, was inconsolable.[31] The bond between him and Drouais was far greater than mere pedagogy. In the early 1790s, during his time in Rome, Girodet did his best to match Drouais's example of independent behavior as well as his characteristic expressions of contempt for the Academy and its teaching.[32] The most acute problem that he faced was how to imitate Drouais's example of independence— and his transformation of the academic nude into an emblem of that independence—without falling into a dependent imitation of his predecessor.

At first glance, it would seem, the two figures could not be more unlike and still share the same genre. Unlike the tense, activated body of the Drouais *Athlete,* Girodet's languishing shepherd seems utterly sealed, closed and beyond time, a body that gives back to narcissistic desire its primitive dream of bliss in death. His compulsion to give this body an appearance of ever-youthful freshness led him to one spectacularly failed experiment: so that the painting would look forever as if it had just left the easel of its youthful maker, he mixed a large measure of olive oil in with the surface layer of pigment. The painting was to go on show in the student exhibition beginning August 25; in July he wrote despairingly to Gérard that the surface was never going to dry. He had to scrape it off and in a few weeks produce the astonishingly seamless skin to which the otherworldly effect of the painting owes so much.[33]

But that skin of the painting, which by a simple metaphor stands for the flawless surface of its subject, is one way that Girodet, as much as Drouais before him, is following the code of the hero's body. His Endymion wins the love of an initially hostile goddess (the fiercely *chaste* Diana) exactly as Rinaldo had charmed the supernatural Armida. He may have had every personal reason to want to produce a figure of timeless beauty and erotic charge, and to have others see him through it, but just wanting it would not have been enough to produce this result. Like a captive whose every struggle against his bonds draws them more tightly around him, Girodet's every effort to distinguish himself from Drouais makes his rival more the meaningful absence in the work, the essential location of the oppositional terms of reference that give force to each distinctive feature and quality in the *Endymion.*

And this play of opposition is articulated almost entirely through a shared rhetorical syntax of the heroic body.

To grasp the degree to which the markedly original overall character of the *Endymion* can be generated through a systematic reversal of the *Athlete's* distinctive features, we could even create a table:

Athlete	*Endymion*
Suffused with muscular tension	Drained of tension
Disfigured	Physically flawless
Suffering	In a state of bliss
Resisting an unyielding environment	Yielding to pliant, enveloping environment
Left without human aid	Embraced by divine devotion
Ready with his weapons	Has discarded weapons
Hyperconscious	Never conscious
Described with unnatural clarity	Described with a diffuse but natural obscurity

Having derived the broad characteristics of his figure from a systematic opposition to Drouais's example, Girodet was then able—and this is the genius of the painting—to incorporate the play of opposing qualities into the very syntax of representing the ideal nude. The effect of a radiantly integrated body is won from a difficult manipulation of the code of the nude that preserves the internal complexity of potential appropriate to the hero.

The outline of the figure, for example, while firm and complete at first glance, refuses wholeness as we follow its linear course. The integration of the body with its surrounding atmosphere is an effect dependent on a continuously shifting play between clarity and obscurity of outline; the harder, highlighted areas are just hard enough to prevent the body from submerging itself in the haze; the soft, shadowed ones just sufficient to prevent the body coming free from its surrounding matrix. The body is legible as a whole, and so is the entire painted surface, because of this oscillating, unfixed play of difference.

Accompanying this play of line are unexpected reversals in the normal scale and relative presence of the body's parts: the features of the face are hardly present; they offer not so much a profile as a compression of the face into a narrow illuminated zone, contrasted with the large, almost grotesque area of neck in emphatic shadow. This insistence on reversal extends to the accompanying Zephyr/Eros figure, which is rendered in such a way that the edges of his body are drawn with light rather than dark tones that normally indicate the recession and disappearance of three-dimensional form; shadow moves from the edge of the body to its center. And then there is the largest division of light and shade, the one that divides the body into its upper and lower zones. The desire of the goddess, reduced to moonlight and removed from any obvious gender location of its own, is displaced from the privileged phallic location of male desire, allowing the question of Endymion's sexual identity to be suspended. The sharp line of shadow cuts in a horizontal line directly across the swelling curve of the hip and just above the genital zone. The male Eros, who stands in for the absent woman, opens the way to the moonlight with a look of malicious pleasure. His simultaneous provision and denial of light is the largest display of pure difference in the painting. It generates less a castration of the male body—as some have seen it[34]—than a perpetual displacement of its stability of gender.

It is that systematic instability which organizes the separate qualities of the figure—the elongated and tapering legs, the ringlets of hair, the compressed Greek profile, the abandonment of consciousness—into its pervasive effect of androgyny. But to see this "androgyny" as only or mainly about sexual desire—its confusion, multiplication, or cancellation—is to impose a present-day limitation of reading on the body. It is to fail to see the other boundary crossings that are simultaneously at work in it: youth and age; inexperience and maturity; the timeless and the instantaneously immediate. It is a body that is removed from life yet never decays; that is subject to perpetual repetitions of sensual pleasure yet is never exhausted by them; that is trained like an athlete of antiquity for war yet remains forever untouched by

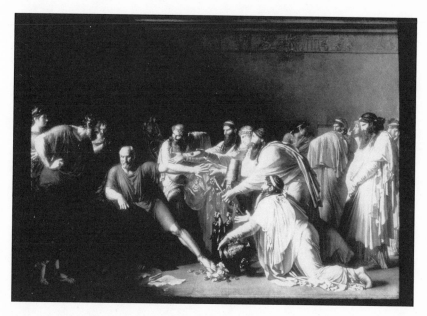

Fig. 11. Anne-Louis Girodet, *Hippocrates Refusing the Gifts of Artaxerxes*, 1792, 99.5 × 135 cm., Paris, Faculté de Médecine

violence, knowing death only in the midst of ecstatic animation of the nerves, muscles, blood, and skin. These are the components of its construction of the human ideal, which is then situated between two poles of observable, nonhuman nature: the impalpable energy of light and the substantial, tactile presence of botanical and entomological specimens.

The startling originality and apparently non-Davidian character of the *Endymion* should thus be understood as a move in the same game begun by Drouais, with every encouragement from David. The project of negation, because ruled by the power of the identical code, enfolds him in an embrace of continuity. Though the painting was certainly an effort to surpass and distinguish himself from Drouais's example in this genre, it involved no permanent separation from the mainstream work of the studio, still less from the political ideals embodied in that work. It was indeed *after* the *Endymion* that Girodet produced the most purely Davidian composition of his career, *Hippocrates Refusing the Gifts of Artaxerxes* (Paris, Ecole de Médecine) (fig. 11). Outside of the crucible that the academic nude had become, he displayed his lineage, artistic and political, without apology. Here, as in David's *Socrates*, an exemplary Greek sage surrounded by disciples makes a declaration of patriotic devotion: no amount of riches would make him heal the enemy when his own people were in danger.

Some months after he completed the *Hippocrates*, Girodet wrote to the National Convention in Paris, on behalf of his fellow students in Rome, promising that they were ready to live out the patriotism allegorized in that painting:

> The citizen-pupils [of the Rome Academy] will hold dear the happy day that brought them to the nourishing breast of their country; guided by their love of her, would they ever forget for a moment that their duty is to perpetuate from age to age the memory of virtuous deeds? Happy if they can play their part by planting in the hearts of their fellow citizens the sentiments with which they themselves are inspired; happier still if, having rendered to our country the homage of their talents, they can spill their blood in her defense.[35]

This document, signed in a body by the students of the Academy but composed by Girodet, played its part in a growing conflict between the French artists and the Papacy in the autumn of 1792. In the first months of the Republic, Rome, more than Paris, forced the issue of what it meant to be a Jacobin artist. It was largely a war of symbols, but symbols that counted for real forms of power and the risk of life and death. In the midst of it, Girodet was represented by his ardent Revolutionary rhetoric in the political discourse of Paris. This brings us to the second part of the pupil's example to the master. By the summer of 1793, shortly before the display of the *Endymion* in the Salon, his representation would take on heroic proportions in the shape of an extraordinary story— in the literal sense of manufactured text—that was available to anyone in Paris and that was specifically addressed to David. In effect, the older artist, as he faced the task of memorializing Bara, was on the receiving end of two powerful messages from Girodet— two forms of difficult and challenging loyalty—one in paint and the other in a political narrative of heroic action. Before discussing aspects of David's actual translation of the *Endymion*'s ephebic body type into that of the boy-martyr, it will be important to establish the circumstances linked to the young artist's example of personal courage on the stage provided by the ancient cradle of republican liberty.

*   *   *

The text in question was a pamphlet, dated June 1793, entitled *The Death of Bassville, or, The Conspiracy of Pius VI Unmasked.*[36] Its author was Michel Cubières-Palméyzeau, a veteran of the literary underground who had put himself forward in Year I as an enthusiastic Jacobin publicist with ties to the Commune of Paris (which subsidized the pamphlet). Its subject was what might well be counted, before Le Peletier and Marat, the first martyrdom of the new Republic, that of Hugou de Bassville, the de facto if irregular French envoy to the Papal States, who had been murdered in Rome by an ultra-Catholic mob on the previous 13 January.[37] Both the factual circumstances of Bassville's assassination and the way that it was reported would have affected the interpretation, in that volatile moment, of any painting by Girodet.

The text begins, "You know, my dear master . . .," at which point an asterisk directs the reader to this explanatory note:

> This is not the author who is speaking, but a young French artist, a pupil of David, a resident of Rome at the time of Bassville's murder, and an eyewitness of the facts that he will relate. The author believed it appropriate to render this account in the first person in his voice in order to lend to the narration greater fluency, vividness, and fire.[38]

There are a number of reasons why Girodet would have presented himself as a suitable narrator, in whom this impetuosity, spirit, and veracity would have been plausible. The first is that the catalyst for the murder was the making of an image in which Girodet had a direct hand. This was a female personification of liberty, an early Marianne, the central emblem of the arms of the Republic as improvised by the students in Rome. After the declaration of the French Republic in September 1792, the Papacy had withdrawn diplomatic recognition from the French mission in Rome. Only a caretaker consular presence remained. Harassment of French citizens in Rome by Swiss soldiers and Catholic zealots increased, tacitly or not so tacitly encouraged by the church authorities. Toward the end of the year, Bassville arrived from Naples, where the French fleet held the port. Though charged only with

the task of gathering information, he soon assumed control of
French diplomacy, insisting on an assertive Republican presence
and making repeated peremptory demands for concessions from
the Papacy. The director of the Academy had by this time resigned,
and in his absence, Bassville made the Academy his virtual head-
quarters. At that moment in Paris, David took the opportunity
to demand a removal—more than that, an auto-da-fé—of all
royalist symbols and insignia in the Rome Academy.[39] And the
order was given that the arms of the Republic were to be hung
above the portal of the Academy in place of the fleur-de-lis.
David's insistence on this point may have come from ignorance,
but what he was proposing was a reckless endangerment of the
lives of the students. For the issue of the arms of the Republic
coming to grace the Academy was precisely the one that brought
the wrath of the Papacy down on their heads.

The impertinent Bassville had been tolerated, it seems, as
long as he had the fleet at his back, but in December it was
surprised by a storm while leaving port and largely disabled. After
that, some kind of violent retaliation in Rome was probably inevitable; there was no longer any restraint on the popular clergy
and the formation of anti-Republican mobs. Bassville, by January,
had taken the precaution of removing most of the pupils of the
Academy to Florence or Naples, both still friendly to France. He
still remained, at grave and growing personal risk, intent on showing the Republican colors.

The fictional Girodet declares that "it was I who traced in
silence the figure of liberty; and the dangers grew around me; it
is you then, they said to me with harsh irony, who should make
this marvelous figure."[40] The last statement is presumably directed
to hostile Romans, whom he goes on to address:

> Yes, it was I, vile slaves, unworthy of the name of Roman, which
> you have disgraced and made an object of contempt for peoples
> everywhere; yes, it was none other than I, and know that if I
> tried to paint it, I would know still better how to defend it.
>
> This celestial figure was not yet finished, when the Pope,
> fearing the effect that one sight of it could produce, prohibited
> its display.

The basic facts related here are correct. Girodet was one of
only four French students left at the Academy, and the primary

responsibility for the arms fell to him. The Pope and his chief minister had made a particular issue of the change in national insignia. Bassville, on 13 January, paid with his life for that project when a mob attacked his carriage and, pursuing his party into the French consular quarters, murdered him. At the same time, a crowd had gathered around the Academy to prevent forcibly any Republican displays. Cubières's text relates it this way:

> We were just ready to finish the features of our adored mistress; we were giving the last touches of the brush to her forceful features, when we hear a rumbling sound in the street; it grows louder, increasing by degrees, and soon enough a lawless rabble, composed of provocateurs, escaped convicts, brigands and assassins, bursts into the Academy in confusion. They spread throughout the courtyards, rooms, and staircases, smashing in a few moments all the doors and windows, turning over the statues, mutilating the paintings, tearing and treading them underfoot, and leaving behind only a vast heap of debris out of masterpieces of painting and sculpture. . . .
>
> We heard all of this, our brushes still in hand and hands suspended in the air [while] the assassins had no more than twenty steps to mount to slaughter us beneath the very eyes of Liberty herself.[41]

Now let me switch from this text to another account of the same event:

> We still had brushes in hand when the furious rabble burst in, and instantly reduced the doors, windows, and panes to dust. They had only twenty steps to mount in order to assassinate us; . . . we had to descend a hundred steps under the blows of rifle butts to reach the street, where we found ourselves abandoned and without aid in the midst of this rabble thirsty for our blood. . . .
>
> The tortuous streets and our cool heads saved us for the moment. Escaping this danger and believing that I was taking all precautions, I proceeded to hurl myself into further peril: I ran to the house of Bassville at the very moment of his murder. . . . I ducked into an Italian house two steps from there and stayed inside until nightfall. I was foolhardy enough then to return to the Academy, which had become the Palace of Priam. The mob was ready to put it to the torch.

Thanks, says this writer, to a lucky encounter with a loyal former
model, he escaped the wrath of the mob a second time (hearing
as he went into hiding their shouts of "Vive le pape! Vive la
Madone! Périssent les Français!").

This overlapping narrative comes from one of Girodet's own
letters to his foster father Trioson.[42] His private account anticipates
the public one concocted by Cubières, and this remains the case
right through to the description of his eventually reaching a safe
refuge in Naples (after days of travel on foot and an encounter
with storms and murderous brigands in the Pontine marshes). The
public representation of Girodet as Jacobin hero was continuous
with the one he created for his intimates and for himself.[43] And
with the orthodoxly Davidian *Hippocrates* still in Italy, the only
available embodiment of that representation in paint was the
Endymion.

If it came to stand for him as an alter ego in Paris, that
ascription of meaning would not have been arbitrary; it would
have made sense for reasons other than the evident narcissistic
self-identification present in it. First, that reading accorded with
the ideological association, founded in the aesthetic writings of
Winckelmann, between the physical perfection achieved by the
ancients and their free society of equal, active citizens. Girodet's
vision of male physical perfection could carry all the more authority
because it emanated directly from a privileged site of republican
virtue.[44] As Cubières has him saying at one point, in words consistent with the artist's actual letter to the Convention,

> We have crowned [the bust of Brutus] with leaves of laurel and
> oak; we have made libation after libation in its honor. . . . Is it
> a crime to inaugurate the image of Brutus in the country of
> his birth and at the very moment when we believed that we
> could see his ghost walking among us?[45]

Second, that vision of physical perfection carried with it a statement of precocious originality in style and conception that was
motivated by the same antiauthoritarian stance—youth against
age, the free citizen against lackeys of despotism—initiated by
David and Drouais. Their countercultural stance had transformed
the reading of history painting in such a way that the virtue
inherent in a picture was to be found as much or more in its form

as in the actions depicted. Arresting and powerful form, moreover, was seen to proceed from the virtue of the embattled artist; the work and the creator had been made inseparable.

The events in Rome of 1792–93 brought these two strands of ideology together: the politically utopian veneration of antiquity was joined with idealization of the artist as enemy of despotism and man of action. And it all centered on Girodet, making his *Endymion* potentially the most persuasive demonstration to date of Winckelmann's vaguely theorized link between the physical perfection of the ancients and the free conditions of their society.

*   *   *

It may be then that the account given so far—of David's habitual dependence on his student's work, and on Girodet's in particular, of the emancipatory ambitions invested in the *Endymion*'s originality, of the aura of revolutionary heroics surrounding Girodet's name—can go some way to explain David's choice of an idealized nude ephebe for his last martyr portrait. But such an explanation, if left there, would make David's reading a superficial one; it would say little about the specific character of the *Bara*, particularly the eerie effacement of the genitals that accompanies the girlish body shape and child's face. Do these features represent independent departures on David's part, or can they too be included in the dialogue between master and pupil?

Here, as in the consideration of either painting individually, to begin with the appearance of "androgyny," as if this were a settled quality, would be a mistake. To approach the level of discerning apprehension that David would have brought to his student's work—and to avoid the dangers of anachronism—we need to set aside the effect of a closed, complete image and attend to the mechanisms in the painting that produce it. The *Endymion*'s inspired interplay of conceptual oppositions would have corresponded to the difficult combination of ideas and conditions bound up in the Bara commission. How was David to move from the celebration of mature martyrs—Le Peletier and Marat—who were significant historical actors, known personally to the artist, to an unknown boy? How was he to ennoble what was at best a trivially unlucky act of bravado—one that may in fact have had no actual revolutionary motivation? How was he to find unstereotypical form for the abstract stereotypes of outraged innocence and the sacrifice of youth with which he was forced to work, following Robespierre's unreal dictum that "the French alone have thirteen-year-old heroes"?[46] The *Endymion* had made the flawless ephebe a plausible vehicle for this kind of complexity of meaning.

Large problems of translation, of course, remained. David could no more appropriate the *Endymion* prototype directly than Girodet could have done with that of Drouais's *Athlete*. Questions of original stylistic signature aside, the story of Bara's death had to be depicted with an immediacy and total visibility that made the frozen stillness and obscurity of Endymion's nocturnal bower unusable. The nervous scumbling with which the body and its setting alike are rendered amounts to an appropriation of the glassy atmospheric unity of figure and ground achieved by Girodet. The reversal of technique—from sealed to porous, one might say— allows the master to make the pupil's innovation his own.[47]

But when it came to the suppression of the genitals—doubly imperative in light of the mandate that David represent outraged innocence and the special object of a *mother*'s love—the overall illumination and blond light deprived him of the device of veiling shadow. David's response was to take the boy's body and break it in two, simultaneously to figure its suffering and to downplay its sex. And it is here that the trouble with the image begins. The body of Bara is twisted unnaturally at its center; that, along with the shadowed abdomen, is the mark of the body's violation, the bayonet wound to the midsection that killed the boy (this device directly recalls Drouais's *Athlete*). Part of what produces the body's unnatural twist is the curious position of the legs, the upper one behind the lower. As the boy seems to be rolling over onto his chest, the expected position of the legs would be the reverse of this.

The logic for the anomalous arrangement comes from an identifiable substitution of a direct classical analogue to the *Endymion:* for this area David has borrowed the hips and legs of the Borghese *Hermaphrodite,* but as seen from the rear, not from the front (fig. 12). The derivation of the design of the *Marat* from the contour of the Virgin in Girodet's *Pietà* showed a tendency on David's part to abstract and displace patterns of line from other works of art. Here the entire upper contour of Bara's body, particularly the raised hip, is determined by a similar superimposition of the two-

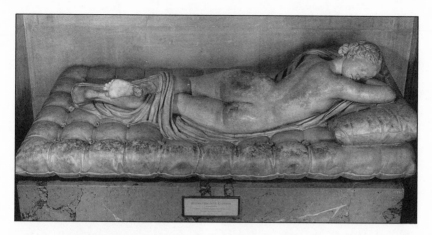

Fig. 12. *Hermaphrodite,* marble, Paris, Louvre

dimensional contour of the *Hermaphrodite,* while the strangely effaced treatment of the genitals follows the pattern of lines created by the lower buttocks and inner thighs of the antique statue. This borrowed undecidability of gender, overlaying the representation of an unseen but mortal wound, leads to an eerie undecidability of point of view: a simultaneous transparency and reversal at the primary locus of erotic sensation.

Much of the strangeness of the image is derived from this clash of two incompatible bodies in one. Wound, absent genitalia, and anus become conflated in a way that leaves the painting undecidably positioned between public and private interest, between the sayable and the unsayable.[48] Girodet's *Endymion* had been the result of an adroit set of moves within the established codings of the hero's body, motivated by an intense wish to construct a self distinct from the luminous Drouais and therefore maximally distanced from the latter's approach to the nude figure. David struggles here to retain his mastery by taking possession of both prototypes at once, to accommodate the heroic endurance of pain within the erotically replete conflation of *Endymion* and the Hellenistic *Hermaphrodite.* But this condensation of their distinct positions within the visual codes of the nude hero generates dissonance, even cacophony, smoothed into a provisional consistency by a thousand touches of the hand.

The logic of substitution and reversal that guided David's handling of Girodet's ephebic prototype, while comprehensible,

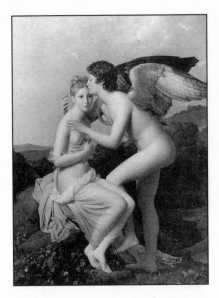

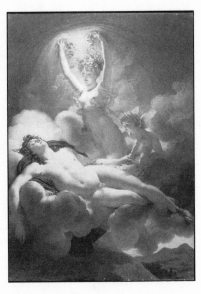

Fig. 13. François Gérard, *Cupid
and Psyche*, 1798, oil on canvas,
186 × 132 cm., Paris, Louvre

Fig. 14. Guérin, *Aurora and
Cephalus*, 1811, oil on canvas,
254 × 186 cm., Leningrad, Hermitage

was thus no guarantee of legibility. The *Endymion*, itself the
product of substitution and reversal of the distinctive features of
a previous prototype, could be said ultimately to have suffered a
similar fate, but for different reasons. The painting had evolved
along a course that was engaged and politicized in its motivation,
but the logic of that course meant that the painting was more
and more invested in reference to the realm of art, to the negation
of the overt effects—if not the inner logic—of David's and
Drouais's challenging precedents. In the atmosphere of political
amnesia fostered under the Directory, those precedents lost their
force, lost their ability to activate the differential meanings re-
coverable in the *Endymion*. Girodet's community had stopped
speaking the same language.

   In a way, the less attractive, private component of his practice
is factored out following the fall of Robespierre. In his *Cupid and
Psyche* of 1799 (Paris, Louvre), Girodet's old studio companion
Gérard led the way in capturing the *Endymion*'s sealed envelope
of flesh and delivering it to a strain of precious eroticism that
sought a place beyond the vicissitudes of political orthodoxy (fig.

13). In the wake of Gérard's initiative came a chain of languishing androgynes openly dependent on Girodet's example, including Broc's *Death of Hyacinth* (Poitiers, Musée Sainte-Croix) and the *Iris and Morpheus* and *Aurora and Cephalus* (both Leningrad, Hermitage) of the inevitable Guérin, the artist who most faithfully attended to the prevailing winds (fig. 14). When the languages of the Revolution broke down, the painting could be taken and used as a token of the refusal of public meanings altogether. The interpretation offered here does not pretend that the private and subjective meanings we see as naturally inhering in Girodet's *Endymion* are not present. His antagonism toward David, his jealous resentment of Drouais's priority, were powerfully overdetermined. But between 1790 and 1793, he had a public context available in which they could make another kind of sense.

III. THE PRIVATE AND THE PUBLIC

Patrice Higonnet

Joint Suicide in Eighteenth-Century French
Literature and Revolutionary Politics

I

MANY PEOPLE KILLED THEMSELVES DURING THE FRENCH REVOLUTION:
Montagnards like Romme, Goujon, and Soubrany; Girondins like
Clavière, Buzot, and Roland; *enragés* like Roux; and Communists
like Babeuf. As did, for that matter, many moderates and royalists
like Chamfort and Le Peletier's assassin, Pâris. And the fascinated
spectators of this dramatic solution to man's earthly condition
included, it often seemed, the entire elite of the revolutionized
French nation. The *patriotes* of 1793 assumed as a matter of course,
for example, that even the imprisoned king would try to end his
days: Louis XVI, a devout Christian, had no such intention; but
it is revealing that his captors should have thought he did.

The *discours suicidaire* of the 1780s is vast. Even the minor
question of its explicit roots is an expansive matter. Of obvious
relevance to that narrow issue are ancient literary texts (Plato,
Cicero, Plutarch) and stoic philosophy generally. But many other
suicidal models were present in the minds of French men and
women in 1789, ranging from English drama, with Addison's *Cato*
of 1713, to contemporary texts by Montesquieu, Voltaire, Rousseau, and Goethe. No less memorable was a long and rich icono-
graphic tradition of male (Cato) and female (Lucretia) self-
destruction, renewed during the last decades of the Ancien Régime
by Sébastien Adam, Beaufort, Chasles, Coypel, Fragonard, Hallé,
Angelica Kaufman, Perrin, Scottin, and many others. The death

of Socrates alone galvanized the pictorial energies of Dandré-Bardon, Challe, Sané, Peyron, and Jacques-Louis David (1748–1825), himself a failed suicide who had authored in 1773 a baroque treatment of the deaths of Seneca and his wife Pauline. And that Roman story had broad resonance in turn: the fate of Nero's former tutor was for the *philosophes* a parable of the scholar's fate in troubled times that Diderot developed at some length.

In short, the problem of voluntary death is of scope, and this dimension will warrant—or so we will assume—our narrower concern in these few pages, namely, the more limited theme in both literature and politics of *joint* suicide. We will leave aside the more accessible and in any case ideologically quite different problematic of "single person suicides" (examples of which abound in both literature and history) to focus on those rarer instances of chosen death that involve both self and "other."[1]

In literature as against history, joint and voluntary death had already achieved notorious consistency long before the Revolution in *La Nouvelle Héloïse* of 1761, with its two celebrated letters on chosen death. In the first, deeply felt, Saint-Preux justifies suicide. In the second, lamely phrased, an Englishman, Milord Edouard, forcefully but inadequately condemns what was often known in eighteenth-century France as an English malady.

Rousseau, in these pages, considers chosen death from a number of perspectives, including that of joint suicide:

> O what a pleasure for two sincere friends voluntarily to end their days in each other's arms, to intermingle their latest breath, and at the same instant to give up the soul they shared in common! What pain, what regret can infect their last moments? What do they quit by taking leave of the world? They go together; they quit nothing.[2]

Saint-Preux directs this proposal to his male friend, Milord Edouard, but the interesting grammatical indeterminacy of "*amis*" allows us to suppose that the perfect sentimental suicide would have ideally involved Julie instead, as develops in due course:

> But to be by her side, to see her, to touch her, and whilst I almost enjoyed her again, to find her lost to me for ever; this

was what threw me into such fits of fury and rage, as by degrees agitated me even to despair. My mind soon began to conceive deadly projects, and in a transport, which I yet tremble to think of, I was violently tempted to throw her with myself into the waves, and to end my days and tedious torments in her arms. This horrid temptation grew so strong at last, that I was obliged to walk to the other end of the boat.[3]

It is suggestive that Rousseau may have originally intended to close this most influential novel of the age on this very note, that is, with a murder/suicide.[4]

That, he did not do. But this world-literary task was taken up by Nicolas-Germain Léonard. Born in 1744 in the Guadeloupe where he again resided between 1787 and 1792, Léonard died in Nantes on 6 January 1793. While at Liège, where he was posted for a decade as a diplomat, Léonard composed in 1773 *Le Tombeau des deux amants,* a work reminiscent of his 1771 verse elaboration of Rousseau's two letters on suicide, a publication that he entitled *Epître à un ami sur le dégoût de la vie.* It was at Liège also that Léonard published in 1783 his extremely well-received novel, *Lettres de deux amants habitants de Lyon,* a title that was clearly meant to echo the subtitle of Rousseau's *Héloïse, Lettres de deux amants habitans d'une petite ville au pied des Alpes.*[5]

Rousseau's suicidal *Héloïse* had its source in Jean-Jacques's imagination, but Léonard's more mundane text had its origin in a "fait divers," a joint suicide that had taken place at Lyon in 1770, and that, revealingly, had in its own right achieved considerable notoriety.[6] Although by no means the first[7] or last[8] incident of this kind, it was the first such double suicide to become a durable literary event.[9] Rousseau, who may have been residing at Lyon at the time it took place, wrote an epitaph for the young couple:

> Ci-gissent [sic] deux Amans; l'un pour l'autre ils vécurent,
> L'un pour l'autre ils sont morts, et les Loix en murmurent.
> La simple pitié n'y trouve qu'un forfait;
> Le sentiment admire, et la raison se tait.[10]

Typically, however, Voltaire's reason was less mute than Rousseau's. He mentioned the event in his *Correspondance,* albeit ambiguously. In one letter, Voltaire did compare this modern double suicide to the classical story of Petus and Arria (Pete, non dolet!) as he did again in his *Questions sur l'Encyclopédie*. In another letter, however, he added that he would like to know more about the true motivation of the deed: "It seems to me that the reasons given for it are not worth very much."[11]

The episode was widely discussed. Voltaire wrote that "the entire city of Lyon has witnessed it," and it must have struck his own imagination as well since he included a long description of it in his *Questions sur l'Encyclopédie*, which he happened to be working on that summer. In May 1770, the *Journal Encyclopédique* of Bouillon also ran a story on this "scène affreuse."[12] The event had many other literary echoes, of which Léonard's book, duly translated into English, was, however, and by far, the most widely known.[13] Léonard improved on the original. Voltaire had already ennobled the dramatis personae in the *Questions* (the young man had been, he wrote "very well known, handsome, well built, likable, [and] very talented")[14] but Léonard went much further. In his book, the young woman, Marie Thérèse Loret, who in actuality had been the twenty-year-old daughter of an innkeeper, is transmogrified into Thérèse *de* Saint-Cyran.[15] Faldoni, her lover—in actual fact a sickly thirty-year-old fencing master—is also "aristocratized" as "a well-born young man, ill favored by fortune." Like Saint-Preux, Léonard's fictional Faldoni is the victim of unfeeling race-proud prejudice. He fights a novelistic duel with the arrogant brother of Thérèse. The theme had decided appeal, and De Pezey's moralistic *Les Tableaux,* with its fourteen illustrated situations (which ranged from charity and self-sacrifice to voyeurism and seduction), included an elaborate description of the two lovers, whose story "has been carried forth by a thousand voices to all the corners of Europe from the banks of the Rhône which served as its theater."[16]

Many other pre-Revolutionary and literary variants of this same apolitical, sentimental, and sacrificial theme could be cited here. Thomas, for example, in his celebrated *Essai sur le caractère, les moeurs et l'esprit des femmes dans les différents siècles,* approvingly cites Plutarch's account of a woman who had to poison herself to be able to murder her husband's murderer: "I lived only to avenge my husband . . . ," she explains to the dying assassin who has wedded her. "That has been done. As for you, instead of a nuptial couch, ask that they prepare your tomb."[17]

Conceptually, however, such texts add little to either Rousseau's inspiration or to Léonard's elaboration of the theme; and on the basis essentially of these two epistolary texts, we can point to the emergence of a particular literary genre: two young innocents, obsessed by themselves and each other, disclose the whole of their private, unembellished, and hopeless love to the voyeuristic reader. They show to the pre-Revolutionary reading public that a joint, reflected death is preferable to separate, disjointed, haphazard lives. Joint death in love is preferable, they say, to alienating, individuated life in the world as it stands. Private self-destruction creates the fulfillment that is denied by a corrupted public life.

The *practical* effect of these various literary productions must, of course, be considered separately. That this literary genre, though widely esteemed, ever inspired any actual joint suicides in "real life" is very much to be doubted. In the early 1780s, a friend of Mme de Charrière and an acquaintance of Clavière, the twenty-nine-year-old Swiss and Calvinist minister Chaillet (born 1751), did indeed consider joint suicide with his friend Mademoiselle Du Pasquier (born 1756). He had read *La Nouvelle Héloïse* in 1769 ("Oh! Rousseau! Your book is the favorite work of sensitive hearts!") and in 1777, he had also read (and purchased) *Werther:* "Heaven be praised! I have *Werther!* I have bought it. It is mine." In a suicide and farewell note (never sent) he asked that his copy of *Werther* not be handed down to a stranger but burned. He also explained to his "cold friends" that he planned to die not from impatience, or madness, or to escape from the woes of life, but because long and serious meditation had convinced him that as far as he was concerned, such was "the good and wise will of God in Jesus Christ for me."[18]

But in fact, and quite typically, the young Chaillet did not kill himself. (He lived to be seventy-two.) His "non-death" has of course its comic side. In 1812, Julien-Louis Geoffroy, a celebrated drama critic and former Revolutionary journalist who worked during the First Empire to revive classical literary taste, commented on that very subject in his review of a much criticized and soon to be parodied theatrical version of Léonard's book, a play entitled *Célestine and Faldoni* by Jean-Batiste Augustin

Hapdé that was performed at the Odéon in June 1812.[19] "Some respectable people," snickered Geoffroy, "fear that this drama will make amorous suicides fashionable. Let them rest at ease. This example will not be contagious in Paris: although it might work up some southern heads, the progress of civilization opposes such a mania."[20]

Like Chaillet's survival, however, Geoffroy's superficial wit becomes more interesting if we translate its racist terms to say that before and after the Revolutionary upheaval, neither the literary myth of double suicide nor the fame of the *amants de Lyon* could exert a decisive appeal.

Rousseau and Léonard no doubt elicited many tears, but before 1789, nothing much could come of them. Only the Revolution could transform a *fait divers* (however celebrated) or a novelistic, cultural value (or fad), however appealing, into a serious vocation of public sacrifice.

II

After 1789, joint suicide as such was not perceived as a patriotic act. Just as Revolutionary Jacobinism drastically simplified the varieties of pre-Revolutionary and enlightened thought, so did the Revolution winnow among antecedent models of self-destruction. In this ideological triage, joint and sentimental suicide was well beyond the boundaries of Jacobin orthodoxy.

This fall from Revolutionary grace is not surprising. From 1792 to 1795, all progressive political groups did indeed approve of chosen death, but only of *patriotic* and heroic chosen death. For obvious reasons, sentimental suicide in its "untranscended" forms had become in these years irrelevant politically. Jacobinism did begin in 1789 with the rights of the individual, including the right to take one's life for whatever reason: Marat (1743–93,) Lequinio (1755–1814), and Carnot (1753–1823) argued for it on those grounds. But when Jacobinism drifted in the spring of 1794 toward a radical extension of the public sphere, privately motivated voluntary, sentimentalized death suddenly seemed purposeless.

For pre-Revolutionary Christian theologians, whether Catholic like the abbé Barruel or Protestant like Jean Dumas, the bodies of men belonged not to man but, invariably, to God, a filiation of proprietorship that sidestepped the complicated question of suicidal martyrdom, an issue which had puckishly fascinated many Enlightenment polemicists including Voltaire and Diderot.

The Jacobins replicated in some ways the arguments of the Christian divines. They too did not think that men or women owned their bodies.[21] After 1789, God obviously no longer signified, but corporeal property remained an issue. For the Jacobins, men's bodies now belonged to the French nation, just as the bodies of women belonged not to themselves, but to their Republican heroic husbands.

In this context, to die with one's lover, or worse yet, *for* one's lover, was obvious proof of an inappropriate and even *aristocrate* frame of mind. In the apolitical literature of the Old Regime, fictitious men and women of sensibility could imagine their joint and sentimental voluntary deaths as acts of private social protest that would galvanize the reading public. (Suicides were commonly reported in the press before 1789.) But in the explicitly politicized and embattled world of 1793, men certainly—and women also— were required to be not just more practical and stoic but far more civic-minded: in 1795, Romme, the future *martyr de prairial,* wrote about himself to his mother that he had brought "to my prison the love of the public good." But to his wife, he wrote instead (after asking her for a volume of Rousseau's works) to remind her that her body belonged to their (Republican) child to be:

> Think of the child that you are carrying in your womb. Grief,
> if you yielded to it, might preclude a happy birth. Do all you
> can to conserve a fruit worthy of our love of equality.[22]

René Dumas, a vice-president of the Revolutionary Tribunal, explained this same social arithmetic to the suicide-prone Adam Lux, a doomed admirer of Charlotte Corday: "I wish to remind you that a good citizen spills his blood only for the fatherland or for his own liberty." And revealingly, Lux's instinct was to justify his self-destructive inclination by placing it squarely within the context of the Tribunal's Jacobinical perspective: "I wished to [kill myself] because I wished to be free."[23]

In Jacobin orthodoxy, liberty and death went hand in hand. The prospect of annihilation made the dream of liberty more sublime. But public responsibilities always had precedent over private desires: "A Republican woman," explains a character in Briois's play *La Mort du jeune Barra,* "owns nothing. Her property, her children, her husband, everything belongs to her homeland. [Tout est à son pays.]"[24] As Cécile explained about her appropriately named lover Victor in a play by Aristide Valcour, performed at the Opéra Comique in April 1794:

> If my lover succumbed, Cécile would weep over his death. But she would have the courage to outlive him. She would be brave enough to give her hand in marriage to one of his companions. What is the happiness of one individual when set against the salvation of the Republic?[25]

More nobly, Mme Roland, who conceived herself to be both passionate and virile, testified to the same hierachy of private and public sentiment in a letter addressed to her aforementioned friend Gilbert Romme:

> I do not know if you are in love, but I do know that in our circumstances, a good and honest man can only follow love's torch if he has kindled his passion on the altar of the fatherland.[26]

Beaurepaire's patriotic suicide at Verdun in September 1792 was much praised, as were later the near-suicides of Bara and Viala and many others. But a good citizen, though he might exemplarily kill himself for the Revolution, was required to choose life for the Republic over self-indulgent and sentimental death. Suicide as such was neither good nor bad. Everything depended on the reading of chosen death that the victim left for posterity.

Politics and passion were ordinarily disassociated in Revolutionary self-destruction, even for women. Mary Wollstonecraft— who was as politicized a private person as one could hope to find—did not link the private and the public in the melancholic suicide which she envisaged at Le Havre in 1794 and which she attempted in London in April 1796. Likewise, the attempted self-destruction of Lodoiska in August 1797 after the death of the Girondin novelist Jean-Baptiste Louvet (1760–97) was a private rather than a public drama. The same could probably be said of the voluntary deaths of the wives of two executed husbands, Clavière and Rabaut-Saint-Etienne, about which we do not know very much. As far as we can tell, these are merely the suicides of people too discouraged to live. The death on 11th Thermidor of Robespierre's older friend and landlady, Mme Duplay, is similarly problematic.

The same apolitical effect appears, finally, in the case of the terrorist and future Thermidorian "réacteur," Tallien: it was after having received a peremptory note from Thérésa Cabarrus ("Tomorrow I appear before the Revolutionary Tribunal. I shall die grief-struck at the thought of belonging to someone as cowardly as you have been") that Tallien went off to the Convention, armed with a dagger, and ready (he later explained) to kill either Robespierre or himself. But once again, this proposed suicide is quite beside the point, despite its superficial relevance.

With the conspicuous exception therefore of Adam Lux (to which we shall return), the history of the Revolution does not provide us with any significant and directly politicized joint suicide. Two or three instances or approximations of such deaths can, it is true, be cited. Of these, the most conspicuous of is that of Philippe Lebas (1764–94). A few days before 9th Thermidor, Robespierre's close friend did indeed write to his wife: "If it were not a crime, I would blow your brains out and kill my own self. At least, we would die together."[27] The thought of their unborn child held him back, however, and Lebas, when he killed himself on the morning of 10th Thermidor, did not kill his wife.

The case of the Dunel family in the Faubourg Saint-Antoine in 1795 deserves mention as well: after the failure of the *journée* of prairial, Madame Dunel embraced her husband, "wrapped her arms around his neck and without further ado said that she hoped they could all perish together." Dunel then poisoned his entire family and tried (unsuccessfully) to gas himself.[28] The death of "la femme Boutry" and her husband is similarly relevant. When the police of the Faubourg Saint-Antoine came to secure her arrest, Boutry, her husband, fired a pistol into his own mouth.[29] But these, again, are isolated and opaque instances.

The only significant exception to the unyielding if informal Jacobin interdict on simultaneously sentimental and politicized suicide is, therefore, that of the Franco-German Adam Lux.[30] Born in Mayence in 1765 (and consequently only twenty-eight years old in 1793), Lux was trained in both medicine and philosophy. As is so often true, private and public concerns probably meshed in this case: it is of interest that Lux in 1792 had already urged his nephew to strengthen his resolve while still young. Only such early training, he explained, would enable the young man to understand the virile (and suicidal?) message of Rousseau, Cato, and Socrates.[31]

In March 1793, a few months after the French occupation of his home city, Lux was sent together with Georg Forster by the Mayençais Jacobins to Paris to request the annexation of their city to the *Grande Nation*. Like many foreigners, Lux fell in with the Girondins, whose political marginalization during the spring of 1793 he took to be the downfall of Republicanism in its purest form. As a signal to the misguided French nation, Lux decided to kill himself. He asked the Girondins for their assistance. (Politely, they refused it.) The supposed sequels of his unrealized suicide were lovingly detailed: Lux asked to be buried at Ermenonville, between the temple of philosophy and the grave of Rousseau. To drive his point home, Lux also asked that his grave bear as an inscription: "Here lies Adam Lux, disciple of Jean-Jacques Rousseau."

A few weeks later, on 6 June 1793, in a speech that he vainly hoped to deliver to the Convention, Lux explained why he still wished to die by his own hand:

> the triumph of crime has convinced me that I should sacrifice my blood and finish my innocent life with a death that will be more useful to liberty than my life ever could be. That is my first motive. The second is to honor the memory of my master Jean-Jacques Rousseau with an act of patriotism that will be above all slander and suspicion. . . . The resolution that I have taken could only be that of an independent spirit. I belong to the public good. I am free of all factions.[32]

It was, however, the execution of Charlotte Corday (which Lux witnessed and took to be the effect of her suicidal will) that crystallized his resolve, as he explained in a pamphlet dated 19 July 1793. (Marat had died on 13 July; and Charlotte, four days later.) In words which echoed in part a treatise on enthusiasm that he had written some years before, Lux, who witnessed Corday's death, described his sudden rapture:

I saw this unchangeable sweetness in the midst of barbarian howls. This gaze, so sweet and penetrating! these lively, humid sparks which flashed in her beautiful eyes. . . . She climbed the scaffold . . . she expired . . . and her great soul rose to the bosom of the Catos and the Brutuses.[33]

Arrested on 23 July on account of this tract, Lux was duly condemned on 4 November 1793 by the Revolutionary Tribunal, somewhat puzzled, it may be added, by his suicidal vocation. He was executed that same day.

Lux's fate is certainly of interest. Nonetheless, it serves primarily to underscore the rarity of joint and eroticized suicides during the French Revolution. Indeed, in the spring of 1793, the feminist playwright Olympe de Gouges (1748–93) even ironically proposed to Robespierre a politically parodic version of this heretofore literarily popular denouement. They should, she thought, drown together in the Seine:

I propose that we bathe together in the Seine. And in order to wash away completely the stains with which you have soiled yourself since the 10th of August, we will tie to our feet cannon balls of sixteen or twenty four pounds, and we will hurl ourselves together in this watery waste. Your death will calm men's minds, and the sacrifice of my pure life will disarm the heavens.[34]

So great in fact was the Revolutionary interdict on the direct politicization of joint and voluntary death that the most curious aspect of this *problématique* may well have been, as it were, a "non joint suicide," namely, that of Manon Roland (1754–93), whose self-destructive impulses figure prominently in Dorinda Outram's recent book, *The Body and the French Revolution.*[35]

While in prison, Manon Roland very seriously envisaged chosen death. She went so far as to compose some of these notes which suicides often write to those whom they leave behind: "Forgive me," she wrote to her older husband, Jean-Marie Roland (1734–93), who was to drive a sword through his heart when he heard of his wife's death, "Forgive me, respectable man, for having disposed of a life which I had consecrated to you." And again, to her younger and platonic lover, Buzot (1760–94), "Die free, as you knew how to live."[36]

Significantly, however, her final decision was to die on the guillotine rather than by her own hand. The reason for this must lie in the nature of her goal and of its relationship to Revolutionary orthodoxy. Mme Roland might well have committed suicide if her intent had been to correct public opinion, as Lux consciously intended by an act that he viewed as aggressively exemplary. But her purpose being instead to defy rather than to correct her enemies, it made more sense for her to accept death unflinchingly and in public than to seek it by her own hand. Manon Roland might have killed herself with her lover Buzot if she had thought politics irrelevant (as had the *amants de Lyon*). Conversely, she could also have taken her own life if she had thought it possible for her to affect the political climate of the times (as did Adam Lux). But she thought neither of these two things.

Because she was dying as a political person, but more against than for the People, a joint or politicized suicide (as hers would have had to be) made no sense. Her decision not to kill herself, and especially not to kill herself with her lover Buzot (who took his life a few months later), was fully in the logic of her defiant situation.

The extreme disfavor into which the idea of joint suicide fell so quickly after 1789 is suggestive. We can after all easily imagine hypothetical circumstances and public *mises-en-scène* in which joint and sentimental suicide might have had political significance: a young soldier and his betrothed, for example, would blow themselves up so as not to surrender to invading enemies. We can conceive either of multiple suicides that would have been staged by the actors to allow appropriation by the Revolutionary state (if the participants had been victims of counter-Revolution) or, conversely, of suicides that would be shaped to bolster the Revolutionary myth of betrayed fervor, of Jacobins misunderstood by a still-deluded-but-about-to-come-to-its-senses mob. What Lux tried to achieve by himself, for example, might have been staged by a suicidal pair.

Such cooperation is all the more imaginable for the fact, ably described by Dominique Godineau, that militant feminists were often married to militant sans-culottes,[37] and it is clear enough that very young and married couples of all kinds operated as political teams after 1789: the Rolands and the Desmoulins (Camille [1760–94] and Lucile [1770–94]) come to mind; as do Lebas and his wife Elizabeth Duplay; Mme de Staël (1766–1817) and Benjamin Constant (1767–1830); or for that matter Louis XVI (1754–93) and Marie-Antoinette (1755–93). But such partnerships, though they often led to death, never resulted in a pattern of joint and chosen death.

To explain this nonappearance, the argument moves back to the persistent if often overshadowed anticorporatist individualism that was so typical of Jacobean ideology. For although individualism, as has been pointed out, was in 1794 wholly subsumed by the Jacobins under the rubric of nation, the rights of the private self were never—in principle—abandoned. (We can likewise remember that Robespierre, though dictatorial in his practice, never gave thought to dissolving the Convention in order to rule autocratically as Marat had suggested.)

In the metaphysics of the French Revolution, the individual, even in 1794, stood unmediated in his relation to the Nation and the State. This was as true during the Terror as it had been in 1791 with the Le Chapelier law, or in 1789 with the Declaration of the Rights of Man. All associations remained illegal—in 1794 especially—and the Jacobin clubs themselves invariably denied accusations of particularism. They were, as they endlessly explained, not truly "clubs" at all. They were, they said, only the true representatives of the entire nation. Their view, restated in modern and Habermasian language, was that they expressed the entire nation's revolutionary and crystallizing desire for an all-encompassing public sphere.

Jacobinism, even in its most totalitarian moments, remained violently anticorporatist and economically individualist. It did not hesitate to order the division of common lands that even poorer peasants seldom wanted. It never denied the primacy of individual values, even if it sought to realize them completely within the compass of an unfederated, one, and indivisible Republic. Symbolically, the dying (and often suicidal) Revolutionary hero did certainly and obviously sacrifice his entire self to the motherland, but in so doing, he also fulfilled the deepest yearnings of his truest being. It was his public death that allowed him to realize his most private self.

In this interlocking and excluding context, a joint suicide, that is to say, the creation of a mediating cell between the individual and the nation, could never be allowed, even if its purpose was to self-destruct and thus to further the cause of the grateful nation. The theme of joint suicide, so popular in the literature of the Enlightenment, could not be transposed into Revolutionary politics directly.

This failure has obvious eloquence. It speaks to the deeper and complex nature of the entire Jacobin worldview.

III

Ruled out in its untranscended form, joint suicide could, however, and most easily so, reappear in a *sublimated* context. Jacobinism could not encompass explicitly sentimental and joint suicide. But the pre-Revolutionary suicidal sensibility to which Rousseau and Léonard had given fictional consistency did find indirect Revolutionary expression in two quite different ways.

The first involved individuals who had had suicidally sentimental impulses before 1789 and who now expressed that yearning in the more abstract and highly politicized context of Revolutionary fervor. Biographically, it is possible to identify a few individuals who first developed the theme of sentimental suicide before the Revolution as men of letters, and then, during the Revolution, felt a politicized suicidal urge to kill themselves on behalf of a newly imagined "other," namely, the embattled nation. Writers concerned with suicide before 1789 kill themselves in 1793 or 1795, not with or for a loved one, but with and for the nation.

The first of these prosopographical cases is that of "l'ami du Peuple." The issue reaches back to 1770–72 when Marat (1743–93), who was still then a young man, had, during his stay in England, penned a novel entitled *Les Aventures du comte Potowski,* an epistolary work in ninety letters, only published in 1847, where the theme of suicide figures prominently.[38] For Marat's Stalinist biographer Massin, this book is a failure ("un livre raté")[39] and in truth, Marat's opus has its problems. The plot is egregiously banal: Gustave, Comte Potowski, is in love with Lucile de Sobieski, who like him belongs to the highest nobility. Their travails are many but all will end well in a "chaste hymen": "all my wishes are fullfilled. Lucile is now mine."

For all its weaknesses, however, Marat's text still holds our attention. First, it is a philo-Polish novel, and, of necessity, highly politicized. Like Burke (Marat and Burke both at that time radical Whigs of a determined kind), Marat defends a martyred Poland. Catherine the Great is not handled gently. She is a tyrant. Of her dealings with her Russian subjects, Marat writes as Montesquieu did of the Chinese empire: "Does she not drive them forward by terror? Does she not keep them from ever breathing freely? Is not a sword for ever suspended over the heads of those who might be indiscreet?"[40]

Second, Marat's text also evinces a sustained interest in suicide. Thus Gustave, mistakenly thinking himself to have been betrayed by Lucile, decides to immolate his rival and then to take his own life. Sigismond, his jaded friend from Warsaw, is not taken with this possible denouement: "To cut your throat for a woman? That's a bit violent; although many have done it for less."[41] Later, thinking Lucile to be dead, Gustave again thinks of chosen death:

> Oh! my soul! I cannot go on. . . . Grief consumes for me all the advantages of life. In the depths of my despair, I feel the endless tearings of eternal separation. I feel myself dying by degrees, and grief shortens my remaining days. Cruel fate! take away this breath of life which still gives me life. I no longer have the strength to suffer.[42]

Gustave often yearns to die by his own hand, and so does Lucile: "Death would have reunited me to my lover," she writes. "How I envy his fate! He has been freed from the miseries of this world, and I am still mourning."[43] True enough, Marat does not precisely eulogize a joint and sentimental suicide, but he comes close to it.

Suicide lurks in the pages of Marat's novel, and it is also the subtext of a sacrificial and Revolutionary career whose intertext is the literary theme of voluntary death. Marat's *Plan de législation criminelle,* first published in 1774 and republished in 1790, includes an individualist defense of suicide. Then, too, in 1793, pistol in hand, Marat threatened to kill himself on the very floor of the Convention. Massin describes this as a purely theatrical gesture, but a more thoughtful interpretation might present it as a revealing moment in a journalistic career that was suicidally intense. Marat needed mortal enemies, and in the spring of 1793, after the murder of Le Peletier, such a wish could no longer remain unfulfilled. A clear parallel exists, incidentally, between Marat's suicidal behavior and that of his murderess, quite conscious for her part also of the inevitable consequences of her act. She too was an avid Republican and a reader of Plutarch's lives. Like Marat, Corday intended to sacrifice herself for the public good. "Les extrêmes se touchent": opposites attract each other. In this case, both victim and avenger accepted and even sought their deaths.

Goujon's case is another prosopographical instance of literary and sentimental suicide transposed after 1789 to the plane of sacrificial politics. A friend of Romme, Goujon was, like him, a *martyr de prairial*, that is, one of the left-wing Montagnards who were condemned to death for having sided with insurrectionary sans-culottes in 1795. Goujon, like Marat, had written a play on the theme of sentimental suicide, *Damon et Phintias, ou les vertus de la liberté*, known to us episodically through some passages in the *Souvenirs* of his brother-in-law, Tissot. These excerpts are very short, but they allow us to infer that the aesthetic of Goujon's work was reminiscent of the sentimental effusion of both *La Nou-velle Héloïse* and the *Amants de Lyon:*

> Do not force me to go on living after I have lost you. What would I become? Answer: would not life be a burden to me? Yes, if you have to die, I shall spill my own blood next to yours. We have both worked for good. We have nothing to regret. Death's scythe glistens above our heads, but in vain; and vainly does it threaten us with inevitable blows. He who waits for death without remorse knows how to face it without fear.

Or again, as Damon explains to Phintias, "Death is sweet for me. I want it. I desire it. I crave it at this very moment."[44]

This was in 1790–91. By 1795, Goujon's yearning for chosen death had taken shape as a desire for politically motivated self-destruction. His statement to the Thermidorean tribunal after the abortive sans-culotte insurrection was suicidally defiant:

> I will find refuge in his bosom [a reference to the Supreme Being] and will be content to have left this earth of misery and

oppression, where virtue succumbs, where crime insolently gathers unto itself the power and the glory, at the price of innocent blood.

His celebrated *Hymne à la liberté,* written in prison at Morlaix, was similar in its tone:

> De nos jours immolons le reste
> A nos frères, à nos amis;
> Avant que des fers ennemis
> Les chargent d'un joug trop funeste.
> Pour défendre la vérité,
> Des méchants bravons la furie.
> Mourons tous pour l'Egalité,
> Sans elle il n'est plus de patrie.
> Liberté. . . .
> Découvre aux siècles à venir
> Tout l'éclat de notre innocence;
> Dis-leur que nous dûmes mourir
> Pour te conserver à la France.[45]

IV

The issue of transposed double suicide, however, goes well beyond the private lives of suicidally inclined Revolutionary actors and authors. It involves far more important issues. Indeed, the transposition of politicized and sentimental suicide is at the intersection of Jacobin definitions of the self and the nation. It also speaks to the relation of gender to the Revolutionary idea of nation.

René Favre, John McManners, and Richard Andrews, in their excellent books and articles on the theme of death in the thought of the Enlightenment, have presented the suicides (or near-suicides) of men like General Beaurepaire at Verdun in September 1792, Babeuf in 1797 at Vendôme, and Dr. Bach at the foot of the statue of Liberty on the Place de la Révolution after 18th Brumaire as "heroic suicides."[46] Here, the hero sacrifices his life for a grateful nation that is at least potentially triumphant: the case of the young Bara's voluntary death, especially as reconstructed by Robespierre in the spring of 1794, is perhaps the ideal type of this heroic and exemplary death. The message here is of conjointed apotheosis. The hero dies. The nation lives to remember him.

But what can be sensed in Romme and Goujon—and perhaps even in the later speeches of Robespierre and Saint-Just as well—is closer to the "sentimental" and joint suicide of Léonard's book than to the exemplary death of Socrates and Cato, of Bara and Viala.

The deathly statement of the martyrs—of Romme, Goujon, and their friends—has a subtle logic. Passing their weapon from hand to hand, the *martyrs de prairial*, who serially stabbed themselves in the dock after they had been condemned, are indeed visible and heroic victims. But they are also involved in a joint and covert suicide of love (to each other and the nation) and of hatred, perhaps even in a joint suicide of homosocial love and hatred.

Both Jacobin actor and feminized loved one (that is to say, the nation) are on the edge of extinction. Goujon's tone in 1795 is not of heroic example but of disappointed and amorous self-immolation. Here, the pre-Revolutionary and literary beloved, that is, the female lover (who is also the disappointing other), becomes a politicized, but still feminized ideal: the Nation. With the *martyrs de prairial*, the male legislator espouses the nation in a common death. Goujon dies by his own hand, since Liberty has allowed herself to die as well. The death of the *martyrs de prairial*, that is, of innocence betrayed, as was the passion of Thérèse and Faldoni, is now set in a totalizing political register, impassioned still, but deeply embittered also.

In the canvases of David, man, who is public, acts heroically. His body and his wounds belong to the united nation. Woman, who defines herself by reference to man, is supine. She is incapable of public self-sacrifice. The actors are male. The nation is female, a duality which incidentally brings us back to the posthumous fate of Charlotte Corday: by inverting the Enlightened and Revolutionary interpretation of femininity, her criminal resolve doubly gave offense. From her judges' point of view, her deed was not just parricidal. It was a kind of cross-dressing as well, a virile act whose ironic complement was Marat's naked and "demasculinized" bathing body.

Gendered heroism is explicit in *The Oath of the Horatii*, but it is an implicit and suicidal theme also in the suicide of the *martyrs de prairial*. In 1795, united and self-destructive heroes die a fraternal death as a reproach to the beloved (and secretly despised) female nation.

Romme's private life speaks perhaps to that same homosocial theme: though long a bachelor, Romme did finally marry in 1794 at the age of forty-four, but in a particular way, by asking his Parisian *section* to find for him as a wife the widow of a fallen soldier. One can ask who was the bride of Romme: the widow whom the nation has assigned to him, or her former and fallen husband.

V

Like the causes that explain the disfavor of explicit joint suicide (however politicized), those that explain the prestige of transposed joint suicide are hardly fortuitous. Some of them, to be sure, are mundane and not specific to the French Revolution at all. A craving for immortality is no doubt of some relevance: paradoxically, it is the fear of death that pushes toward death. It is by dying together that the *Amants de Lyon* will live forever. A theatrical Cato declaiming on the relevance of his death to the life (and memory of the nation) made this point explicitly:

> Ainsi, même en mourant, utile à ma patrie
> J'aurai vu couronner les travaux de ma vie
> Et jamais sans mon nom, le mot de liberté
> Par les ages futurs ne sera répété.[47]

Before 1789, sentimental suicide engendered that same notoriety that politicized suicide entailed during the Revolution.

The rhetorical style of the entire epoch, with its "mode of excess," as Peter Brooks has so appropriately labeled it, is also clearly relevant. Literary deaths before 1789, like political deaths after 1789, were carefully staged to elicit admiration.[48] Marat's suicidal novel, for example, made repeated use of sublime devices. Revolutionary heroism galvanizes and surprises, as does, of course, suicide and especially joint suicides. The literary sublime hinges on surprise, fear, or even disgust; and these are the qualities which suicide often evokes as well. It is likewise suggestive that the supposed effect of the guillotine on bystanders was often described in terms reminiscent of the pre-Revolutionary concerns of the

philosophes on the effects on pregnant women of the brutalized
and displayed bodies of suicides.

A yearning for melancholic absolutes is another entry in the
same rhetorical agenda. "Gabriel ou la mort," exclaimed Sophie
de Monnier, one of Mirabeau's many mistresses, a young woman
who killed herself in 1789. In the Revolutionary context of 1792–
95, in the "République de l'absolu," to use the terms of Victor
Hugo, chosen death is a privileged solution. It is a proof of
passionate involvement and an experience also of ultimate and
absolute suffering. "Might it be," Feucher wrote in 1786 in his
Réflexions d'un jeune homme, "that the soul has only one way
of feeling, and that pain is its only attribute? Everything seems
to prove it,"[49] a literary judgment that found its political echo in
Robespierre's letter to Pétion in 1792: "I have come to suspect
that the true heroes are not those who triumph but who suffer."[50]

In the highly staged suicides of the *martyrs de prairial* in 1795,
chosen death is a manifestation of "excess," but its presentation
also speaks to the persistent Revolutionary concern for the representation and physicalization, however particular, of the Jacobin
worldview.

For Romme, Goujon, and Soubrany, a public and voluntary
death is a lived (as it were) allegory, a "metaphysical moment"
in the life (and death) of liberty and of its homosocial heroes, a
moment whose meaning derived in large part from the representational styles of the epoch. The martyrs' staged suicide in the
dock replicates in lived politics the allegorical and frozen canvases
of Regnault, Vien, Girodet, or David. Angus Fletcher has re-
minded us of the implications of allegory, of its "apocalyptic
function" and its aesthetic surface, "which implies an authoritative, thematic, 'correct' reading." Allegory expects that the
reader/spectator must either accept its coded message or rebel.
The contrast is obvious between allegory (and Jacobin suicide) on
the one hand and either comedy (the Ancien Régime) or tragedy
(*sans-culottisme.*)

In these last two and forthright contexts, the hero stands, as
I. A. Richards put it, "without subterfuge,"[51] but allegory by
contrast is of its essence "an art of subterfuge," where codes and
messages stand between the spectator and sublimated reality.[52]
The Jacobin suicides allegorically represent the General (and styl-

ized) Will of the French nation. Through speeches and visual representations, they allegorically legitimize by their death the dying General Will of the *grande Nation*. Their staged and frozen images prove the existence of the Rousseauistic Will even to those who invent the images, and even as it dies.

The politicization and staging of joint suicide is an archetypal instance of the process through which self-referential Jacobinism acquired practical consistency: on his symbolic and self-immolated body the politicized lover of the Revolution allegorically inscribes the existence of the (failed and female) nation. The *martyr de prairial's* chosen death speaks to the force of Jacobin politics, just as the statue of Hercules represents it also. The self-appointed martyr's choice of "la Liberté dans la mort," of liberty in death, gives to the victim a sense of aesthetic wholeness. It proves to his audience the truth of the public Jacobin principle within which the hero has inserted his private, disastrous, seemingly excessive truth. Thus, to an episodic private and public story that would have no meaning, the self-obsessed and moralized Jacobin prefers a theatrical, allegorized, and coherent, if death-giving, narrative.

Another type of explanation shifts the argument, initially at least, away from rhetoric and public styles of representation toward the more private domain of modern psychiatric speculation on the cause of self-destruction.

For Freud, suicide is an inverted form of narcissism. Chosen death binds love and self-love to death. The would-be suicide turns against himself a death wish originally directed to another, as appears from the fact that many suicides seem to believe that they will not truly die. Joint suicide winds that ratchet one notch tighter. It stands at the intersection of love and hate. The suicide/ murderer—who is invariably the male protagonist—simultaneously loves and detests the other. In both *La Nouvelle Héloïse* and *Les Amants de Lyon*, the heroine is noble but ultimately distant and unattainable. For Saint-Preux, Julie is hatefully maternal and virtuous: "to feel her for ever lost to me. It was this that threw me into fits of rage and fury, which progressively drove me to despair." The words of Adam Lux are likewise strangely evocative of this same theme: "I rejoiced in her superiority," he writes of Charlotte Corday, "for is it not just that the adored object should always be raised above the adorer?" Suicidal love levels this barrier through the destruction of the loved object.

We can now move back from the private to the public: Freud's explanation is wholly apolitical, of course; but the power of the French Revolution lay precisely in its unbounded ability to make the personal into the political.

The *martyrs de prairial* lived—and died—for people just as Saint-Preux wished to live—and die—with and for Julie. (It is in fact the civic and spiritual consciousness of these irreducible Montagnards which in 1795 placed them above rather than against the Communist concern for material equality that was to blossom as Babouvism.)

But their idealized passion is also (for Goujon especially) a disappointed love. Like all double suicides, the allegorized, "excessive" death pact of the *martyrs de prairial* conveys a frozen message of love, disillusion, and hate. The feminization of the nation, like the masculinization of the hero, has unsettling implications for those whose attitude toward conventionally defined sexual roles is ambiguous. In the politicized and sublimated joint suicides of 1795, as in the message of *l'esprit révolutionnaire*, the private and the public are entirely fused. But in some instances at least, joint and sublimated suicides of love and hate are the end point of a logic that was difficult to sustain.

Pre-Revolutionary literary precedent (i.e., the statements of Léonard and Rousseau) suggested a sentimental solution to a genuine social malaise. In a second phase, after 1789, Jacobinism transformed and politicized these same values, and this transition, it can be added, was all the more feasible because the literary theme of joint suicide was in its details prepolitical. Conveniently, the *Amants de Lyon* of 1783 had included passages on the evil of the *lettres de cachet* and on the reprehensible contrast between the poverty of the just and the riches of the unjust. The social message of *La Nouvelle Héloïse* or of Marat's novel does not need to be belabored.

The difference, of course, is that in pre-Revolutionary literature, sentimentalized and suicidal actors were the idealized, sexualized (and fictional) victims of prejudice in the civil sphere. After 1789, suicidal lovers rise above their immediate private social or erotic concerns. They become the expression of the nation's public sphere. Their private and literary yearning for self-destruction is not only ideologically transformed, it is actualized as well. Now the suicides really die.

VI

The history of politicized sentimental suicide, though significant, was also very short, and Mme de Staël brought the cycle to a close in her novel *Delphine* (1802), set in 1790–92, a text that revolves around the opinions of an independent and outspoken heroine who dies in September 1792, shortly before the proclamation of the First Republic.

Margaret Higonnet has shown how Delphine's personal conflict (she loves a married aristocrat of Spanish birth and of passionate but reactionary temperament) is presented by Staël as a subset of the other and larger social civil war of men and women.[53] This war between the sexes parallels in turn the political civil war of the French nation of her time. The novel is played out on interlocking levels since Delphine, the fated victim of social prejudice, also defends the Revolution, which Léonce disdains. Delphine's autonomous social behavior violates his traditionalist political principles as well as his social codes. The suicidal conclusion of Staël's book is in the logic of these situations: Léonce is unable to resolve his varying dilemmas and will choose to end his life as an émigré before a firing squad after having vainly tried to end it on the battlefield. The conflict between his desire for Delphine (now become a defrocked nun) and his duty can have no other exit. In the first version of the book, Delphine takes poison so as to die at the same time as Léonce.

Critically, however, Staël's imagined pattern inverts the mechanism present in both the case of Adam Lux and in the sublimated deaths of the *martyrs de prairial*. For Staël, Revolution and Jacobinism are not in any way synonymous. Her hero and heroine do not die for state and nation. Their fate certainly parallels, but it does not replicate, the innermost Jacobin history of the Revolution. Though set in a political time frame, the voluntary deaths of Staël's two lovers resemble those of the *Amants de Lyon* far more than those of the *martyrs de prairial*. True, we can understand the fate of Staël's heroes only by reference to the political debates of the times; but Delphine and Léonce in 1802 are outside Jacobin discourse. Like Thérèse and Faldoni in 1783, they are the victims of social wrong more than of politics, the vicissitudes of which only serve to illustrate their private drama. Delphine's first enemy is the pre-Revolutionary constraint of fashionable society ("le monde"). Delphine and Léonce do not stage their deaths as public dramas, and they do not seek to give to their private fates a public message. The sentimental novel of the 1780s, which was dramatically transposed and politicized in the deaths of the *martyrs de prairial* in 1795, has now again with Staël in 1802 become explicit but depoliticized.

And what holds for the first version of *Delphine* published in 1802 appears in spades in the second version of the novel, rewritten by Staël and posthumously published by her son in 1817. In this new conclusion, Léonce still finds chosen death (in the Vendée in 1793 rather than on the eve of Valmy), but Delphine no longer kills herself. Rejected by Léonce, she dies of inanition, and more precisely of Christian inanition as a martyr to sentiment:

> feeling herself to be weakening, she asked one of her serving women to read her some of her favored passages from the Psalms, from the Gospels, and from some religious writers. All the passages she chose were full of sweetness and compassion.[54]

"La Révolution est finie." Looking backward, the death of Delphine and Léonce in 1802 marks a sudden decline of the politicized theme of joint suicide that Jacobinism had brought to the fore in 1792–95. Looking forward, these two literary and suicidal victims herald the romanticized and wholly apolitical suicide in 1811 of Heinrich von Kleist and Henriette Vogel, much criticized, as it happens, by Mme de Staël. With their deaths (and her disavowal of them) begins an altogether new phase in the cultural history of joint and chosen death.

Jacques Revel

Marie-Antoinette in Her Fictions:
The Staging of Hatred

THIS PAPER SUMMARIZES AND DISCUSSES CERTAIN ASPECTS OF A MUCH larger research project on Marie-Antoinette—more precisely, on the character of the queen as it was constructed and interminably reformulated in the abundant pamphlet literature devoted to her. For a long time, this category of texts was largely neglected and disdained, neglected because disdained. It is true that most of the pamphlets are very mediocre literature, if we can even use the word literature to describe them. They are most often anonymous, crudely composed and written, and, unquestionably, very unreliable sources of information. In short, their reputation is nothing less than suspect.

This undoubtedly explains why these pamphlets have been exclusively treated as *curiosa* for such a long time: third-rate literature, if not worse, that collectors of marginal—and, if possible, pornographic—writings ferreted out and preserved in the deep secret of their libraries during the nineteenth century. Besides these bibliophiles, a few self-proclaimed "specialists" published a small portion of this material at the turn of the century, at the apogee of the Third Republic, under the highly fallacious pretext of establishing the ultimate truth about Marie-Antoinette. In a very different way and in the name of opposed political values, Hector Fleischmann and Henry d'Almeras (under several pseudonyms) were the first editors of this licentious literature. They nevertheless have the merit of having left behind them bibliographical instruments that are very useful, even if not entirely reliable. These editions can, in turn, be regarded as specific moments of the ambiguous legend, of the strange mixture of ostensible moralism and verbal abuse, that has accompanied the memory of the queen for two hundred years.

The renewed interest in these pamphlets after such a long period of suspicion and semiclandestinity is therefore all the more remarkable. Recently, historians and literary critics seem to be considering these documents as having something to teach us and no longer as simple curiosities. Meanwhile, however, the approach has profoundly changed. No one even pretends to use them as primary sources containing factual—even if dubious—information on Marie-Antoinette and her entourage. Rather, they are considered the support for a set of representations that may have something to tell us about the categories, the values, and the stereotypes that informed the proliferating collective discourse about the queen. And, because Marie-Antoinette was both a royal person and a woman, it is not surprising that the analysis focused at the outset on categories of gender and on the manipulation of these categories at the end of the eighteenth century. A literary critic, Chantal Thomas, has just published a study of the "nefarious" queen, La Reine scélérate, that consists essentially of a series of free variations, sometimes suggestive, sometimes anachronistic, on the theme of antifeminism during the Revolutionary period.[1] Lynn Hunt has attempted to reconstruct the articulation of the "many bodies of Marie-Antoinette," primarily from the sexual body to the body politic. She sees in the explosion of this violent and, above all, pornographic, writing about the queen the expression of a "fundamental anxiety about queenship as the most extreme form of women invading the public sphere" and, at the same time, a brutal reaction to the mounting fear of sexual indifferentiation that informed the representations of the Revolutionary period.[2] Sarah Maza suggests a similar interpretation in her rereading of the famous episode of the queen's necklace.[3] To the extent that it reflects on the last decade of the Ancien Régime, her analysis tends to show that the reaction that both she and Hunt evoke must be related not only to what Hunt calls the "homosocial" Republican ideal of virtue but to an even older preoccupation. In fact, the origin of the motifs that associate a confusion of genders with the threat of an invasion of the public sphere by women probably dates from the 1750s, during the reign of Louis XV.

My own perspective is different, even if it often intersects with the concerns and methods of these authors. My primary interest is in the long process of privatization and degradation of royalty in France during the last half-century of the absolute monarchy, in the waxing and waning of a collective movement of desacralization that affected French sovereigns from Louis XV to Marie-Antoinette.[4] A recent case study investigating how the persona of Louis XV emerges from the interplay of collective representations around an incident in the spring of 1750 allows me to pinpoint the first signs of this decisive transformation. However, Louis XV and Marie-Antoinette were not the first French sovereigns to encounter such attacks. To name just a few of the most famous: Henri III during the time of the League; the queen-mother Anne of Austria and her prime minister and lover, Cardinal Mazarin, during the Fronde; Louis XIV himself, at the turn of the eighteenth century—all had been the object of pamphlet campaigns denouncing their conduct, chiefly their sexual conduct. It is true that before the mid-eighteenth century, this kind of denunciation never seems seriously to question or even explicitly to address the function of royalty but, instead, concentrates on the moral character of the person and on the duties it transgresses. In the pamphlets to be discussed here, however, the private and public roles of sovereigns are inextricably bound together—which explains why privatization becomes the form par excellence to degrade the king or queen's image. This marked difference helps us to focus on the question: why did the register of pornography become politically expedient at the end of the Ancien Régime? An answer to this question would help us to understand better the quantitative explosion of pamphlet literature, its success, and its durable effects.

In this paper, I want to restrict myself to a more limited set of questions: how can one explain that these pamphlets could fuel so many beliefs—or, better yet, form the basis of so many certainties? Why did they prove to be so dangerously effective? For whoever works today with this literature, these questions hardly demand justification. The pamphlets are marked by permanent verbal excess. Their pretension to "realism" is obviously unreal-

istic; approximations and contradictions are rampant. They are
obviously works of fiction. But these fictions have been able to
present themselves as both credible and effective. My analysis will
therefore center on the production of *certainties,* which is one of
the most difficult dimensions to understand in a literature of this
type. I would like to suggest that these pamphlets have collectively
proposed a kind of textual staging of Marie-Antoinette and that
they have done so by utilizing specific themes and devices that
made acceptable and plausible the representations of the queen
thus circulated. They created a paper queen that, early on, in fact
well before the Revolution, gradually replaced the "real" queen,
until the latter was completely eclipsed.

Up to this point, I have used the term "pamphlets" and I
will continue to do so throughout this paper. But like many
historians who use this word, I am referring to a fairly large range
of texts. Some were handwritten, and these have mostly been lost;
others were printed and were therefore more easily preserved. There
are songs, very short plays, eight- to sixteen-page satires (by far
the most frequent), but also book-length works such as the *Essai
historique sur la vie de Marie-Antoinette* (first published in one
volume, then augmented to two, and frequently reprinted), or
the famous *Vie privée, libertine et scandaleuse de Marie-
Antoinette d'Autriche.* At this point, we still know very little
about the publishing history of this literature that, under the
Ancien Régime, eluded not only the system of privileges but also
the various controls that burdened the book trade; thus, we often
only know of this literature through chance findings in the police
archives.[5] Except for the very first years, around 1780, the conditions of production of pamphlet literature remain largely unknown. It seems assured that in the earlier period small groups
of specialists headquartered in London, or the Netherlands, or
sometimes even in Paris (in spite of the great risk of such a
location), had been responsible for a production that was often
financed by important people of the court and probably by Louis
XVI's own brother, the Count of Provence, the future Louis XVIII.
We know for certain that the campaign to defame Marie-
Antoinette sprang up in the mid-1770s from within the court. A
famous text describes idiosyncratically how the pamphlet circuit
then became established:

A timorous courtier puts [the rumors] in verse and couplets and, via the Minister of Flunkeys, has them delivered to the central market. From there, they come into the hands of the artisan who, in turn, brings them back to the noblemen who forged them and who, without losing any time, go to *l'Oeil de Boeuf* and, whispering in each other's ears in the most consummate hypocritical tone, ask: "Have you read them? Here they are. They are circulating amidst the people of Paris." Such is the origin and such is the route of these wretched little verses that, the very same day, spread those abominable anecdotes about people of known virtue throughout Paris and at court; the truth of which anecdotes is almost always founded on contemptible hearsay and never on eyewitness reports.[6]

But later, and particularly during the Revolutionary period, things become less certain. For the most part, we know little of the authors and their publishers; both are often equally masked behind imaginary names. At best we can guess that the range of possibilities was very wide. Some texts are visibly the work of authors whose style and taste were shaped by high literature and who are actually ironic and capable specialists in the perversion of genres. Again, this is particularly the case in the early pamphlets, such as in the classic *Amours de Charlot et de Toinette* that evokes, as early as 1779, the supposed frolics of the queen and her brother-in-law, the Count of Artois; or, ten years later, in *Le Godemiché royal,* where obscenity is elegantly expressed with classical reminiscences and with parodic citations that only a literate public could decipher. Take, for example, these Racinian verses put in the mouth of Hébée (*sic*), the too eager confidante of Juno–Marie-Antoinette:

> Quel étrange discours! mon âme en est émue;
> Quoi! vous régnez, Madame, et n'êtes point foutue!
> Je méprise le trône et tous ses vains honneurs;
> Un vit vaut seul un sceptre: au diable les faveurs
> Et tout ce que le sort aveuglément nous donne . . .

> [What strange discourse! my soul is touched;
> What! you reign, Madame, and aren't yet fucked!
> I scorn the throne and its vain honors;
> A prick alone is worth a scepter: to hell with favors
> And all that chance blindly hands us.][7]

Other texts, on the contrary, are written in a colloquial language—which certainly does not mean that they are of popular
origin. The recourse to parody is still plausible: the *Père Duchesne*
at that time provides the most brilliant example. The variable
quality of the printed texts seems to me just as significant as their
stylistic diversity. Some were published carefully; others, far more
numerous, are very approximate—full of typographical errors
(spelling or other), repetitions, omissions. They are visibly issued
from an inexpensive editorial process, much like certain volumes
of the *Bibliothèque bleue* in the seventeenth and eighteenth centuries. The necessity of controlling prices during the short editorial
life of many of these satirical works and the precarious conditions
in which they were realized certainly can account for these faults.[8]

One could describe in more detail the diversity of this pamphlet literature. It seems to me nevertheless legitimate to treat it
as a whole, if only because the pamphlets were viewed in this
way by contemporaries. They definitely do not constitute a genre
in the strictest sense as do, for example, the legal briefs of the
same era analyzed by Maza. Rather, these texts should be considered like pieces of a vast puzzle in the making. To say the
least, the pamphlets borrow much from each other, from simple
allusions to whole (usually unacknowledged) citations. Even if it
is likely that they circulated in quite different audiences—which
still remains to be proved—together, these pamphlets refer to a
repertoire of common references, to a body of "knowledge" that
they simultaneously bring into existence. They can, therefore, be
taken as the elements of a single and tight network of intertextuality. A good example is the classical, and quasi-obsessional,
comparison of Marie-Antoinette to Catherine de Médicis, who can
safely be assumed to have incarnated a sort of negative heroine
in popular memory. But Marie-Antoinette was also compared to
both Frédégonde and Messalina, who probably did not evoke much
in popular culture. The complete series of these bad queens is as
likely to be found in the "literary" pamphlets—which is not
surprising—as in popular *libelles* or texts affecting a popular style.
The series therefore functions only because it is perceived as a
citation taken from a thesaurus of commonly accepted references.
It does not need to refer to something else because it is in itself

a principle of knowledge. The whole corpus constitutes its own proof.

Naturally, we do not know much about the manner in which these texts were received by their public. Nothing would be more dangerous than to formulate hypotheses about the sociology of readers from a given style of writing. The problem has often been put forth in terms of an anonymous or collective literature destined for a larger public, as is the case with the chapbooks of the *Bibliothèque bleue,* with the *mazarinades* as well as with today's newspapers.[9] The present case is even more complex because pamphlet writing combines, in a consistently ambiguous manner, transgression with moralism, while simultaneously calling for an ambiguous attitude on the part of the reader. However, we know at least that the contents of the pamphlets circulated widely, whether via direct reading (the printings were limited but could have been repeated) or via a play of citations relayed by written words or transmitted orally. We know this from indirect witnesses: for example, very early in the Revolution, the Parisian mob (especially on 5 and 6 October 1789, during the march on Versailles) appropriated themes and formulas that were already those of the pamphlets denouncing the queen; or, again, one observes that the black legend of Marie-Antoinette was widely diffused in the provinces: taking their cue literally from the pamphlets, the popular societies that congratulated the Convention after her execution also tagged her as a Messalina, a bloodthirsty tigress, a female monster. Our only certainty is this: the queen was the object of a general hatred to which these texts greatly contributed.

THE LAW OF EXCESS

Four principal themes run through this literature, echoing each other partially. They are : (1) the uncontrolled sexuality of Marie-Antoinette, a very prominent theme in nine pamphlets out of ten; (2) her irreducibly foreign character—she is "the Austrian"—and her declared hatred of France and the French; (3) her political ambition; and (4) her pretension to conduct her life as she wishes and, in particular, to create a private space for herself. Leaving aside for the moment the way in which these themes are orchestrated in the pamphlets, let us note that none of these categories is truly surprising. They massively echo a general commentary that accompanied Marie-Antoinette during all of her reign and of which I shall recall here only the most general characteristics:

The queen's sexuality. Everything began, it is known, with the long years of the royal couple's sterility where the responsibility was attributed early on to the impotence or the awkwardness of Louis. This private problem obviously could not stay within the private sphere since it concerned royalty and was, therefore, a matter of state. The absence of an heir concerned primarily the reigning sovereigns, Louis XV and Marie-Thérèse, who had expended efforts to establish a new European order through the alliance of their dynasties. But it also concerned the royal family, particularly the brothers of Louis, Provence and Artois, who could hope for a dynastic promotion thanks to the sterility of their older brother. Besides the royal family, the political milieu, the ambassadors, and the entire court were interested in following the vicissitudes of the young couple. Day after day, for seven years, the state of the queen was thus the object of public commentary; it gave grounds to prognostications and, of course, to derision. In this painful affair, roles were soon distributed. To Louis was attributed impotence, weakness, and ridicule. Marie-Antoinette was cast as enterprising and dangerous. These roles were obviously related to each other: it is because Louis was weak that his wife had to represent a threat. And she had to be threatening especially in the domain where she was both humiliated and frustrated: sexuality. Since it had been impossible to make of her a woman and a mother, she had necessarily to be a slave to inexhaustible sexual desire.

The Austrian. Once again, everything rests on elements that are originally plausible. The marriage of Louis and Marie-Antoinette was, as already mentioned, the linchpin of a reversal of European alliances. It was concluded at a time when the cruel memories of the Seven Years' War were still fresh in the minds of contemporaries and it provoked much hostility, especially at court and even within the royal family. The queen's aunts and Madame du Barry, the official mistress of Louis XV, thus found themselves united with others in a fairly heterogeneous anti-Austrian coalition to whom Marie-Antoinette—or at least what she represented—was not welcome. But there is more. Marie-

Thérèse, and Joseph II after her, had always expected that the new French queen would exert a favorable influence on the foreign affairs of her adopted country. The correspondence of the empress with her daughter, and especially that of Count Mercy-Argenteau, the man in charge of watching over Austrian interests at Versailles, amply documents this hope. The results of their interventions were doubtless extremely limited, owing as much to the inconsistency and awkwardness of Marie-Antoinette as to Louis's apparently early suspicions. These interventions did exist, however. They were known at court and even beyond the court, and they were subject to a commentary which soon presented the young queen as the agent of foreign interests hostile to the kingdom and, possibly, to the king.

Political ambition. This theme is obviously tied to the preceding theme. Because Marie-Antoinette was thought to have an energy and a force of character found lacking in her husband, she was soon suspected of wanting to exercise a personal influence on the political affairs of the kingdom. This influence was, in reality, probably fairly limited, except in the very last moments of the Ancien Régime and then during the first months of the Revolution, when she was at the head of the faction that urged political intransigence. For the rest, her interventions were primarily dictated by whim and were expressed in an alternating game of favor or disfavor; they consisted for the most part in obtaining advantages—titles, charges, pensions, gifts—for her friends. But however limited the tangible results, they rendered credible the certainty that the queen was intervening in politics and that, in this area, she was playing her own game. The radicalization of the period 1787–89 certainly gave more credence to these suspicions.

Finally, the pretension to live her life as she wanted to and to impose a *private sphere* at the heart of the court points once again to well-known facts. Even though the Versailles of Louis XVI and Marie-Antoinette rekindled the grandeur and prestige that had dissipated during the last twenty to twenty-five years of Louis XV's reign, the queen asserted from very early on a right to organize a private space, symbolized by the Trianon, apart from the official world of public representation. There, she claimed to escape from the constraints of court life and to realize, with friends of her own choice, a self-regulating sociability. She was forgetting, just as Louis XV had already done before her, the old unwritten maxim that royalty has no right to private life. It was also to open herself up to suspicions, gossip, and slander: that which one aimed to protect from public view was obviously hidden for very good reasons. After the legend of the *Parc aux Cerfs,* the rumor of the Trianon invented an uninterrupted orgy in its groves and alcoves and a search for the systematic transgression of the most elementary moral values. This echoes naturally the first theme.

If I have recalled these few factual elements, it is not so much to suggest that the pamphletary discourse about Marie-Antoinette could be true, but to recall that this discourse plays with elements of reality and draws from them its plausibility. All of the points elaborated above provided grounds for debates, they fostered a vast commentary, they acquired their own richness. In order to be believable, every rumor must combine a certain measure of reality with some imaginary element, and this is evidently the case here. It is useful again at this point to remember that most of the hostile rumors against the queen originated from Versailles. They were surely manipulated by court factions that opposed each other in their strategies or, simply, in their more immediate interests. At court each detail, each quip, was the object of endless observation and collective commentary; but these details had also to refer to verifiable or, at least, plausible situations. The rumors then spread and, probably by the late 1770s, they reached the city, where they found another public. This public, which, as I have said before, we know very little about, was much further removed from the life at Versailles and therefore less subject to the principle of plausibility. Again, the plausible is not the real—but it must be able to be accepted as reality. In the city, comments about the queen could proliferate endlessly, and imagination was given much freer rein. At court, rumors had to conform to the rules of the local game, to enter an established network of references, citations, and allusions that gave them purchase—in short, join a network of intertextuality even though the intertext was founded on gossip only.

The apparently contradictory aspects of this staging can help us better to understand its mechanisms. They are contradictory inasmuch as they associate on the one hand the traits that were traditionally associated with the image of the queen—what I characterized above as the plausible elements in pamphletary fiction—and, on the other hand, traits that seem only to point to a general principle of emphasis pushed to the extreme and, sometimes, to the absurd. On the one hand, authors wanted to accredit what they insinuated; on the other, they seemed to surrender to verbal intoxication to the point of questioning the possibility of such accreditation.

A few examples will illustrate this double mechanism. It is in all that touches on the representation of the queen's sexuality that these examples are most significant. Marie-Antoinette was young and she was beautiful, and the failure of her marriage had for a long time been a public failure. It is not surprising that rumor gave her lovers. The count of Artois, the king's youngest brother, was a scatterbrain given to gallantry. He was often seen in the queen's company, in particular in those private fringes that were shielded from the court's rules and fostered many questions and suspicions. It certainly was bold to suspect a love affair between them, but, after all, it was in the order of things, which, of course, does not signify that such a liaison ever existed. Thus, the theme of the erotic pamphlet *Les Amours de Charlot et de Toinette,* published for the first time in 1779 and destined for great success, contains nothing surprising. What is surprising, however, is the manner in which, from two fundamental principles (the sexual demands of the queen and her incestuous relationship with Artois), the text of the pamphlet gives birth to a proliferation of variations that become largely independent of the initial motif. Certainly, incest already gave the intrigue an exceptional character. But here Marie-Antoinette's sexual dissatisfaction is soon transformed into an incessant nymphomaniac voracity that aimed at men, women, solitary pleasure, and, for good measure, animals. This "fureur utérine" stimulates a good portion of the pamphletary production concerning the queen. Each pamphlet rearranges these basic elements according to the requirements of its plot, or, more often, simply to outbid its competitors. A similar text, *La Vie privée, libertine et scandaleuse de Marie-Antoinette . . . ,* suggests, without apparent fear of self-contradiction, first, that, to the queen's appetite, women are only appetizers and men the main course, and then, the contrary. The contradiction here is of little importance. What counts, however, is the principle of variation and, especially, the quest for the superlative and for excess which normally translates into an evocation of large-scale, collective, complicated, sexual games. Another example of this outbidding is found in *Le Godemiché royal*, where the same process is used to transform Louis XVI—generally described as a sleepy, impotent man—into a homosexual who rebuffs the queen's advances. In terms of pornography, the rule is always to find better, stronger stuff. Hence the importance of accumulation, of the series, of cipher, that do not aim to produce an effect of reality but rather to impose a rhetorical model of development. The confession of *Marie-Antoinette dans l'embarras* provides a good illustration: "At the age of ten and a half, led astray by a 'fureur utérine' that I could not control, and all the more surprising considering its rarity in the climate where I was born, I amused myself successively with ten or twelve countesses from Lombardy, Florence and Milan who, in truth, made me experience the most delicious voluptuousness, but who exhausted me to the point where I almost perished."[10] This is, as one may surmise, the beginning of a long litany ruled by the superlative.

Incest, like nymphomania, is another favorite choice of this rhetorical production of the imaginary. Because the queen is suspected of being her brother-in-law's mistress, she can be accused of worse. *La Vie privée* does not hesitate to propose that she was the lover of her own brother, Joseph; of her sisters, too, while still in Vienna; and of Louis XV upon her arrival at Versailles. Further, everything began even earlier: did she not have her first sexual experiences with her father, while she was still in her mother's womb? In this context Hébert's accusation during her trial in October 1793, charging her of indulging in incestuous games with the Dauphin in the Temple, becomes more plausible. This last accusation, as we know, proved to be ineffective; it was perceived as monstrous, or at least as abusive to the point of not being admissible. One may imagine also that pamphlet readers did not necessarily believe all these accusations of the queen's depravity. But the problem, in all likelihood, lies elsewhere. What the pamphlets suggest is less facts than a series of imbrications: the quasi-indefinite possibility of formal variations that would end up creating a paper queen with an autonomous reality and a superior effectiveness. The fiction that they all contribute to construct can constantly be enriched by new details that are authorized only by the text already constituted. The more the collective text proliferates, the less its need to take root in "reality." It produces another reality that, although it is verbal, ends up nonetheless imposing a way of speaking of Marie-Antoinette that relegates her royal person to the background.

This process of hypersexualization of the queen is not the only example of the autonomy of textual representations. Another motif, not entirely unrelated, is the intimate, private sphere of the queen. I have already mentioned that the search for a private space was a constant in the life of Marie-Antoinette and that this search also produced its own share of rumors. Thus, it is not surprising to note that most of the scenes described in the pamphlets are situated in private places: the queen's apartments or those of her entourage—the boudoir, the royal sofa; the famous groves of Versailles, rendered notorious after the tragicomic mishaps of the Necklace Affair; the château's terrace, that Marie-Antoinette managed to reserve for a short time for a small circle of intimates. Once again, requirements of minimal plausibility are thus satisfied.

But the theme of privacy becomes subject in its turn to autonomous proliferation. On the one hand, privacy suggests secrecy. It is at the origin of new imaginary exercises about what happens but is not seen, about what happens when one does not see. The theme of sexual frenzy reappears at this point, as well as that of political conspiracy.[11] What is plotted in the queen's private space is always dangerous for the people, for the nation, for the Revolution. These intrigues are mysterious, but the authors of pamphlets denounce them by claiming the support of proofs that are themselves marked with the stamp of secrecy and privacy: the account of a chambermaid, a lost correspondence, even secret articles of a conspiracy hatched by the queen—an organization that superimposes itself upon the erotic network encircling Marie-Antoinette.[12] On the other hand, the register of privacy implies daily or ordinary life—a domain that is normally not compatible with the representation of royalty. In this case, the staging of the private sphere is at the origin of a degradation of the representation that it renders trivial, even ridiculous. Thus, in several pamphlets from 1792 to 1793, the "royal household" is the object of a treatment that approaches that of the farce, with strong "popular" connotations. Louis is a drunken idiot, the queen a violent shrew, and the argument between these two fallen sovereigns usually concludes with a brawl.[13]

Thus, it is not the presence of the private that is surprising in the pamphlets. That is normal in the view of what contemporaries knew (or thought they knew) of the queen's life. What is proper to pamphletary writing, however, is the capacity of autonomous proliferation of a theme which tends to reformulate entirely the reality it attempts to describe. The formal process of free amplification evokes, in many regards, the contradictory demands of the art of caricature: the motif or subject represented must be recognizable, but it must also submit to the greatest deformation possible.[14]

REALISM AND PARODY

This brings us back to the problem of the rhetorical processes at work in this literature. The pamphlets rely on a very large, open gamut of narrative techniques that range from essays (historical or political) to short stories, from dialogues to epic poems, from correspondences to documentaries. Besides these differences, what these texts have in common is a flaunted pretension to truth with the affirmation that they hold in their possession irrefutable proofs. Many present themselves as being grounded on unpublished sources or as being themselves original sources. Here the diversity of solutions is very large. For example, *La Vie privée, libertine et scandaleuse* that I have often mentioned cites a letter from Marie-Thérèse, Empress of Austria, that calls upon her daughter Marie-Antoinette to devote all her efforts to the ruin of France. The *Essai sur la vie de Marie-Antoinette* provides another letter of the same origin, but this time, it instructs the queen in sexual depravation and reminds her of the incredible power she will exercise by using her sexual favors to accomplish her sinister schemes.

All of this literature produces proofs in a quasi-obsessional fashion. It can go so far as to present itself as a massive documentary file. This is the case of *Marie-Antoinette dans l'embarras*, composed of a dossier of letters between Louis XVI, the queen,

La Fayette, and two secondary protagonists who consult together about politics and intrigue. But these sources themselves require a means of accreditation. In this same pamphlet, the king begins with a declaration that constitutes a general introduction to the dossier at the same time as it seals its status: "I would sincerely like to throw back the curtain behind which I have for such a long time hidden the wrongs that Marie-Antoinette is accused of, but the ice must be broken so that, if they unfortunately prove true, I can deliver to the Pope the evidence that will permit me to receive his holy permission to repudiate her."[15] Elsewhere, a third party might produce testimonies he collected through zeal, indiscretion, or chance. *L'Orgie royale,* an opera-proverb of 1788, is thus observed and reported by a guard who claims to have seen "everything" through a keyhole and then drawn up the chronicle. These are all classical devices. Obviously readers were capable of recognizing them as such (although this is an affirmation one can venture only with caution, as the strategies used by the scandal sheets of the twentieth century are there to remind us). Nevertheless, I do not believe that the forms of accreditation inscribed in the text of the pamphlets were indifferent or gratuitous. They certainly did not guarantee the existence of a particular reality, but that this reality was produced according to admissible forms, forms that respected minimal conventions implicitly agreed upon between the author of the pamphlet and his reader.

But this appeal to reality is only half of the picture. One has the impression that as soon as it is founded formally, this reality is disorganized and dismantled through a series of systematic procedures. The first of these has been described above and so needs only to be recalled briefly here.

The principle of overemphasis, of which I have stressed the importance, serves here to play the effect of reality to the point of absurdity, to the point where it contradicts itself. Take the example of *Les Embarras de Marie-Antoinette,* the pseudocorrespondence where the protagonists supposedly reveal the secrets of their hearts. A genre scene is inserted in the text—a dialogue skit that confronts Marie-Antoinette; the count of Provence, her brother-in-law; and his mistress, the countess Balbi. The dialogue is conceived as a sort of board game. Set against Provence and the countess, who ceaselessly quote the turpitudes and crimes of the most scandalous heroines of history—Queen Margot, Catherine de Médicis, Frédégonde—the queen must, as in a quiz, beat her opponents by inventing newer and more detestable performances. These fictions, which allow actors to reveal the truth about their characters, derive from classical literary conventions, but the emphasis given to them connects them, rather, to puppet shows or to games of verbal one-upmanship (like jousting with lies, those contests in irrealist imagination). Even the construction of the fictive scene contradicts the effect of reality that it aims to suggest. After Marie-Antoinette cataloged her imaginary exploits, what can possibly be the status of a "political" declaration such as the one that the pamphlet puts in her mouth:

> It has been such a long time that our handiwork has merited the most general disdain that I now feel obligated to admit it was good to annul all titles of nobility, titles that are all the more ridiculous since it has been undeniably proved that virtue is not transmitted by birth. What is this I say? I wager that of the seven to eight thousand gentlemen that were counted in France before last June, there are more than eighty-nine percent who owe their existence to lackeys, to plowboys, to artisans of the most obscure class.[16]

A second characteristic aspect seems to be the mixing of genres that are hardly compatible. *Les Embarras de Marie-Antoinette* has just provided us with an example. The text juxtaposes a fictive correspondence and a dialogue skit, the tone of a supposedly intimate correspondence indiscreetly revealed, and the self-ostentation characteristic of the stage, even if it is a private stage. Without a doubt, what the two genres have in common is precisely the recourse to fictions that should disclose the truth about the characters. But the discordance that exists between the different registers of fiction provokes, rather than an *effet de réel*, an *effet de dé-réalisation*. It is as if the pamphlet text sought less to be believed than to impose an accumulation of fictional modes. The same text also proposes two obscene prints with Marie-Antoinette as the central figure. The second, which ends with satire, corresponds fairly well to the general thematic of the *Embarras:* it concerns the description of an orgy in a complicated—and, to tell the truth, hardly credible—arrangement of entangled bodies. The first print, placed on the frontispiece and therefore presumably designed to attract the reader, represents the queen offering herself, under the eyes of other soldiers, to a guard who is dressed from head to toe. The legend delicately comments: "Bravo, Bravo! the Queen is penetrated by Patriotism." The print has very little to do with the contents of the pamphlet. Nor is it destined to create belief in the reality implied by all this literature—the wickedness and the perversity of Marie-Antoinette. This fundamental conviction is in fact expressed throughout the levels of discontinuous and heterogeneous representation. Once again, in the production of the reader's assent, the accumulation of juxtaposed signs remains the privileged technique of demonstration.

A final aspect, and perhaps the most important, is the systematic recourse to a parodic style of writing that is exercised in almost all the pamphlets. Parody can be exercised in established genres: history, as in *La Vie privée, licencieuse et scandaleuse* or in the *Essai historique sur Marie-Antoinette;* romance as in *Les Amours de Charlot et de Toinette;* classical tragedy as in *Le Godemiché royal;* comedy proverb and opera as in *Le Branle des Capucins,* "short artistocratic-comic-laughable opera in two acts," or in *L'Autrichienne en goguettes ou l'Orgie royale,* "opera-proverb composed by a Garde-du-corps and published since the Freedom of the Press, orchestrated by the Queen"; popular farce and vaudeville in *Le Ménage royal en déroute,* in the *Nouvelle scène tragicomique et nullement héroïqe entre M. Louis Bourbon, maître serrurier au Temple, et Madame Marie-Antoinette, sa femme . . . ,* among many other texts in the same vein; canonical forms such as the numerous variations on the *Testament de Marie-Antoinette* or the *Adieux de Marie-Antoinette à ses mignons et à ses mignonnes;* legal texts, like *La Requête de la Reine à NNSS du Tribunal de police de l'Hôtel de Ville de Paris* in which Marie-Antoinette supposedly demands the accusation and condemnation of Camille Desmoulins, guilty of making an attempt against royal dignity in his writings.

This parodic effort, with the ironic distance it implies, is also found in the style of personal testimonies. Just as in children's shows, the heroes of pamphlet literature give the plot away. When bad, their baseness is obvious. *La Confession de Marie-Antoinette, ci-devant Reine de France,* a confession that gave rise to multiple variants, well illustrates this strategy since the queen, under the pretext of inspiring the French to sympathize with her lot, takes sixteen pages to detail her love affairs and her schemes. This bout of sincerity is however just as quickly contradicted by the satire's conclusion: "I have just, people of France, proved to you my honesty, by confessing that which among you is called weakness, libertinism, vice, turpitude, and is known among the high-born as virtue, noble character, heroism. Think about what you have to do, according to the plan that I have conceived, and that will be executed, in spite of all the precautions you might take, because all of your leaders are in my pocket."[17] In the fictive correspondence gathered in *Marie-Antoinette dans l'Embarras,* La Fayette, the queen's presumed lover, takes care to mark in italics the key words of his duplicity in the letter he addresses to Louis XVI: "It would have been so nice to satisfy, at least in part, the troubles of your Majesty's concern, in order to show *my entire devotion, my probity* and *my integrity,* when her Majesty confides in me some important fact."[18] The authors of the pamphlets do not hope to enhance credibility with these techniques. They are conforming to an already constituted representation which they can overdraw without any fear of exaggeration since their only rule is, once again, that the character remain identifiable underneath the caricature.

If this analysis is correct, my original question becomes even more pressing. Why and how were these pamphlets able to produce certainty among their readers (or those to whom their readers communicated the contents in part or in whole)? If this literature simultaneously conveys elements of plausibility and elements that question the reality it aims to create, how can they be so effective?

An initial response might orient us to the characterization of modes of reading and, more largely, to specific uses for these pamphlets. To those who read them today extensively and without pausing, they seem, as I have said, mostly boring. But besides being subjective, this impression is perhaps linked to a type of appropriation that is not anticipated by the text. As was probably the case for many of the chapbooks of the *Bibliothèque bleue,* and as is the case for widely distributed newspapers today, these texts were probably not conceived in view of extensive and continuous reading. Did they even need a beginning, an end, a plot? The elusiveness of narrative structures one observes in most cases, the repetition of the same situations, the continuity of the commentary, the limited number of protagonists suggest other types of organization and reading. It is as if, taken together, these pamphlets constituted a vast repertory of anecdotes and *exempla,* as if they were illustrations of a truth that was taken for granted and had been formulated elsewhere. In fact, these texts function via an accumulation of scenes that are largely interchangeable and whose quantity and intensity alone give each of them its own particular characteristics.

To speak of *exempla* is to suppose the existence of a subtext that it is the function of these pamphlets to represent. In the particular case of Marie-Antoinette, nothing requires, in fact, demonstration. Everything is already known (or at least within the register of evidence) and has for a long time been the object of implicit recognition. Making that recognition explicit only adds formal variations to this network of certitudes. At this point, the apparent contradiction that seems to be lodged at the heart of pamphlet writing can be clarified: the text must clearly fit into a known repertory, but it must, as much as possible, be distinguished by particular traits that it generally finds in the realm of excess. Here again, we find a technique similar to that of caricature.

From this results one final consequence. Pamphletary fiction is to itself its own authority. It constructs its own reality, and each text refers not to facts outside itself but to the collection of pamphlets taken as a whole. The collection thus produces a coherent network of intertextuality, organized in citations, references, allusions, in a lexicon and an arsenal of shared syntactical and formal resources from which it is always possible—and, in fact, necessary—to borrow, and from which each single text draws its credibility and the illusion of reality on which it rests.

If these propositions seem acceptable, they invite us to reexamine in depth the political and social content of these pamphlets, as well as their implications. In the meantime, one thing is certain: well before the person of Marie-Antoinette was placed in jeopardy and then eliminated, it had long been devoured by its fictional representations.

Translated by Terri J. Nelson and Bernadette Fort

IV.   POST-REVOLUTIONARY FICTIONS

David Simpson

The Revolution That Will Not Finish: Mythologies of Method in Britain

1989 WAS A BUMPER YEAR FOR HISTORIANS OF THE FRENCH REVOLUTION, many of whom found themselves flying from conference to conference, and occasionally from television studio to newspaper office, delivering the latest opinions on the events and legacies of 1789. Ironically, much of this energy, especially in the United States, has been devoted to a demonstration of the degree to which we may finally allow ourselves to believe, as if awakening from some bloody nightmare of history into a new dawn of common sense, that the revolution is over: *la révolution est finie*. This published consensus is particularly appealing to Frenchmen of centrist and center-right political inclinations—most notably and influentially, Professor François Furet—who are visibly relieved at what they see as the hegemony, in contemporary France, of a liberal market economy working to efface the traditional polarities associated with the rhetoric of class struggle and the heyday of the PCF. They argue, not implausibly, that there has been a decisive shift in the language and consciousness informing French political life, a shift that renders archaic any recourse to the alliances of the last two hundred years, all of which have themselves been condemned to repeat the terms of a debate established in 1789 and unshaken until quite recently.

There seems little doubt that the terms of the political argument are indeed changing, as indeed I would argue that they always have been changing. These arguments somewhat resemble those about realignment that come around with every presidential election in the United States. They similarly presuppose a national mentality that has been set in one direction or another, while mostly leaving aside any reckoning of the huge nonvoting population and of politics outside the major parties. The realignment debates are at least mostly positivist and quantificatory: they try to describe things as they are according to a mathematical model that is self-consciously reductive. The assertions that the French Revolution is finished are of a different order: they suggest not only that things have changed, but that they have changed once and for all, thus passing polemically from a model of how things are to one inscribing how they must always be, or not be. Only the most uncritical belief in the power of the extant political discourse to circumscribe or manage "real history"—the uncontrollable, unpredictable events that have always been a part of any complex account of history, and of almost all experience of history—can allow itself to assert, as if analytically, how things must be in the future. Moreover, the exposition of the present discursive paradigm on which these predictions are based is itself highly selective and even wishful. The belief in the stability of the present political alliances, and of the national and global economies on which they must be at least partly based, is perhaps possible only if one generalizes the perspective of the upper middle and ruling sorts in a few privileged national enclaves, ignoring at once the tensions within those subcultures and the pressures that may affect them from outside. Thus it would seem wise, even prudent, to exercise some skepticism over just what has "ended," and how, whether it be the French Revolution, whatever that was, or the much invoked bogeyman of "communism," or, in the splendid coinage of Dan Rather standing before the Berlin Wall, "Marxist-Leninist-Stalinism." Or, indeed, the democratic majority in the United States, and all the analogues we encounter in an international anglophone press more and more dominated by a few people and a narrow range of vested interests.

I offer these rather general speculations by way of a prelude to an account of one legacy of 1789 that has certainly not disappeared, and may indeed even have been strengthened by the turn in the priorities of the countercultural Left associated with postmodernism: the denigration of method, and of a certain kind of theory. *Method* and *theory* are not, of course, synonyms. *Meth-*

od most usefully describes an achieved analytical or descriptive procedure that produces results and has a practical (or indeed speculative) outcome, while *theory* has an altogether more indecisive semantic aura, suggesting the sort of speculation that goes beyond what is already known into the sphere of the prospective and hypothetical. The suspicion of method as a radical political-educational strategy that informed conservative opposition to Ramism and then to certain factions in the English Revolution of the 1640s was premised on the assumption that methodical practices were established and available, potentially to all and sundry. After 1789 or thereabouts, the conservative element (along with some nonconservative elements) in the anglophone tradition is much more habituated to a denial of theory, the speculative, hypothetical gesture to which the "empirical method," indeed, is often proposed as a healthy antidote, one particularly British and also, by way of various mediations, often also American. The French Revolution did much to discredit English tolerance for systematic thought in general and for the mathematical paradigm in particular (in nonmathematical contexts). "Method" and "theory" have since tended to appear as synonymous in popular and popular academic speech, denoting systematic mental procedures aspiring to some high degree of logicality. In this way, that which is arguably most rigorous (method) becomes associated with what is imaged as most abstract or illusory (theory), and neither is deemed properly responsive to or descriptive of the gloriously fertile muddle that is "human nature." It has been above all the business of "literature" to present this human nature with its best self-image; while in political life it requires supervision by experience and common sense rather than by schema or principle. It requires, in other words, governance by an established patrician class whose continuity is assured by its own prequalifications—since only those already in office can have had experience and learned common sense.

This essay will focus principally on the 1790s in Britain, and on the reactions to the French Revolution and to its perceived espousal of method, system, and theory as guiding principles in describing human nature and fashioning political structures. Well before the Terror, these inclinations had been imagined by the British as peculiarly French, and as hopelessly out of line with the world as it is, or as it was thought to be from within the mythology of the British national character. Edmund Burke's *Reflections on the Revolution in France,* perhaps the most famous of all British responses to that event, is dominated by a general hostility to those "systems" which a "cabal, calling itself philosophic," has sponsored in French political life.[1] Burke, in fact, stands as an exemplary ancestor of that now-familiar Anglo-American suspicion of "French theory"—a phrase, by the way, that is there in Arthur Young long before it is repeated by our colleagues in humanities departments in the 1970s.[2] This "theory" was imaged as a common cause among the *philosophes* and as the efficient cause of the social and legislative changes happening from 1789 on. It has continued to function ever since as the mark of alien violence and implausible intellectuality. In a monumental essay of 1968, "Components of the National Culture," Perry Anderson sought to explain the relative scarcity of intellectuals in British public life, and the peculiar inflections of those who did appear. He noted, with considerable conviction, that the "British bourgeoisie had learned to fear the meaning of 'general ideas' during the French Revolution: after Burke, it never forgot the lesson."[3] And Burke it was who stood forth as the spokesman of a nationalist alternative to clear and distinct ideas. In his own prose style, he celebrates confusion and copiousness: "I beg leave to throw out my thoughts, and express my feelings, just as they arise in my mind, with very little attention to formal method" (p. 92). In his arguments, he scorns all rational paradigms, despising the "geometrical and arithmetical constitution" (p. 144), emphasizing instead the priority of intuition over logic and discernment over definition (p. 153). Politics and mathematics should have nothing to do with one another. In politics, only the "method of nature" should be followed (p. 120): social and political life is imaged as a living organism (or sometimes a family) composed of variously active and harmlessly redundant elements all shuffling through time in a harmonious aggregate and at an instinctively slow rate of adaptation. This "nature" that is the state does not yield up its secrets to the coldhearted theorist (for theory is always cold) but only to wise passiveness. It cannot be contained within the "metaphysics of an undergraduate, and the mathematics and arithmetic of an exciseman" (p. 299) but must be left in the care of the world-wise patrician whose experience and prudence preclude any giving way to the extravagances of theory. Burke is one of the leading prophets of that much celebrated and much reviled doctrine, Anglo-Saxon empiricism. Here it is again, in the words of Arthur Young, the self-styled English yeoman:

> I have been too long a farmer to be governed by any thing but events; I have a constitutional abhorrence of theory; of all trust in abstract reasoning; and consequently a reliance merely on experience, in other words, on events, the only principle worthy of an experimenter. [*The Example of France*, pp. 2–3]

No matter that these images of the Revolution put about by Burke and Young and others like them were challenged by those who might have claimed a rather deeper immersion in the sphere of the empirical. De Pont himself, the original addressee of Burke's text, responded that "these economists, these philanthropists, these philosophers, upon whom you speak with so much asperity," have done much more for the cause of liberty than "those knights errant, whose extinction you deplore."[4] And William Belsham spoke for many others in accusing Burke of mistaking "the plan rejected for the plan adopted" in France, and in modestly pointing out that the proposed new *départements* were by no means "square compartments geometrically exact" but had been decided upon by much local consultation and compromise.[5] No matter, again, that various of the mathematically inspired reforms discussed in 1789 had been either proposed or initiated in the last years of the Old Regime. For Burke, everything began anew, and began tragically.

On the other side, there was an equally extreme emphasis on theory, method, and system as the keys to good order and political health. Here is George Rous:

> We are conscious of no crime when we rejoice in the sacrifice of Gothic prejudices, at the shrine of reason, by a great and enlightened nation; and we wait with anxious expectation the result of this grand experiment of scientific legislation.[6]

And Joel Barlow looked to France as about to provide firm evidence that *"Theory* and *Practice"* need not any longer remain "eternal enemies" in the "highest concerns of man."[7] Some commentators did point out that neither theory nor practice is by definition the property of the Left or the Right of the political spectrum. Thomas Cooper observed that Burke himself had a theory, "the THEORY of *Privileged Orders,*" and a system, insofar as he was "the systematic opponent of every Species of Reform."[8] And John Thelwall focused his considerable polemical talents in demonstrating that even Burke used the inexorable syllogism (the tool of the cold logician), however "disjointed" and "artfully divided" its parts might be.[9] But these qualifications did not much inform a debate that presented theory and system as championed by the Left and despised by the Right. Similarly, Thelwall's careful attempt to dispute the relation between philosophy and political violence fell largely upon deaf ears. His *Sober Reflections* reached a much smaller readership than did Burke's more inflammatory ones; so too did his argument that Jacobinism suffered from a lack of philosophy rather than an excess of it. For Thelwall, Robespierre was not at all the incarnation of the philosophic spirit but the symptom of its near-total extinction: "During the reign of his desolating tyranny, philosophy was silenced, science was proscribed, and daring speculation soared no more."[10]

Despite these perspectives, then, the popular political imagination continued to believe in theory and practice, method and contingency, as the respective insignia of Left and Right. In accounting for this, we need look no further than the languages of the protagonists themselves, who do indeed declare these affiliations and make these claims. But this alone does not explain why they seem to have been so widely believed. In explaining the belief, a number of truisms about the late Enlightenment seem to continue to hold: scientific and fideistic thought had often been in tension with one another; rationalism had claimed for itself a politically leveling function; natural rights had been seen to be related in inverse proportion to positive laws. Much of the urgency of the British debate in the 1790s may be attributed to nothing more complex than the symbolically charged events of the revolutionary period: a new assembly, a set of constitutions, a Bastille leveled, a king executed. But the British debate took on the profile that it did for a number of residual as well as immediate reasons. I do not mean to suggest that there was some preestablished discourse into which the events in France had to fit; but I will suggest that there was a rhetoric of national identity, indeed of national*ism*, that identified being "English" with being against theory, against method, against rules and systems, and in favor of practicality, tolerance, compromise, and common sense, all the things that a methodized paradigm most visibly threatens. This in-place image of national identity, one which had been solidifying at least since the Restoration of 1660, was massively reinforced by the events of the French Revolution, which were produced to prove that theory in intellectual life inevitably resulted in terror and violence in public life.

I cannot here attempt any comprehensive account of the English predisposition against method and theory before 1789. But let me offer at least some critical instances. We have already noted John Thelwall spotting the syllogism, the logician's "mark of Cain," buried in the sublime and self-consciously disorderly pronouncements of Edmund Burke's prose. Capel Lofft, another of Burke's critics, described the ideal of simplicity in political systems as depending on their being exempt from "unnecessary, disconnected, unduly united, or disproportioned parts."[11] Paine himself, in the *Rights of Man*, praised the Declaration of Rights because its first three articles comprehended "in general terms" everything that came after them.[12] I doubt that any of these writers—Thelwall, Lofft, or Paine—had the name of Ramus even in the back of their minds. But they were responding, at a distance and in a highly mediated way, to the terms of a conflict in the sixteenth- and seventeenth-century academy generated by Ramus and by Ramism's attack on the received practice of pedagogy. Generations of scholars have managed to render this conflict into a "dry as dust" chapter in the history of ideas; but it was much more urgent at the time. Wherever one explores the debate over Ramism and method in post-Renaissance Europe, one picks up the scent of political dispute and declared social crisis. It is not hard to see why. Any system that purports to describe human behavior and the world order along autonomously rationalist lines tends to entail the redundancy of institutions and the assault on habits; more radically, it may describe them as positively pernicious. This is the threat that Burke perceived from the British and French radicals. As soon as human nature is posited as naturally progressive in itself, out go monarchs, aristocrats, placemen, and the entire

apparatus of class discipline, along with the ideological language
that justifies it—all the attributes of what Burke thought of as
"Merrie England," but which Paine preferred to think of as "Old
Corruption."

Something similar was at stake in the early quarrels over Ramism. Ramus was a Protestant martyr, murdered on St. Bartho-
lomew's Day, 1572, and an educational reformer, both in the
limited sphere of the universities and in the wider world of printed
books. He wanted to revivify higher education by abolishing si-
necures and replacing private disputations by public lectures; he
wanted more books printed in the vernacular; and he radically
revised the contents of those books, both typographically and,
most important of all, by abbreviating the traditional logic into
a ready and easy manual potentially accessible to all who could
read their native language and were possessed of a modicum of
natural reason. Academics in the European universities in the
sixteenth and seventeenth centuries fought even more violently
over Ramism than their modern successors have battled over Derrida and others like him. And, while the political applications
and determinations of contemporary literary and other "theory"
remain to say the least variable, Ramism in Britain was clearly
identified with a potential broadening of the educational franchise. Its claim for the orderly nature of the ordinary, uneducated
intelligence placed reason outside the control of the official educational apparatus, while its commitment to the vernacular and
to the needs of an artisan middle class appeared as both a symptom
and a cause of a perceived dissolution of class boundaries. The
Ramist logic was explicitly pragmatic, oriented toward being in
the world (and, some said, to the particular world of the Protestant
entrepreneur). I do not mean pragmatic in the more limited modern sense; its utilitarianism was in objective correspondence with
the world as it is in itself. There was, for Ramus, no distinction
between how the mind worked (when stripped of the Scholastic
obfuscations describing it) and how the world was ordered. Both
worked by a single method, applicable to all forms of inquiry,
and dependent less on education than on natural facility. The
easiness of this single method allowed for a much larger part of
the population than before to be thought of as intelligent. The
priority of the general, axiomatic principle over the particular

instance rendered nugatory all claims of age, experience, and authority (exactly as Paine would challenge Burke). The Ramist education was, in its time, cheap, efficient, quick, and complete. Thus Ramus himself was able to propose a reform of the institution of the university: fewer professors, who would be paid directly by the state; public rather than private lectures; teaching in the vernacular rather than in Latin (and in an orthographically reformed vernacular at that). Ramists claimed to teach the whole of Aristotle's logic in a text reduced to about one-tenth the length of the original.[13] Now, anyone of "indifferent capacitie" could "with a little paines" gain some knowledge of that "necessary Science."[14] Fage's 1632 version of the *Dialectica* is explicit in its populist educational ideal:

> God reason taught, and man he did inspire
> With faculties, which Logicke doth require.
> The matter precepts, forme Methodicall,
> The end is reasons use, to teach th'unlearned all.[15]

Abraham Fraunce satirizes the orthodox Aristotelian response in terms that seem the less hyperbolic the more one reads of this debate:

> Ramus rules abroade, Ramus at home, and who but Ramus?
> Antiquity is nothing but Dunsicality.... Newfangled, young-headed, harebrayne boyes needes be Maysters that neuer were Schollers; prate of methode, who neuer knew order; rayle against Aristotle assoone as they are crept out of the shell. Hereby it comes to passe that euery Cobler can cogge a Syllogisme, euery Carter crake of Propositions. Hereby is Logike prophaned, and lyeth prostitute, remooued out of her Sanctuary, robbed of her honour, left of her louers, rauyshed of straungers, and made common to all, which before was proper to Schoolemen, and only consecrated to Philosophers.[16]

Not for nothing were many of the Puritans avowed Ramists.[17]

Ramism was an eclectic rather than a monolithic doctrine, and elements that are alternately Platonist and Aristotelian, hermetic and rationalist, protoscientific and antiscientific, can be and have been traced in it. But it seems to have been consistently the property of reformist subcultures, and as such appears in different incarnations within them. Even John Wesley wrote a logic, and his movement may have been given its name not just by analogy to medical practices but also and as much through a recognition of its similar social correlatives to those of the Ramist and Puritan precursors.[18] Ramism was not the only critical residuum in the debate about method in the 1790s, but its aims and principles can be recognized in the language of the theorists, just as Baconian inductivism provided Burke and his allies with an alternative vocabulary. Much of eighteenth-century scientific and political theory plays between Ramism and Baconianism, in variously mediated ways, ways that tell us much about the precise receptions of those theories. For it was the Baconian paradigm that became the norm for scientific discourse, even in the French tradition. And Bacon hated Ramus, that "man of bold disposition, and famous for methods and short ways which people like," and the author of the fantasy that any mere logic could be "subtle enough to deal with nature."[19] In place of a priori theory and system, Bacon offered inductive observation corrected by experiment: "For God forbid that we should give out a dream of our own imaginations for a pattern of the world" (pp. 32–33). Nothing could seem more English, and more prototypically Burkean. Baconian method, unlike the received (and Ramist) logic, moves from parts to wholes, inductively. Its social-political ramifications were developed and specified in Thomas Sprat's important *History of the Royal Society* (1667), which worked hard to propose and defend the friendliness of Baconian science to the existing religious and social order. For Sprat, it is the artisan class that can pursue science properly and inductively. The aggregate of that class offsets the prejudicial effects of their individual specializations, and that aggregate remains under the guidance of a patrician class of "gentlemen, free and unconfin'd"; that is, males of sufficient income and education to be above the temptations of interest and the psychological deformations of particular occupations or regimes of experimentation.[20] Sprat almost overgoes Burke, by anticipation, in his eulogy of an experimental method that is to be entrusted to wise guardians rather than to abstract rules, one that is

> never to be a *fix'd* and *settled* Art, and never to be limited by constant Rules . . . [it is] like that which is called *Decence* in humane life . . . never wholly to be reduc'd to *standing Precepts;* and may almost as easily be *obtain'd,* as defin'd. [P. 90]

As a salutary message designed to gloss over the civil strife of the 1640s and 1650s by an ethic of benign (but authoritarian) inclusiveness, Sprat's *History* could hardly have been bettered. Forswearing abstract "method" and "*Speculative Opinions*" (pp.116,118), it proposes a system of checks and balances (discussion and experiment), an analogue for scientific practice of the evolutionary rather than the revolutionary model of political change. It might thus have put to rest the invocation of the "great Creator Reason" in the words of the Digger leader Gerrard Winstanley: a creator who "spoke not one word . . . that one branch of mankind should rule over another," and who is "not yet risen up to rule as king."[21] Sprat made Bacon safe, if he was not already safe, for the reconstituted political and commercial order after 1660 and 1688. So too was Newtonian method absorbed into the rhetoric of normality.[22] But, as with Newtonianism, we would be missing much by regarding Baconian method as an integral and insulated entity able to preserve through time and place its inventor's original disdain for (in this case) Ramus and Ramism. Condillac, who, along with Condorcet and Rousseau, had the most direct influence of all the *philosophes* on legislation after 1789, presents Bacon as his hero. His *Logic* is purely Baconian in its determination to begin "*not* with definitions, axioms and principles" but "by observing the lessons which nature gives us."[23] At the same time, it is a *logic;* and it clearly revivifies the Ramist legacy of belief in a single method, and one that, being based in nature, is "actually known to everyone" (p.73). The voice of radical Ramism is heard again in Condillac's claim that "there are people with accurate minds who do not seem to have studied anything" (p. 83), while many of the learned go wrong, and not least because of their vested interests in whatever has been established by "superstitions, by governments, and by bad philosophy" (p. 205). Similarly, D'Alembert's preliminary discourse to the *Encyclopédie* professes strict Baconian doctrine, and praises Bacon as above all the "enemy of system," while the two editors go on to invert the Baconian primacy of imagination over reason,[24] and Diderot in his own voice revalidates geometry as the paradigm of a properly methodical knowledge—a paradigm that should extend beyond the sciences and even into theology.[25]

Diderot and D'Alembert, even as they praise to the skies the inductive or Baconian method, thus seem to nudge it firmly in the direction of the rational-mathematical model.[26] And with Condorcet, it is Descartes who is brought back as the heroic precursor, the one who "brought philosophy back to reason" by reminding us that it must be derived entirely from "primary and evident truths which we can discover by observing the operations of the human mind."[27] Condorcet again restates the rationalist (and Ramist) belief in the mind as able to project the necessary order of the world out of itself. He also, like his British contemporary Joseph Priestley, had the Ramist's faith in charts, analytical schemata able to represent much in little, and in such a way that "men who have not been sufficiently educated" could "master them when the need arises" (pp. 277–78). And, once again, Condorcet was a believer in the single method (p. 290).

Perhaps I am now rehearsing familiar material, and have done enough to suggest, albeit somewhat reductively, that the philosophes were doing something different with the Baconian paradigm even when they were claiming to uphold it (as Condorcet, however, did not). As late as 1816, Coleridge would claim that "speculative philosophy" was a significant contributory cause of the French Revolution, and that theoretical abstraction and political violence would always go hand in hand.[28] Much of Coleridge's own career was in fact given over to an attempt to reclaim the vocabulary of method for the conservative cause (whose chief antagonists, after 1815, were the utilitarians). He for one remained quite sure that the "pale-featur'd SAGE'S trembling hand" could be "Strong as an Host of armed Deities."[29] In the same spirit, John Thelwall would probably have convinced no one, in the speech he had prepared to deliver upon his acquittal from treason charges in 1794, that the pen he planned to hold aloft was "the only artillery I ever meant to make use of."[30] Intellectuals, philosophers, and men of letters were feared by conservative Britain in the 1790s exactly as they were exponents of method, theory, and system. And, of course, the radicals themselves made massive claims for the power of truth and in particular its appearance in print. Godwin, Paine, Mackintosh, and a host of others, however they disagreed on the finer points within the radical portfolio, all believed that the mists of superstition could not but be dispersed by the power of the printed word. Truth had only to be in readable form in order, eventually, to be believed.[31]

The question then arises: if method, theory, and system were the declared affiliations of the political Left, while custom and intuition were those of the Right, what place remained for the practitioners of "polite" literature? On the one hand, there was the puritan plain style. Catherine Macaulay declared for it in disdaining Burke's "ornaments of stile" and his "fascinating charms of eloquence," those features of his writing which meant that he could only ever address the "*passions* instead of the *reason* of mankind."[32] Mackintosh also found Burke's rhetoric to be the offspring of a "prolific imagination" and an "ardent and deluded sensibility" (*Vindiciae Gallicae*, p. v). As Thomas Paine saw in the new "true method" nothing less than an end to the "age of fictions" (*Works*, 2:510), so David Williams dismissed the establishment politicians as merely literary talents: "Their fancies or imaginations are not balanced by science, or by that high and exalted reason which is formed by the calm and patient study of philosophy, a profound acquaintance with history, and the strict discipline of mathematics."[33] But literature, of course, was widely supposed to be dealing quite properly in sensibility, imagination, fancy, and fiction. Insofar as it was in this sense thought to appeal to that part of the mind not appeased by method and system, it was implicitly in loose alliance with the antitheoretical Right. Writers who seem to have sought to find a middle way thus found themselves mired in a definite discursive confusion. Blake's *Book of Urizen*, for instance, argues against the exponents of a single method ("one Law"), whom we may reasonably identify as the radical post-Ramists; but it does so without reproducing anything resembling the Burkean rhetoric of limited self-development within a patrician-governed culture of custom and habit. Blake for one would have wanted to reclaim the values of a "prolific imagination" for an at least countercultural and perhaps radical cause; but we can now see how difficult it must have been for any contemporary audience to understand such a position at a time when the political associations of method and imagination were so clearly preestablished. Wordsworth, not dissimilarly, tried to combine the Burkean emphasis on the passions (over reason) with a democratic universalism in writing an appeal to the passions of all persons, in their essential state (by which he meant when uninfluenced by class distinction, customary difference, and special interest). Here too what was essentially a mediated and eclectic paradigm—something of Paine, something of Burke—failed to find an audience that responded to its peculiarly embedded poetic-political economy, although its democratic tendency was clearly perceived by those who spoke out in defense of the *decorum* that *Lyrical Ballads* so visibly challenged.[34] When the literary and scientific models came most explicitly together, as in the writings of Erasmus Darwin, which sought precisely to "inlist Imagination under the banner of Science" and to guide it away from "looser" toward "stricter" analogies,[35] the conservative literati stood forth to defend the borders of "literature" against such miscegenation—and most of all against the extension of a scientific culture (pagan and erotically liberating) to ordinary readers and to women. Richard Polwhele, in deploring the trend whereby the female writer now only draws "Each precept cold from sceptic Reason's vase," looks back to a time when the feminine and the literary were united in a common devotion to leisure and consolation, rather than theory and stimulation:

> Ah! Once the female Muse, to NATURE true,
> The unvalued store from FANCY, FEELING drew;
> Won, from the grasp of woe, the roseate hours,
> Cheer'd life's dim vale, and strew'd the grave with flowers.[36]

Much of the argument about and between the female authors of the 1790s—and there were many of them—was occasioned by the prospect of a rationalist female, one who broke ranks with both genre and gender codes in proposing a *literature* that was not restricted to fancy, feeling, and the strewing of flowers upon graves. The argument continued, and it informed the increasing separation of literature from science that the late nineteenth- and early twentieth-century reorganization of university faculties put into institutional practice. The cult of irony and paradox that captured, for instance, the imaginations of college English teachers (some of them) from the 1920s on was a sort of methodical antimethod; at once an adaptation of and a trenchant alternative to the culture of science as it was then perceived. It was also a revalidation of the importance of a subculture of elite, qualified readers, a protest against what was seen as "mass culture," and thus a removal of the literary from the sphere of ordinary persons in a state of vivid sensation. The production and discussion of literature in this way moved ever further from its Wordsworthian moment, further away from any potential incarnation in a "book that all may read."[37] "Literature," to deserve the name, became a special language, the product of a special mind, and available only to an exceptional critical intelligence. It could not take on the mantle of method and theory, for that had been given over to scientists (in England) and to Frenchmen (and eventually, also, to Germans). At the same time, literary criticism at least had to propose some vocabulary exact enough to support a professional academic subculture.

Anglo-American cultural and educational history owes this, among other things, to the legacy of 1789, which clearly reinforced (though it did not invent) a nationalist stereotype of liberal-minded, antisystematic Englishness. The national literature had to reflect this paradigm, most frequently and tediously in the figure of Shakespeare, and the national criticism has traditionally been arrested at the *pons asinorum* made up of the two equal and opposite angles of system and intuition, reason and imagination. As a secondary discourse visibly parasitic on literature, criticism must establish itself as different enough to appear otherwise than redundant. Hence it must dally with a language of self-consciousness, method, and scientificity. But as an antiscientific cultural imperative, affirming the values of undivided mental labor and the "human" dimension, literary criticism must defy the perceived rationalism of mathematical and scientific method, and the cold conclusions of metaphysicians and technocrats. Hence all these tears, over "theory," over "politics," over race, gender, and everything else that is seen as invading a discipline that has in fact never had any clearly marked borders and has ever been able to define itself only as "not" something else. The nationalist mythology has ensured that "theory" has remained the business of the French (and sometimes the Germans), and has continued to reiterate its tendencies toward violent reductiveness, even when that theory is explicitly antirationalist and antisystematic. In this way and in this context the Revolution of 1789 is not at all finished but continues to underpin a living mythology for those critics and cultural analysts who follow in Burke's footsteps and continue to identify "theory" as a violent imposition upon an essential and variable humanity and its literature.

These are "fictions," of course, but very active ones, as the conservative rewritings of the French Revolution remain popular and thick with allusions to the dangers of guiding practice by theory. The conference for which this essay was prepared, and whose proceedings are the basis of this volume, was brilliantly titled to appeal to a critical and historiographic community living through poststructuralism, with its corrosive effects on notions of essence, substance, and reference, and through postmodernism, with its emphatic distrust of totalities and rational models. *Fictions of the French Revolution* permits us any number of negotiations around the notion of fictionality, and even more around the little word *of.* Words can be things, to echo Mirabeau (and Wordsworth). Consider, for instance, the afterlife of the term "revolution" itself. The British claim a glorious and an industrial, but never a social or political revolution. The events of the 1640s have been designated a "civil war," while the shoring up of the establishment in 1688 is a revolution in the conserving sense—a turning back to things as they were, or should have been. Words do embody some knowledge and suppress others. But the suppression, if we take the trouble to look into it, is usually visible and describable. There is little evidence for the existence, at any point, of a historically monolithic discourse that is capable of complete epistemological hegemony, even when it is supported by a near-monopoly of institutional power. At the same time, the dice are always loaded. In the rowdy exchanges between the Burkes and the Paines of the 1790s, different voices were hardly heard: the nativist dissenting platforms of Price and Priestley (for nationalism was appropriated by the Right), the much more radical ideas of Thomas Spence (the Winstanley of the 1790s), these never gained the discursive high ground in the debate over the revolution. No more did the complex narratives of such observers as Mary Wollstonecraft and Helen Maria Williams—complex because obliged to set the ideal of a rationalist explanation against the daily evidences of shifts in direction and disjunctions between practice and profession within the "revolution." These versions of the history of the times had little effect on the mythologies of "system as violence" that reappeared in the late 1790s with the "Illuminati" scare—a phenomenon that seems to have had more to do with ruling class concern over the state of Ireland than with any recrudescent desire to understand why the French Revolution really happened. Marxist theories of why 1789 happened have taken rather a drubbing lately—by no means entirely undeserved. Marxist theories of what was made of 1789 once it had happened have yet to have their day (and we must begin, again, with *The Eighteenth Brumaire of Louis Bonaparte*). The beginning of that task must be the recovery of the varieties of explanatory languages—fictions, perhaps—and the explanation of why some of them were much more popular than others. To ignore the varieties is to accept the version of history written by the winners, and to reify any model of a possible future. It is to repress the evidence for what we may still think of as a class struggle, even as the very term "class" comes under massive and necessary scrutiny for its inadequacy in describing the changing nature of conflicts both within and outside the nation-states. As those of us in literary criticism and beyond continue to argue over "theory" without any very profound awareness of what we mean or why we have been trained to mean it, this history remains an important and a living one. After 1789, English literature was even more doggedly English in its suspicion of systems and theories, and arguably more anti-cosmopolitan.[38] In this way we all live with the fictions of the French Revolution, in much the same way that Perry Anderson described back in 1968. At a time when the British ruling party is once again trying to narrow the educational franchise, and radically so, literary criticism is once again obliged to stand up and be counted in a variety of ways. It has as much to fear from being deemed useless as from being found dangerous and therefore to be repressed. In the United States, the politics of theory is just as urgent in relation to an educational movement that proposes an uncritical familiarity with the history of the majority culture as the core of cultural identity, at exactly the moment when that majority is more (demographically) unstable than before. We remain embroiled in the legacies of 1789, but mostly without being aware of any connections between then and now. Perhaps our major fiction about the French and their revolution is that it was theirs, and theirs only (whatever it was); and that we, comfortable

within a ruralist-nationalist idiom of the customary, are entitled
to think of "our" way of doing things as different and preferable,
as if there were indeed an "us" entitled to articulate that
language.

François Furet

The Tyranny of Revolutionary Memory

I

FOR THE PAST TWO HUNDRED YEARS THE FRENCH REVOLUTION HAS been the sole heritage of French public life, and even those who opposed it could lay claim to no other past. This is in a sense obvious, since the Revolution was the political matrix of all of France's political families; but that heritage has proved a rather unmanageable one, as illustrated by the chaotic nature of French constitutional history. In France, in contrast to the American case, the idea of revolution and the idea of the past are not easily reconciled, for the first idea—that of revolution—unceasingly eclipses the second and eradicates the continuous aspect of constitutional thought.

This is so for two reasons: the first is that the Revolution, in giving such a spectacular role to political voluntarism, divided national history into two parts. The men of eighty-nine wished to sever themselves from the past and to found a new social contract. After breaking with aristocratic society and rejecting the concept of the king's sovereignty, they were rapidly brought into conflict with the Church and French traditional religion. With the Year I, in 1792, they started the history of their nation completely anew. The obviously fictitious side of such an ambition detracts nothing from the force it held over people's imaginations at the time: the rejection of the Ancien Régime struck a chord in every Frenchman, even those who would have wished things were otherwise. Once the Revolution had occurred, its opponents could hardly call for a return to the times that had produced it. The counter-Revolutionary Right, which would have liked to celebrate tradition, was as bereft of the past as was the Revolutionary camp that had condemned it. For all intents and purposes, they were also thrown back upon that exclusive heritage which began in 1789; but since they were the ones who had denounced it, they had recourse only to sentiments and memories—something little-suited to the definition of institutions or even policies.

At least the Revolutionary camp could have had the potential advantage of being able to construct, over time, a tradition and a history. It was, however, the opposite that really happened, since they were ceaselessly racked with internal divisions and their quarrels for succession tore the patrimony of 1789 into bits. No one was ever able to direct the course of events for more than a few months' time and the Revolution passed through the lives of its heroes setting them against one another with inexpiable hatred. Even the famous Year I, when it was at last decreed to begin with the twenty-first of September in 1792 in order to appropriate historical time, began only with the Republic, relegating the first and greatest years of the Revolution to the Ancien Régime along with the king. This epoch was followed by a time when the Republicans were divided into Girondins, Montagnards, Sans-Culottes, Dantonistes, Hébertistes, Robespierristes, and, at the end of the series, Thermidorians. This was the second impediment to the Revolution's becoming a patrimony: it was internally divided and had spilled the blood of its partisans as well as its enemies.

Furthermore, another idea was born of these battles, which differed from the one that had appeared in 1789. The first idea was that the Ancien Régime was to be overthrown and replaced by a new order founded exclusively upon the law. From 1792 on, however, the Revolution soon abandoned that ambition. After the fall of the Girondins on 2 June 1793, the Revolutionaries set up the "Revolutionary government," indefinitely adjourning its constitution. This tautology—that the government of the Revolution was "Revolutionary"—meant that the Revolution had become its own end. The Revolutionary idea henceforth took on a different sense than it had had in 1789 since it came to designate less a rupture or a passage between two social states than a privileged form of action by which the human will took a lasting hold upon the historical world in order to transform it. That image is inseparable from an open-ended drift of political action toward the future: it is a radical negation of all rootedness—including rootedness in its own history—and seals off the possibility of envisioning the establishment of law as its end.

Thus for the French of the nineteenth century, the Revolution was all that remained of their past. Even those who disliked it found that it had robbed them of all that preceded it. As for those who looked with favor on its results but not on its course, there was nothing for them to like—neither before 1789, nor after. And those who lamented the premature end of 9 Thermidor were looking toward the future.

This orientation of heart and mind was very early discernible in the course of events. One need only take the vantage point of the period following 9 Thermidor, that first "end" to the Revolution which was the fall of Robespierre and his dictatorship. The ambition to continue the project of 1789 in order finally to found it in constitutional law came back as an imperative of public opinion. But with this rediscovery of liberty returned, on the one side, the dream of erasing all traces of the Revolution and on the other, the opposite goal of starting it over again.

In order to start the Revolution over again, its course would have to be "edited," excluding once more all the men who wished to end it, from the Monarchiens to the Dantonistes to the Feuillants and the Girondins. One must take up from the heritage of Robespierre and from the course of history interrupted by the bad guys of 9 Thermidor. That was the plan of Babeuf and his friends, who wished to move toward more widespread equality and a communism of agrarian redistribution.[1]

In contrast, the counter-Revolution wished to return to the past, glossing over not only the Terror but also the tabula rasa of 1789: that was where they wished to begin their rewriting of history. But Bonald's rewrite was obligatorily another version of the same tabula rasa.[2] He would design an Ancien Régime along the lines of providential order, even more "philosophical" than the 1789 social contract between men, and he proposed a new abstraction offered in the name of God that would erase the Rights of Man. At the same moment in time, the third idea, that of ending the Revolution, would find its most brilliant interpreter in Benjamin Constant.[3] Constant, lacking a tradition, sought out an ally in long-term continuity: the Republic exists, he said, and it protects all that has been done since 1789 as well as all of those responsible for those actions. But the problem was that that Republic only existed since 1792, and was born of the Terror, whereas the nation's masses, if partisans of the *bien nationaux,* detested the guillotine and the men of the Year II who so tenaciously clung to power.[4] To end the Revolution by the Republic promised to be as impossible a task as to put a king at its head, and the problem of 1796–97 seemed as insoluble as the problem of 1789–91.

The failure of Constant and his friends thus reiterated the message that the Revolution constantly eluded those who wished to end it. Prior to the Year II, it had not yet come to the end of its forces and its forward march. After that date, it had gone too far to be able to contain its own past. At least the Revolution always managed to make of its history a fortress under siege: in Fructidor of the Year V it would recover—without pleasure but without too much pain—its cortege of souvenirs and means— exile, the Terror, a new set of emergency measures. Only Madame de Staël was unhappy, but she too understood that the force of Revolutionary "necessity" was a synonym for unconstitutionality.

Bonaparte would close the theater of the Revolution for some time by chasing all the Revolutionaries from real power, giving them only positions. The personal dictatorship he established conformed both to his character and to the situation: his passion for giving orders relegated the gang of regicides to the shadows. The state he reinvented to his advantage, if along the abstract lines of reason, harked back to the central heritage of the last centuries of the monarchy. But if his state presented over the administrative machine of the kings the advantage of being constituted upon new foundations by a strong, even absolute power, it was a more fragile version of that machine, since it lacked its dynastic cement. An exceptional being, both by virtue of his genius and by the circumstances that had fostered that genius, Bonaparte designated himself at its head, sole master of a state at once despotic and rational (something the French kings had never understood how completely to elaborate). He himself was the only vulnerable element. The old monarchy was weak but hereditary. The new one was strong but temporary and its incontestable character only aggravated its ephemeral aspect. Like an evil spirit, the ghost of the tabula rasa perpetuated itself through the chancy character of the reigning family.

In this way, at least insofar as the modern state governs and administers equal individuals, the Revolution was ended. But it persisted through the crisis in legitimacy it had initiated. Bonaparte certainly understood this, for did he not found a hereditary empire in the manner of kings with a Hapsburg princess? Nonetheless, the only basis for power remained victory and conquest, as though this unprecedented sovereign was condemned continually to repay, as a compensation, the price of his coronation. Perhaps all this was less necessary than he believed. Perhaps the spirit of conquest was more a feature of his character than of the actual situation itself. It remains true, however, that by actively associating those two elements (victory and conquest) Napoleon prolonged, enlarged, and transformed the Revolution instead of extinguishing it. He enriched the already prodigious repertoire of those few years with yet something else: a democracy of the plebiscite. To that, he associated the souvenirs of an extraordinary national adventure, unforgettable if superfluous. He had wished to replace the kings of France but in the end brought them back to the throne in the tow of the enemy, more alien than ever to national history. Once he was defeated, France was empty—cut off from the Ancien Régime by equality and national glory, deprived of the Revolution by the Empire. It returned to a sort of zero-point. After a quarter of a century, the Bourbons and France were once more face-to-face—an odd couple condemned to reinvent a history which would neither be that of the Ancien Régime nor that of the Revolution. Napoleon had understood that impasse at the beginning of his military defeats: "After me, the Revolution, or rather, the ideas that it produced, will resume their course. It will be as though, opening a book at the marker, one were to begin reading again where one had left off."

II

In "beginning to read again" at the page where Bonaparte had undertaken to end the book, the French could not just start off again as if he had never existed. If the emperor's conquests had been but a pointless adventure, the modern state was a lasting trend left by the first consul. The meeting point of the Ancien Régime and the Revolution, it was what assured the position and continuity of national history. At the same time, however, its existence unceasingly sharpened the battle for power. Centralization of the realm by the monarchy had been one of the preconditions—no doubt the principal precondition—for the Revolution. The durable foundation of the Napoleonic administrative state lent the Revolutionary idea a preconstituted goal that facilitated seizures of power while cushioning their shocks. The things about which the French tacitly agreed only worsened their divisions, but helped them to attenuate the consequences of those divisions. Thus the revolutions of the nineteenth century were less immense events—as in 1789—than Parisian happenings. The structure of the nation could give them enough weight to be victorious, but they now lacked in themselves the formidable energy of that quintessential event since that event had already taken place.

They had the power to evoke the past, a past which was unceasingly kept up by an unflagging pedagogy. For the annals of the nation, the Revolution had substituted the immense shadow of its quarter-century and it had become the sole repository for political memories and sentiments. Two hundred years later it is hard to imagine the extent of the intellectual tyranny of that event. For generations it was the sole subject of conversation when discussing public affairs. To the Right, recollection took the form of expiation, and heaven knows that the nineteenth-century Catholics multiplied the occasions for collective repentance! For the Left, those great memories constituted the basis for renewed revolutionary hope: the Convention, the Republic, the regicide, the constitution of 1793, were the ensigns of the future, freshly emerging from the Year II. The nineteenth-century French public scene had the strange characteristic of being both terribly recent and terribly weighed down with history. To understand the extent to which it remained the theater of the Revolution, we need only look at the way religion fared during this time. Napoleon thought he had reconciled the French around the cult of their ancestors, more gallicized than ever. After him, Catholicism once more became, to the contrary, a political issue, the cornerstone of an

Ancien Régime reinvented around the throne and the altar—an unprecedented construction born of the memory of misfortune. French politics in the nineteenth century were thus dominated by what we might call "the imagination of the Revolution," composed of transfigured memories and passions lived over and over again. At the heart of these images was the founding opposition between the partisans and adversaries of 1789. But the nineteenth century also reproduced the divisions caused by the Revolution and which it had unceasingly envisioned in terms of an original rupture. It reinstated the Manichaean cleavages of the earlier model between Orleanists, Republicans, Bonapartists, Jacobins, and Socialists. Just as it was between 1789 and 1799, their object was nonnegotiable since it affected the legitimacy rather than the internal organization or extent of power. The space of national politics thus remained full of radical confrontations.

In fact, revolutionary culture was common to all those participants, Right or Left, insofar as they all sought the regeneration of society, each one claiming that society to be dependent on their own preferred government—a political overinvestment which Marx saw to be the quintessential character of modern France. Even Guizot, the most "liberal"—in the philosophical sense of the term—of the men who governed France in the nineteenth century, superimposed the image of government by Reason on representative government, which was in his eyes the only type of government capable of holding together all the various members of post-Revolutionary society. And as to the others, at base, they all thought to a greater or lesser degree that the social world of free and equal individuals, as it had emerged from the fourth of August in 1789, was incapable of founding a political community on the unitary will of its members only. Robespierre himself was to understand this at the end of his dictatorship when he tried to impose the cult of the Supreme Being. The accent placed by counter-Revolutionary philosophy on a providential order is a sort of reverse insurance against a monarchy which turned out to be so fragile. At the opposite extreme, in the Revolutionary camp, according to men like Michelet, the Republic is the archetypal exorciser of interests and classes, the picture of fraternity and the law, and another religion on the march—the religion of humankind.

In putting the critique of bourgeois individualism at the center of the next revolution, socialist doctrines would add the final touch to this collection of exorcisms of social divisions. They would however revive the great design of 1789, the tabula rasa and constructivist voluntarism, although this time as instruments for going beyond 1789. If the 1789 Revolution rediscovered its meaning, it was in relation to the revolution which was supposed to follow and achieve it. History, the secularized Providence of the nineteenth century, gave its blessing in advance by decreeing that repetition of the French Revolution was inevitable. The socialist revolution would have the advantage over 1789 in that it would wed will to science, and would thus offer the cumulative benefit of the subjective and the objective to its militants. But for the time being, in anticipation of the great change and the workers' emancipation, socialist politics most often took the path traced by Revolutionary politics, multiplying clubs and secret societies, continuing to mount the radical tone, becoming more and more exclusive, and producing utopias which, though related, were nonetheless inimical. In the touching flowering of fraternity that personified 1848, French social constructivism was at its best: released from their origins, which were after all meant to be overtaken, the utopian socialists forgot that they had ever even had a precedent. One of the triumphs of the Revolutionary tradition was that it had erased its own traces. Socialism thus had no past, only a future.

The passion of nineteenth-century Frenchmen to rub out social divisions led to the same result as it did in the late eighteenth century. Their obsession with unity would aggravate their conflicts. The formulae for government that filled the space of national life were conceived less in terms of constitutional adjustments than as a means to achieve the optimum social order: an ambition that would constantly renew the Revolutionary project under the pretext of ending it and which, as can be seen as much in Orleanism as in socialist doctrines, would lend a privileged status to class struggle in political thought. The Revolution unceasingly repaved its path with the idea and sentiment of class. The socialists invented the working class before it had been constituted by capitalist industry and the bourgeoisie never stopped trying to exorcise its retrospective panic of 1793 by shedding the blood of those who were nostalgic for those days in the name of their sense of class domination. The historian cannot help but be struck by the uselessly if deliberately violent manner in which the insurrections of June 1848 were repressed.

Late in the nineteenth century, the Revolution continued, torn between those who wished to obliterate it, to end it, or to start it up again. To such political fundamentalists as the French, the Revolution left little room for constitutional reflection per se or for the minimum of empiricism required in order to study how institutions adjust to the tormented landscape supplied by opinion. The French disliked the monarchy but feared the Republic. They were keen on a centralized state but were unable to withstand its most natural tendency—despotic Bonapartism. A democratic and egalitarian people, they could not manage to maintain in a durable fashion a liberal monarchy, a parliamentary Republic, a referendum Caesarism, or a Jacobin dictatorship. Both a cause and a result of that state of affairs, nineteenth-century political France remained as "literary" as it had been during the preceding century: peopled by writers and philosophers, but lacking great politicians, endowed with Guizot, Tocqueville, Victor Hugo, Lamartine, but without a Bismarck, a Cavour, or a Gladstone. The Revolution continued to cross centuries and men, none of whom were ever able to master its irresistible force. In the end one man, who was neither the most profound nor the most respectable, was able to channel the torrent by virtue of having been long immersed in its waters. But that was perhaps more attributable to chance, to intellectual and spiritual erosion, than to a deliberate constitutional calculation.

That man was, of course, Thiers, the tireless "arranger," the go-between of French politics, who spent his whole life trying to tame the Revolution after having written its history. If he did at last succeed, just before his death, with Gambetta's help, it was not because he did a better job than anyone else of resolving the French constitutional equation, nor because he had even considered the problem in those terms. It was rather because he was a pure practitioner of politics on whom the luck of circumstances had finally smiled. Even the French Revolution grew old in the end, and, with time, its spell over public life had gradually receded. Later on, one could also say that it became more receptive to compromise as the three kinds of regimes that had furnished the national imagination had just collapsed: Bonarpartism had died at Sedan while on its way to winning the battle of succession, the Jacobin republic died with the Commune, condemned by a nation of universal suffrage thenceforth master of Paris; Thiers spared no worker's blood to be rid of that other ghost of the Revolution. Finally, the last pretension to restore the monarchy was dispelled by the Duke of Bordeaux's determination to keep the white flag aloft. These were among the many circumstances that opened up the way to the ecumenical talent of Thiers, who had cast about for a suitable outlet during the entire century. All it took was the rise on his Left—cleverly engineered by Gambetta—of a conservative republicanism—a compromise between the Rights of Man and Auguste Comte—in order to bring together the conditions for a representative Republic that would escape the curse of the First Republic without running the risk of the Second.

Thus in 1875 French politics at last made way for an almost Burkean hodgepodge by virtue of which the Revolution took its place in time. France would escape from the Revolutionary obsession of the best of constitutions by the adoption of the three laws governing the organization of public powers which would prove a durable formula. Circumstantial as they were, those texts did little or nothing to settle the purely constitutional problem left by the Revolutionary tradition: that would have to wait one hundred years more. But they did allow the Republic to assume its place in France's heritage, pacified by universal suffrage and soon to be propagated by French schools.

The rest of the story belongs to the twentieth century. The Third Republic did not put an end to French constitution making, and it is only now that the French political divisions have healed, with the emergence of a stunning national consensus over the institutions of the Fifth Republic. But this consensus had been attained at the price of major innovations within the French democratic tradition: the abandonment of the centrality of the legislative power, a president elected by the people, and a judicial control of constitutionality. This is an altogether different story, to be left for a next encounter.

V.   AFTERWORD

EDITOR'S NOTE

The Northwestern colloquium on "Fictions of the French Revolution" was enhanced by two further cultural events. The Special Collections Department of Northwestern University Library exhibited a variety of documents from its French Revolution Pamphlet Collection, one of the largest such collections in America. On 10 November 1989 the Theatre Department presented the American première of Stanisława Przybyszewska's *The Danton Case*, the first English translation of which had been published in the spring of 1989 by Northwestern University Press. Craig Kinzer's ambitious four-hour staging of this play made a significant contribution to the colloquium. Theater, in so many ways the natural operating mode of Revolutionary actors, forms an important dimension of the subsequent fictionalization of the Revolution. Przybyszewska's play, injecting into the fabric of the French Revolution the concerns and questions of the Bolshevik Revolution, was especially suited to a contemporary Franco-American reflection on fictional cross-fertilization and overlays. In the following essay, Craig Kinzer explains the choices he made as stage director in balancing past and present in his interpretation of the play.

Craig Kinzer

Staging Stanisława Przybyszewska's
The Danton Case

THE FRENCH REVOLUTION HAS BEEN THE SUBJECT OF NUMEROUS
dramatic efforts over the past two centuries but has curiously
resisted successful stage treatment. Of more than one hundred
major stage texts written since 1789, only a handful have found
places in the canon, most notably Büchner's *Danton's Death,* and
Peter Weiss's *Marat/Sade.*[1] Most have disappeared beneath the
shifting waves of theatrical and historical fashion. The theater's
failure to find adequate and successful representation for these
events may be a result of a number of factors both inherent in
the circumstances that gave rise to the texts which did emerge
and to the limitations of the theatrical form itself. Most of the
early dramatic treatments were glorifications of the triumphs of
the Revolution written in pageant form during the period immediately following the fall of the Bastille, or, as in the case of
many nineteenth-century examples, expressions of the historical
interpretation of events that prevailed at the time of production.
These early efforts were mostly jingoistic agitprop and disappeared
quickly. In the case of later treatments, as the dominant interpretation shifted with the times, those dramatic expressions fell
out of fashion. Moreover, the very scope and breadth of the events
of the Revolutionary period may in a sense be too large for the
confines of the theater itself. The wealth of specific detail necessary
for understanding complex events can tend to burden theatrical
production with minutiae and detract from an audience's perception and apprehension of character and the experience of a

compelling dramatic line. Conversely, when individual character is featured at the expense of historical context, audiences unfamiliar with circumstance may lose a sense of the significance of the historical events on which the play is based. The line between "history lesson on stage" and ahistorical character study is a treacherous one.

Büchner's effort is a singular exception to this pattern, and the play's success with contemporary audiences is due in some measure to the particular nature of its historical position. Though written in 1835, the play remained unproduced until Max Reinhardt's staging in 1916 and is a theatrical discovery of the twentieth century. The playwright's vision of historical events runs counter to the prevailing romanticism of his day. While focusing in the Romantic tradition on the exceptional individual, Danton, Büchner goes one step further and dramatically renders that individual almost as victim of the relentless engine of history, without will and at the mercy of fate. In that sense, the play survived the topical circumstances of the Romantic period and has particular appeal to the sensibility of twentieth-century audiences. Moreover, Büchner's relentless and exhaustive examination of one of the period's most fascinating and elusive characters gives the play profound dramatic appeal. *Danton's Death* strikes an effective balance between the private character of Danton and the public events surrounding him. Büchner avoids the "history lesson" trap; only enough historical information necessary for understanding Danton and his actions is included in the play.

Stanisława Przybyszewska's *The Danton Case*, written in 1927, was given its first complete English-language production at Northwestern University in November 1989.[2] In choosing to produce it, we felt that while it possesses some of the pitfalls of earlier efforts to dramatize the Revolution, we had found an exciting theatrical treatment of the period's most fascinating characters and significant events. Burdened with vast amounts of historical detail, the play is nonetheless a compelling examination of complex individuals operating on a vast historical stage, and the playwright's skill at dramatizing both intricate political movement and the internal life of character made it in our view clearly worthy of production. Written as a rejoinder to Büchner's play, *The Danton Case* focuses on the same events—the final confrontation between Robespierre and Danton. And like Büchner, Przybyszewska views those events through an exhaustive examination of the actions of the central figures. *The Danton Case* differs in that it elevates Robespierre, who though significant in Büchner's treatment disappears after Act II, to a dramatic position equal to that of Danton. The tension between these two characters and their struggle for control of the direction of the Revolution form the core of the drama.

Przybyszewska's story begins in a Revolutionary Paris in upheaval, exhausted by war and strained by the constant struggles for power among the factions of the government. Faced with rising public unrest and rumors of a coup d'état against its power base, the Committee of Public Safety, the Jacobin faction argues for the immediate arrest and execution of Danton and his associates. Robespierre, fearing the cost to Revolutionary ideals of such extreme measures, proposes indirect action against the Dantonists by silencing their public voice, Camille Desmoulins's broadside *Le Vieux Cordelier*. The Dantonists retaliate by publicly denouncing the Committee, calling for the arrest of one of their most valued agents, and demanding amnesty and a return to moderation. In the midst of this stalemate, the two leaders agree to meet in private to attempt a reconciliation, a meeting which results in further polarization and Robespierre's conviction that Danton must be eliminated.

From this critical moment, the conflict of the play moves into the public arena. Danton's arrest results in outrage in the National Assembly and calls for the overthrow of the Committee. Robespierre and his associate St. Just, through a combination of subtle manipulation and veiled threat, succeed in neutralizing the delegates and eliminating the convention as a serious adversary. Sensing his power base eroding, Danton determines to take his case to the floor of the Revolutionary Tribunal, where his skill at oratory and public manipulation have a chance at swaying the citizens of Paris to his side and reversing his fortunes in dramatic fashion. The desperate members of the Committee, well aware of the power of Danton's charisma and fearing for their lives, turn to Robespierre for a solution. Using a rumored conspiracy on the part of the Dantonists as a pretext, he instructs the Tribunal to forbid the defendants to speak on their behalf or to call witnesses in their own defense, thereby denying them justice and due process of law. The Dantonists, their last weapon gone, fall to the guillotine. Realizing his efforts to salvage Revolutionary progress will result in a bloodbath, Robespierre faces the inevitable failure of the Revolution and his own imminent downfall.

Przybyszewska's text is embedded in the historical interpretation of the Revolution that prevailed during her lifetime—that of Albert Mathiez, the early twentieth-century Marxist historian whose revisionist view of history attempted to reconstruct Robespierre as true hero of the Revolution. In *The Danton Case*, Robespierre is elevated to the level of tragic hero, sacrificing all personal life and directing all his energies with exhausting single-mindedness for the sake of the public good. In the play's final scene, immediately following the execution of the Dantonists, Robespierre recognizes that the extreme measures taken to preserve the momentum of the Revolution run contrary to the ideals of the Revolution itself. In order to preserve the Revolution, he has had to destroy it. Dictatorship and terror have become an inevitable necessity, and with them the realization "that the people cannot govern themselves—that democracy, the foundation of the civil system, is an illusion." It is Robespierre who is left alone at the end of *The Danton Case*, burdened with a tragic hero's vision of the inevitable failure of Revolutionary ideals.

Przybyszewska was profoundly influenced by the political upheaval in Europe during her lifetime, and the play is a commentary on Revolutionary movements of the early twentieth century. The inexorable movement of egalitarian sentiment toward dictatorship chronicled in *The Danton Case* is a clear parallel to events in Soviet Russia in the 1920s, as well as a presage of the rise of fascism in Germany. The worldwide depression of that time is also a source of dramaturgical comment, and the human suffering of the body politic functions as a driving force in the play from its opening moments. The first scene takes place in front of a bread shop, where a line of Parisians wait for basic foods they know will be in short supply. Their argument over responsibility for their current hardship and the near-riot that ensues serve as a frame and background for the more private drama of Danton and Robespierre. The central players in the game are driven by material necessities of the public, and answerable to them. The crowd subsequently reappears at a number of key points and constitutes a third dramatic force in the play.

The Danton Case, then, examines the relationship between an individual's private choice and the public results of that choice.[3] That examination serves as a window onto that historical moment when democratic revolutions of necessity centralize power in a single figure, and the resulting dictatorship defeats the very impulse that gave birth to it. Working with a vast canvas, Przybyszewska explores both a large-scale political event and the interstices of character. The resulting tension between public and private spaces serves as a strong core for the dramatic event and elevates, I believe, the play to a significant position in dramatic literature.

*   *   *

The task of the director and design team in the Northwestern production was to render in theatrically compelling ways the strengths of Przybyszewska's text while solving some of its difficulties and avoiding its pitfalls. The most significant of these was length. The uncut version of the text runs in excess of five and one-half hours, and much of its length is due to the mountains of historical minutiae it contains. Moreover, while the play has enjoyed a successful stage life in Europe, we worried that American audiences, unused to theater performances longer than two and one-half hours, would find such length unacceptable.[4] We decided to keep cuts to a minimum, preserving as much as possible Przybyszewska's dramatic structure while eliminating overly burdensome historical information. Other cuts were made in an effort to maintain a dramatic balance between the play's protagonists, a balance that the playwright's ideological sympathy for Robespierre on occasion upsets.[5] The challenge here was through careful editing to allow Danton and his point of view a clearer presentation, without denying Robespierre's central position. Rather than altering the play's ideological thrust, giving Danton and the Indulgents a fair hearing allowed our audience to view Robespierre's position as more complex, and I believe made his tragic denouement more compelling. The final production ran four hours, which we found was manageable for our audience, and most of the historical context necessary to Przybyszewska's argument was preserved.

It was further decided to eschew period representation and detail in the setting and costumes. Because the play is embedded in a twentieth-century perspective and therefore not strictly speaking a period piece, and because it uses historical events to make a contemporary comment, we felt that to invest the look of the production with historical accuracy would be to distract the audience's attention away from the currency of the play's issues and onto details not central to its concerns. Once these two decisions had been made, the task of developing a visual and staging approach was necessarily guided by the need to anchor the production visually in a world which reflected the central issues of the play, and reinforced the audience's understanding of the movement and conflict the drama examines.

The costumes for the production were designed with an eye toward mirroring the three distinct and conflicting factions in the play. Danton and the "Indulgents" were clothed in warm colors and natural fabrics, which onstage had a rich, sensuous feel (figs. 1 & 2). Garment lines were flowing and broad, reflecting the hedonistic strain in the Indulgents' political position, and helping the actors embody the striking public postures of the characters. In the play, the actions of individuals within this group are often guided by personal self-interest, so a range of individual detail and idiosyncratic touches, such as Danton's flowing scarf and Camille's dispatch pouch, were added to the costumes. This profane and worldly look was in stark contrast to that designed for the Jacobins, the Committee of Public Safety, and Robespierre in particular (fig. 3). These costumes had an impersonal uniformity, reflecting their professed suppression of individual concerns for the sake of public good, which was at the heart of the Jacobins' political position. Black and white synthetic fabrics were used, colorless and cold. In the case of Robespierre, the "Incorruptible" who has forsaken all personal life for the sake of the Revolution, the costume had a pinched, uncomfortable, almost asexual line, capturing the character's rigidity and fierce determination. The third grouping of characters was the crowd, a force whose power and allegiance are fought over by the first two, and whose successful manipulation by the Jacobins leads to the fall of the

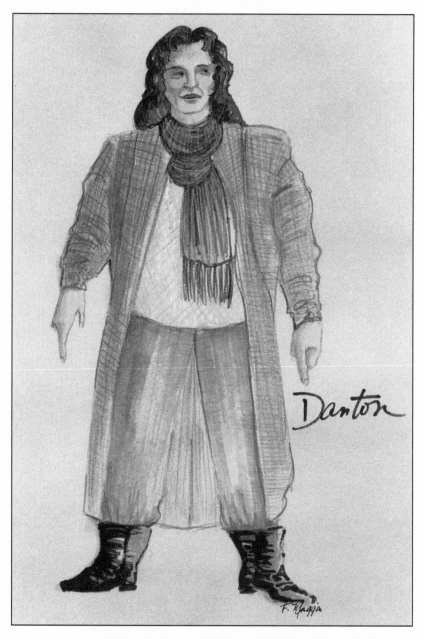

Fig. 1. Georges Danton. Costume sketch from *The Danton Case*; Frances Maggio, designer. Photograph by Dawn Murray.

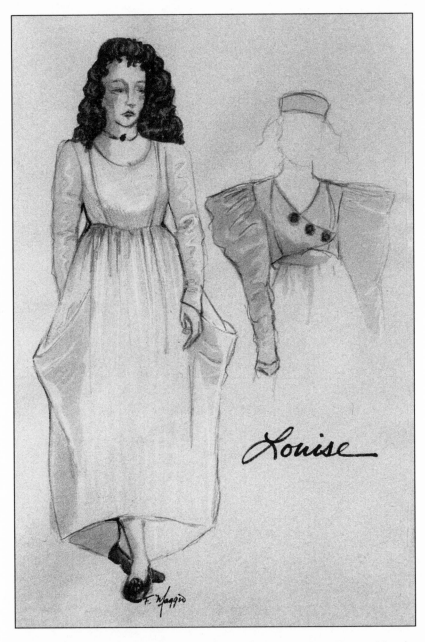

Fig. 2. Louise Danton. Costume sketch from *The Danton Case*; Frances Maggio, designer. Photograph by Dawn Murray.

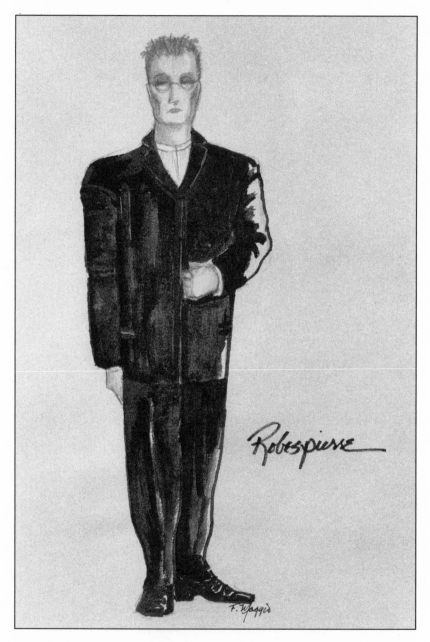

Fig. 3. Robespierre. Costume sketch from *The Danton Case*; Frances Maggio, designer. Photograph by Dawn Murray.

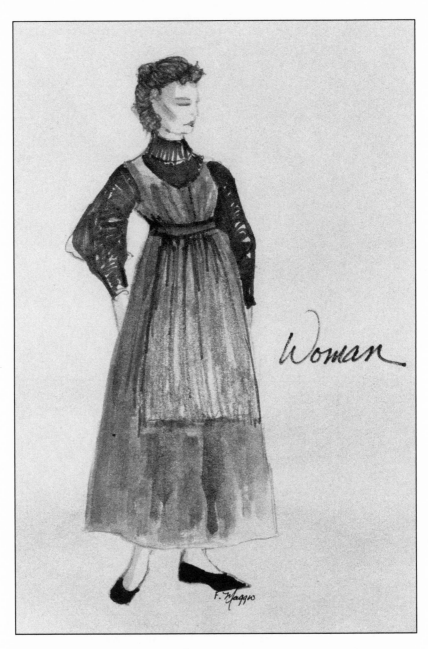

Fig. 4. Woman of the crowd. Costume sketch from *The Danton Case*; Frances Maggio, designer. Photograph by Dawn Murray.

Dantonists (fig. 4). Earth tones and rough, homespun fabrics were used. The color range was close to that of the scenery, so the crowd blended into the surroundings, giving the audience a sense of the vast, almost anonymous power of the play's body politic. Many of the actors in this group played a number of characters, so individual pieces were added to a basic costume, enough to help differentiate character, while keeping the anonymity of the crowd and anchoring the audience in the circumstances of the specific scene.

The Danton Case contains twenty scenes over five acts, and takes place in fourteen distinct locales. The production was staged in a large, 425-seat thrust theater, which dictated that background scenery, such as doors, walls, or windows, could not be effectively used to indicate changes in location. Instead, individual set props were chosen to anchor each specific scene: Robespierre's rooms were defined by a small, spare writing desk and chair; Danton's apartment by a richly upholstered chaise and silver candelabrum; the Committee of Public Safety by a large meeting table and chairs; etc. Small hand props associated with character, such as Robespierre's books and writing implements and Danton's wine goblets, were added. A simple flexible stage composed of several wooden platforms and two upstage sliding panels, which could be rearranged for various scenes, completed the setting.

This spareness of investment in representational detail freed the design team to explore the use of nonrepresentational or symbolic images in scenery and lighting. The images chosen were intended to serve as a framework for the production, referring to larger historical and political issues surrounding the historical drama, and mirroring the movement of the play's central conflict. This essentially imagistic approach allowed us to provide our audience with a "double perspective" on the theatrical event, a simultaneous anchoring of the play in selected referents to historical specificity, and in a nonhistorical, timeless theatrical world of our own creation. In order to generate appropriate images, we viewed the play as a three-part construction, each part containing a number of specific symbols and having its own distinct visual style and patterns of staging. Our choice of symbolic image was guided by our definition of the central conflict in each section.

The first movement of the play begins with the street scene (Act I, scene i in Przybyszewska's text), and concludes with Danton's failed "reconciliation" with Robespierre (II, v). Thematically, this section examines the tension between the private worlds of Danton and Robespierre and the struggle between those two for the allegiances of a number of other characters. Private space was emphasized scenically: entrances into interior scenes were established geographically (i.e., down left into Robespierre's room, up right into Danton's apartment), and used consistently. Lighting was "realistic," indicating time of day, direction, and detail of interior through templates suggesting windows and doorways. The designer used primarily warm colors, treating the human figures three-dimensionally.

Two symbolic images dominated the stage during this opening movement. The first was a large canvas drop, depicting a male figure dispensing justice. This image, taken from a drawing on a broadside of the period, reflected the idea of dictatorship, an issue raised in the first scene by members of the mob (they assume Danton will take on that role) and the subject of much of the political discussion for the rest of the play. Hung upstage in the first scene, it was subsequently handled in a number of ways—as a cloth draping the Committee of Public Saftey's conference table, swagged over the steps in Danton's home, covering the sideboard in the café where Robespierre meets his nemesis—during the remainder of the first section. This figurative idea of dictatorship and the threat it poses to the Revolution thus became a literal presence in each scene of Part I. The second image reflected the power of language, particularly Camille Desmoulins's writings in *Le Vieux Cordelier*, over the sentiments of the mob, and the danger language presents to the Jacobin cause. Robespierre articulates this concern in the final scene of Part I: "My *thought* is powerless against his *poetic* ravings" (italics mine). In the opening scene, piles of paper, pamphlets, and broadsides were placed in various locations on the stage, and referred to by the crowd as the latest subversive publications. As the play progressed, these papers were scattered about the stage, gradually growing in volume and number, and finally surrounding Robespierre and Danton at their meeting at the Café de Foy. As the conflict between factions advances, so does the presence of their weapons on stage. This very presence motivates the extreme actions eventually taken by the Committee.

Part II moves this private conflict into the public area, and the combatants wield institutions in their battle for supremacy. In staging this section, we used elevated platforms for the convention rostrum and trial bench, and the stage floor was reserved for crowd activity and private scenes, thereby establishing a tension between public and private space, and the power of public action as it achieves dominance over individuals. Lighting became colder and more harsh, treating the human form in a less gentle fashion than in Part I. The geography of the stage began to lose familiarity; unlike in Part I, multiple entrances were used in specific scenes, to underscore the increasing chaotic and threatening nature of the public conflict. Characters could be interrupted and discovered at any moment from any direction. As the events move more and more inevitably toward the guillotine, bloodsoaked straw was strewn about the stage and around the feet of the platform which would eventually become Sanson's workplace. Delacroix's figure of Marianne, from *Liberty Leading the People*, was hung directly upstage and served as the visual image central to this section (fig. 5). The effect of this deliberate anachronism was twofold: the idea of liberty is invoked in public discourse by both factions, and is therefore a constant presence in the languages of both text and design. On another level, whether liberty will survive the Terror is a central question of Part II, and to the audience her site on the stage is both overwhelming and precarious.

The power of *The Danton Case* shifts in Part III from public institutions to the relentless momentum of events, and characters are literally crushed under the weight of this power, the force of which has been unleashed by their own machinations. The design team determined that a radical shift in the style of the production was needed, one that would visually equal this turn in the drama's direction. Private space no longer exists; therefore in the staging, reference to realistic locale was eliminated. Scenes bled together, happening almost simultaneously, as characters entered the final vortex of Revolutionary events. In the first scene of Part III, while Robespierre met with the public prosecutor to determine the course of the trial, the Dantonists were already scattered about the stage, dimly lit as if in their prison cells. They remained there in the

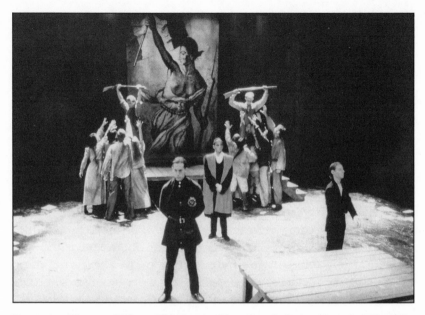

Fig. 5. Act IV, scene iii from *The Danton Case*. Scenic design, Jonathan Darling.
Photograph by Dawn Murray.

following scene, surrounding the Committee during its most critical moment. Following Robespierre's fatal decision to permit no
defense witnesses and thereby deny the Dantonists due process,
Delacroix's Marianne was rudely ripped to the ground by two
soldiers, and the Committee itself was swallowed up in the crowd
rushing onstage for the final battle at the Revolutionary Tribunal.
In the play's final scene, Robespierre sat in a chair alone center
stage, surrounded by the now-executed Dantonists, standing frozen at the perimeter of the stage, staring mutely at the audience.

The two dominant images of the final part of *The Danton
Case* were Marianne, present through Part II and disappearing at
the pivotal moment of Part III, and an enormous bolt of white
fabric hung from the flies upstage. This served as a cyclorama,
onto which various abstract lighting patterns were projected, and
as a radical alteration in the space itself. This injection of bright
color actually changed the scale of the stage space, reflecting the
change in scale of events. Following the verdict of execution the
cloth was unfurled, covering the entire stage floor as well as the
vertical space, and revealing a twenty-foot-square bloodstain center

stage. Events have progressed to the point of bloodbath, and Robespierre, aware of the inevitable carnage that will follow, sits alone in the midst of the very slaughter he has unleashed and which will soon swallow him.

One final staging device central to the concept of our production concerned the crowd. As previously discussed, the body politic is an important third force in the drama, appearing regularly throughout the play and fought over by the protagonists. In this production, the crowd was elevated as a presence beyond what Przybyszewska calls for, and a line paralleling the central narrative was constructed for them. In Part I, the crowd manipulated the stage set to expedite transitions, but did so in the characters they assumed during the first scene. During the shift into the first Committee scene, in addition to moving set pieces, the crowd surrounded the Committee members, pressing petitions into their hands and badgering them with requests and supplications. While the supporters shouted their approval, a young woman shouted quotations from *Le Vieux Cordelier* during the shift into Danton's apartment. The excited spectators were seen on their way to the galleries prior to the confrontation outside the Convention hall. In Part II, this specific character-based behavior diminished as the move from the private to the public realm progressed. Characters began to lose identity; scene shifts became mechanical and unemotional; and at the conclusion of the pivotal Convention scene, when through intimidation and veiled threat Robespierre sways the delegates to his cause, the masses applauded in unison, stripped of personality and free will. In Part III, when the scene shifts no longer occurred, they did not appear until the trial itself, during which, as a result of the Committee's final deception, they turn on Danton and demand his execution. Their final appearance was as an abstract image. As Robespierre delivered his final tragic realization of the impossibility of democracy, their distorted, grotesque silhouette was projected on the white cloth (fig. 6). Robespierre sat immobile and alone, surrounded by the mute foe he had defeated but not vanquished and the people he had attempted to serve but had not satisfied.

As is probably evident, our production of *The Danton Case* took considerable liberties with Przybyszewska's text, particularly

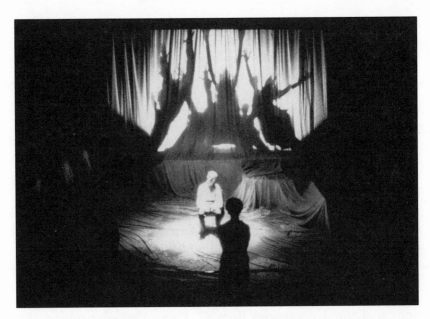

Fig. 6. Act V, scene v from *The Danton Case*. Photograph by Dawn Murray.

in our approach to Part III. The playwright's five-act construction is almost neoclassical, linear and logical in its narrative line. Our staging of the play, with its progression from realism to abstraction, sequentiality to simultaneity, order to chaos, was intended to create for our audience a theatrical experience equivalent to the historical reality of remote events. By availing ourselves of techniques such as montage and imagistic stage design, in their infancy during the playwright's lifetime, I believe that we created a compelling dramatic event, which both explicated a complex piece of history and moved a vast and often unwieldy text effectively onto the stage, and in a sense, beyond the confines of the theater.

One final circumstance aided our efforts, one which every director dreams of but none could hope to stage: On 9 November 1989—the day of the final dress rehearsal of *The Danton Case*—the East German government opened the Berlin Wall. The cycle of modern political revolution, begun in France in 1789 and continued in Russia in 1917, seemed to have come to a kind of completion. On the dressing room callboard, a cast member posted a newspaper photo of the cheering crowds atop the Wall—a radical contrast to the final view of the crowd in our production.

Beneath it was placed a quote from Robespierre's final speech, and a comment:

"Revolution will not survive to achieve its aim this time, or the second, or the fifth time.... The lie will outweigh the upward momentum."
But not forever.

In a fortuitous moment, history, drama, and the stage were fused.

Notes

The French Revolution and the Making of Fictions

I am grateful to Carol Blum, Christopher Herbert, Sarah Maza, and Mary Sheriff for offering helpful comments on this essay, as well as to Jacqueline Berger and Jacqueline Vassiliadis for keeping me abreast of French cultural and commemorative events during the year of the Bicentennial.

1. Frank A. Kafker and James M. Laux, *The French Revolution: Conflicting Interpretations* (New York: Random House, 1968).

2. Cobban's inaugural lecture on "The Myth of the French Revolution" was delivered in 1955 at the University of London. It attacked the prevalent Marxist view that the Revolution was "the substitution of a capitalist bourgeois order for feudalism." See William Doyle, *Origins of the French Revolution* (Oxford: Oxford University Press, 1980), 11–12.

3. Furet's article first appeared in *Les Annales* 2 (1971). It was later integrated in an expanded form into his revisionist manifesto, *Penser la Révolution française* (Paris: Gallimard, 1978). English translation by Elborg Forster: *Interpreting the French Revolution* (Cambridge: University Press, 1981).

4. See Suzanne Gearhart, *The Open Boundary of History and Fiction: A Critical Approach to the French Enlightenment* (Princeton, N.J.: Princeton University Press, 1984), and Lionel Gossman, *Between History and Literature* (Cambridge: Harvard University Press, 1990). This volume gathers essays written by the author between 1971 and 1989.

5. "History and Dialectic," *The Savage Mind* (Chicago: University of Chicago Press, 1970), 257.

6. "Interpretation in History," *Tropics of Discourse* (Baltimore and London: Johns Hopkins University Press, 1978), 58.

7. *Anatomy of Criticism* (New York: Atheneum, 1966), 162.

8. *Metahistory: The Historical Imagination in Nineteenth-Century Europe* (Baltimore and London: Johns Hopkins University Press, 1973), 29 ff.

9. Keeping in mind that for Hegel as well as for Aristotle, poetry was endowed with a cognitive dimension, White adds: "And to call it that in no way detracts from the status of historical narratives as providing a kind of knowledge." "The Historical Text As Literary Artifact," *Tropics of Discourse*, 85.

10. "Interpretation in History," 60–61.

11. *Metahistory*, 29.

12. *Tropics*, 61.

13. Ibid., 98. Fifteen years after the appearance of *Metahistory*, White's theories are still hotly debated by historians reflecting on new theoretical models for historiography. See the stimulating essay by Lloyd S. Kramer, "Literature, Criticism, and Historical Imagination: The Literary Challenge of Hayden White and Dominick LaCapra," *The New Cultural History*, ed. Lynn Hunt (Berkeley: University of California Press, 1989), 97–128.

14. "De l'histoire-récit à l'histoire-problème," *L'Atelier de l'histoire* (Paris: Flammarion, 1982), 73 (my translation).

15. Simon Schama, *Citizens: A Chronicle of the French Revolution* (New York: Knopf, 1989).

16. "Michelet's Gospel of Revolution," *Between History and Literature*, 222–23.

17. See François Furet, "L'histoire quantitative et la construction du fait historique," *Annales ESC* 26:1 (1971): 63–75, repr. in *L'Atelier de l'histoire*.

18. "Le Discours de l'histoire," *Information sur les sciences sociales* 6:4 (1967): 74.

19. Roger Chartier, "Intellectual History or Sociocultural History? The French Trajectories," *Modern European Intellectual History: Reappraisals and New Perspectives*, ed. Dominick LaCapra and Steven L. Kaplan (Ithaca and London: Cornell University Press, 1982), 39–40; and Dominick LaCapra, *Rethinking Intellectual History and Reading Texts: Texts, Contexts, Language* (Ithaca, N.Y.: Cornell University Press, 1983) and *History and Criticism* (Ithaca, N.Y.: Cornell University Press, 1985).

20. "Rethinking Intellectual History and Reading Texts," *Modern European Intellectual History*, 79.

21. *Rousseau and the Republic of Virtue: The Language of Politics in the French Revolution* (Ithaca and London: Cornell University Press, 1986).

22. See Gita May, *De Jean-Jacques Rousseau à Mme Roland* (Geneva: Droz, 1964) and *Madame Roland and the Age of Revolution* (New York: Columbia University Press, 1970); and Dorinda Outram, "Words and Flesh: Mme Roland, the Female Body and the Search for Power," *The Body and the French Revolution: Sex, Class, and Political Culture* (New Haven and London: Yale University Press, 1989).

23. See Jacques Guilhaumou, "Les mille langues du Père Duchêne: La parade de la culture populaire pendant la Révolution," *Dix-huitième siècle* 18 (1986): 143–54.

24. See Outram, *The Body and the French Revolution*, chap. 5.

25. *Interpreting the French Revolution*, 9–10, 14.

26. Ibid., 61–79.

27. Ibid., 12.

28. Keith Michael Baker, ed., *The Political Culture of the Old Regime* (Oxford: Pergamon, 1987), xi. Baker has recently reaffirmed and expanded this definition in *Inventing the French Revolution: Essays on French Political Culture in the Eighteenth Century* (Cambridge: Cambridge University Press, 1990), 4–11. See also Roger Chartier for a lucid overview of the politicization of French culture in the Ancien Régime, *Les Origines culturelles de la Révolution française* (Paris: Editions du Seuil, 1990), 25–28 and 167–203.

29. *Politics, Culture, and Class in the French Revolution* (Berkeley: University of California Press), 14–15.

30. Vol. 1, *The Political Culture of the Old Regime;* vol. 2, *The Political Culture of the French Revolution*, ed. Colin Lucas (Oxford: Pergamon, 1988); vol. 3, *The Transformation of Political Culture, 1789–1848*, ed. François Furet and Mona Ozouf (Oxford: Pergamon, 1989).

31. *Politics, Culture, and Class*, 24.

32. "Regeneration," in *A Critical Dictionary of the French Revolution*, ed. François Furet and Mona Ozouf, trans. Arthur Goldhammer (Cambridge: Harvard University Press, 1989). Also by Mona Ozouf, "La Révolution française et l'idée de l'homme nouveau," *The French Revolution and the Creation of Modern Political Culture*, 2:213–32, and *L'Homme régénéré: essais sur la Révolution française* (Paris: Gallimard, 1989).

33. "Representation," *The French Revolution and the Creation of Modern Political Culture*, 1:469–92.

34. Pierre Rétat, "Forme et discours d'un journal révolutionnaire: les *Révolutions de Paris,"* in Claude Labrosse, Pierre Rétat, and Henri

Duranton, *L'Instrument périodique. La fonction de la presse au XVIIIe siècle* (Lyon: PUL, 1986); Keith Michael Baker, "Revolution," in *The French Revolution and the Creation of Modern Political Culture*, 2:41–62. See also Mona Ozouf, "Revolution," in *A Critical Dictionary*.

35. François Furet and Denis Richet, *La Révolution française* (Paris: Hachette, 1965), 135 (my translation).

36. For an "instrumental" interpretation of festivals in the province, see Claude Mazauric, "La Fête révolutionnaire, manifestation de la politique jacobine. Rouen 1793," *Les fêtes de la Révolution, Actes du Colloque de Clermont-Ferrand 1974* (Paris: Société des études robespierristes, 1977), 181–90.

37. *Festivals and the French Revolution*, trans. Alan Sheridan, with a foreword by Lynn Hunt (Cambridge: Harvard University Press, 1988). See also Ozouf's essays on "La Fête révolutionnaire: le renouvellement de l'imaginaire collectif" and "Le Simulacre et la fête révolutionnaire" in *Les Fêtes de la Révolution*, 303–22 and 323–53.

38. Jean Deprun, "Robespierre, pontife de l'Etre suprême: note sur les aspects sacrificiels d'une fête," *Les Fêtes de la Révolution*, 485–91. Deprun's reference is the 1899 "Essai sur la nature et la fonction du sacrifice" by H. Hubert and M. Mauss in *L'Année sociologique*.

39. Albert Boime, "Jacques-Louis David, Scatological Discourse in the French Revolution, and the Art of Caricature," *French Caricature and the French Revolution, 1789–1799*, ed. James Cuno (Los Angeles: Grunwald Center for the Graphic Arts, 1988), 67–82. Lynn Hunt, "The Political Psychology of Revolutionary Caricatures," ibid., 36.

40. Most noteworthy are Dorinda Outram, *The Body and the French Revolution*, and Joan Landes, "Political Imagery of the French Revolution," *Representing Revolution: French and British Images, 1789–1804* (Amherst, Mass.: Mead Art Museum, Amherst College, 1989), 13–21.

41. The standard reference text is Ernst H. Kantorowicz, *The King's Two Bodies: A Study in Medieval Political Theology* (Princeton, N.J.: Princeton University Press, 1957). For a semiotic approach to the politics of royal representation, see Louis Marin's work on Louis XIV: *Portrait of the King*, trans. Martha H. Houle (Minneapolis: University of Minnesota Press, 1988). On the growing desacralization of royal authority in the eighteenth century, see Dale Van Kley, *The Damiens Affair and the Unravelling of the Old Regime* (Princeton, N.J.: Princeton University Press, 1983), and Jeffrey Merrick, *The Desacralization of the French Monarchy in the Eighteenth Century* (Baton Rouge: Louisiana State University Press, 1990). On the symbolic meaning of regicide for the Revolutionaries, see Michael Walzer, *Regicide and Revolution: Speeches at the Trial of Louis XVI* (Cambridge: Cambridge University Press, 1974).

These views are elegantly summarized in Chartier, *Les Origines culturelles de la Révolution française,* 138–66.

42. "Political Imagery of the French Revolution," 13–21.

43. "The Imagery of Radicalism," *Politics, Culture, and Class,* 87–119. See also Maurice Agulhon, *Marianne into Battle: Republican Imagery and Symbolism in France, 1789–1800,* trans. Janet Lloyd (Cambridge: Cambridge University Press, 1981).

44. *The Body and the French Revolution,* 23.

45. *Discipline and Punish: The Birth of the Prison,* trans. Alan Sheridan (New York: Vintage, 1979), 25.

46. For further development of this idea and its extension in nineteenth-century literature, see Peter Brooks, *The Melodramatic Imagination: Balzac, Henry James, Melodrama, and the Mode of Excess* (New Haven: Yale University Press, 1976).

47. New Haven: Yale University Press, 1985. Older studies of neoclassicism include Hugh Honour, *Neo-Classicism* (Harmondsworth: Penguin, 1968), and Robert Rosenblum, *Transformations In Late Eighteenth-Century Art* (Princeton, N.J.: Princeton University Press, 1967). On Revolutionary art as political propaganda, see David L. Dowd, *Pageant-Master of the Republic: Jacques-Louis David and the French Revolution* (Lincoln: University of Nebraska Press, 1948), and James A. Leith, *The Idea of Art as Propaganda in France, 1750–1799: A Study in the History of Ideas* (Toronto: University of Toronto Press, 1965). Recent studies of David and politics include Robert L. Herbert, *David, Voltaire, "Brutus" and the French Revolution: An Essay in Art and Politics* (London: Penguin, 1972); Régis Michel and Marie-Catherine Sahut, *David: l'art et la politique* (Paris: Gallimard, 1988); and, preeminently, Thomas E. Crow, "The *Oath of the Horatii* in 1785: Painting and Pre-Revolutionary Radicalism in France," *Art History* 1 (1978): 424–71.

48. Jean Starobinski, *1789. Les Emblèmes de la raison* (Paris: Flammarion, 1979), 81. No revolutionary fiction has fired up recent scholarship more than the numerous representations and commemorations of Marat's death in all kinds of media. See *La Mort de Marat,* ed. J.-C. Bonnet (Paris: Flammarion, 1986), and articles in *Images de la Révolution* and *Les Fêtes de la Révolution.*

49. M. P. Foissy-Aufrère et al., *La Mort de Bara: de l'événement au mythe; autour du tableau de Jacques-Louis David* (Avignon: Musée Calvet, 1989), replaces the older study by Joseph C. Sloane: "David, Robespierre, and 'The Death of Bara,'" *Gazette des beaux arts* (Sept. 1969): 143–57. See especially Régis Michel, "Bara: du martyre à l'éphèbe," 41–77.

50. *The Melodramatic Imagination,* 15–16.

51. *The Structural Transformation of the Public Sphere,* trans. Thomas Burger, with Frederick Lawrence (Cambridge, Mass.: MIT Press, 1989).

52. On public opinion, see Keith Michael Baker, "Politics and Public Opinion under the Old Regime: Some Reflections," *Press and Politics in Pre-Revolutionary France,* ed. Jack Censer and Jeremy Popkin (Berkeley: University of California Press, 1987), 204–46; Mona Ozouf, "L'opinion publique," *The French Revolution and the Creation of Modern Political Culture* 1:419–34; and articles by Daniel Gordon, Dena Goodman, and Bernadette Fort in "The French Revolution in Culture," *Eighteenth-Century Studies* 22:3 (Spring 1989, special issue edited by Lynn Hunt). For a stimulating investigation of the open boundary between the private and the public, see Sarah Maza's work on the "causes célèbres" in pre-Revolutionary decades: "Le Tribunal de la nation: Les mémoires judiciaires et l'opinion publique à la fin de l'Ancien Régime," *Annales ESC* 42:1 (1987) and "Domestic Melodrama and Political Ideology: The Case of the Comte de Sanois," *The American Historical Review* 94 (1989): 1249–64.

53. René Favre, *La Mort dans la littérature et la pensée françaises au siècle des Lumières* (Lyon: Presses Universitaires de Lyon, 1979), and John McManners, *Death and the Enlightenment* (Oxford: Clarendon, 1981).

54. *Women and the Public Sphere in the Age of the French Revolution* (Ithaca and London: Cornell University Press, 1988), 12. This is now the authoritative work on this question. Previous studies include Marie Cerati, *Le Club des citoyennes républicaines révolutionnaires* (Paris: Editions sociales, 1966); Darline Gay Levy and Harriet Applewhite, "Women of the Popular Classes in Revolutionary Paris, 1789–95," *Women, War, and Revolution,* ed. C. R. Berkin and C. M. Lovett (New York: Homes & Meier, 1980), 9–36; and, by the same authors, *Women in Revolutionary Paris, 1789–1795: Selected Documents* (Urbana: University of Illinois Press, 1979); and Anette Rosa, *Citoyennes: Les femmes et la Révolution française* (Paris: Messidor, 1988).

55. "The Political Psychology of Revolutionary Caricatures," 39.

56. See Chantal Thomas, *La Reine scélérate: Marie-Antoinette dans les pamphlets* (Paris: Seuil, 1989); Simon Schama, "Body Politics" in *Citizens,* 203–27; Sarah Maza, "The Diamond Necklace Affair Revisited, 1785–1786: The Case of the Missing Queen," *Eroticism and the Body Politic,* ed. Lynn Hunt (Baltimore: Johns Hopkins University Press, 1990).

57. See also Revel's article, "Marie-Antoinette," in *A Critical Dictionary of the French Revolution.*

58. See, e.g., *The Culture of Print: Power and the Uses of Print in Early Modern France*, ed. Roger Chartier, trans. Lydia G. Cochrane (Oxford: Basil Blackwell, 1989).

59. See Marilyn Butler, *Burke, Paine, Godwin, and the Revolution Controversy* (Cambridge: Cambridge University Press, 1984).

60. *The Prelude* (1850), 2:108. See David Simpson, *Wordsworth's Historical Imagination: The Poetry of Displacement* (New York and London: Methuen, 1987).

61. *The Old Regime and the French Revolution*, trans. Stuart Gilbert (Gloucester, Mass.: Peter Smith, 1978), pt. 3, chap. 1, 142.

62. Ibid., 139–42.

63. Paris: Hachette, 1988.

64. "The tradition of all the dead generations weighs like a nightmare on the brain of the living." See François Furet, *Marx et la Révolution française, suivi de Textes de Marx, réunis, présentés et traduits par Lucien Calvié* (Paris: Flammarion, 1986), 245. English trans. by Deborah Kan Furet (Chicago: University of Chicago Press, 1988).

65. *Interpreting the French Revolution*, 5.

66. "The Happy Year" is the title given by François Furet and Denis Richet to the section on the year 1789 in *La Révolution française* (Paris: Hachette, 1965). See also François Furet and Ran Halévi, "L'Année 1789," *Annales ESC* (Jan.-Feb. 1989), 3–23.

The Revolutionary Body

1. Charles Baudelaire, "Notes sur *Les Liaisons dangereuses*," *Oeuvres complètes* (Paris: Bibliothèque de la Pléiade, 1954), 996. I want to thank Sarah Maza for her many helpful comments on this essay. I'm aware that I haven't adequately responded to some of her pertinent queries.

2. On the performatives of Revolutionary oratory, see especially Marc Blanchard, *La Révolution par les mots: Saint Just & cie.* (Paris: Nizet, 1970); in the domain of Revolutionary art, see James H. Rubin, "Disorder/Order: Revolutionary Art as Performative Representation," in *The French Revolution, 1789-1989*, ed. Sandy Petrey (Lubbock, Texas: Texas Tech University Press, 1989), 83–112.

3. Michel Foucault writes, in exposition of the penal reformers of the Revolutionary period: "Aussitôt le crime commis et sans qu'on perde de temps, la punition viendra, mettant en acte le discours de la loi et montrant que le Code, qui lie les idées, lie aussi les réalités." *Surveiller et punir* (Paris: Gallimard, 1975), 112.

188 • NOTES TO PAGES 36-47

4. Saint-Just, "Discours concernant le jugement de Louis XVI" (13 November 1790), in *Oeuvres Choisies* (Paris: Gallimard—Idées Poche, 1968), 78.

5. "Rapport sur la nécessité de déclarer le gouvernement révolutionnaire jusqu'à la paix" (10 October 1793), *Oeuvres choisies,* 169.

6. "Rapport sur les suspects incarcérés" (26 February 1794), *Oeuvres choisies,* 192.

7. Dorinda Outram, *The Body and the French Revolution: Sex, Class, and Political Culture* (New Haven and London: Yale University Press, 1989), 81.

8. See Simon Schama, *Citizens* (New York: Knopf, 1989), esp. chap. 17.

9. I am indebted here to the account of this episode given by Emmet Kennedy in *A Cultural History of the French Revolution* (New Haven: Yale University Press, 1989), 206–12. Kennedy has the great merit of seeing the symbolic significance of this episode.

10. Dorinda Outram, *The Body and the French Revolution,* 127. See also: Lynn Hunt, *Politics, Culture, and Class in the French Revolution* (Berkeley and Los Angeles: University of California Press, 1984); Joan B. Landes, *Women and the Public Sphere in the Age of the French Revolution* (Ithaca and London: Cornell University Press, 1988); Sarah Maza, "Remarks for Yale Symposium, 'Representing the French Revolution,'" 7 October 1989 (unpublished MS).

11. *Le Moniteur Universel,* 19 November 1793, translated and cited in Chantal Thomas, "Heroism in the Feminine: The Examples of Charlotte Corday and Madame Roland," in *The French Revolution, 1789–1989,* 79–80.

12. Cited in Marvin Carlson, *The Theater of the French Revolution* (Ithaca, N.Y.: Cornell University Press, 1966).

13. Charles Nodier, Préface to Guilbert de Pixerécourt, *Théâtre choisi,* 4 vols. (Paris and Nancy, 1841–43).

14. Saint-Just, *Oeuvres choisies,* 327.

15. I quote from the first published edition of *Le Jugement dernier des rois* (Paris: C.-F. Patris, L'an second de la République Française, une et indivisible). Translations are my own. My complete translation of the play is printed in *Yale Review* 78:4 (1990): 583–603.

16. Marmontel, *Supplément* to the *Encyclopédie,* vol. 4, s.v. "Pantomime" (Paris and Amsterdam, 1777). On this question, see *The Melodramatic Imagination: Balzac, Henry James, Melodrama, and the Mode of Excess* (New Haven: Yale University Press, 1976), chap. 3.

17. See Jan Goldstein, *Console and Classify: The French Psychiatric Profession in the Nineteenth Century* (Chicago: University of Chicago Press, 1987).

18. Victor Hugo, *Quatrevingt-treize* (Paris: Garnier/Flammarion, 1965), p. 298. Subsequent references will be given in parentheses in my text.

19. Peter Weiss, *The Persecution and Assassination of Jean-Paul Marat as Performed by the Inmates of the Asylum of Charenton under the Direction of the Marquis de Sade*, English version by Geoffrey Skelton, verse adaptation by Adrian Mitchell (New York: Pocket Books, 1966), 128–29.

Revolutionary Activism and the Cult of Male Beauty in the Studio of David

1. The principal figures here are P. A. Hennequin, J. B. Wicar, and J. G. Drouais. This intimacy could produce strong tensions. Hennequin, in his posthumously published memoirs (*Un peintre sous la Révolution et l'Empire: Mémoires de Ph.-A. Hennequin écrits par lui-même* [Paris, 1933], 57 ff.), speaks of Wicar's jealousy, which led to Hennequin's early expulsion from the studio. On Wicar, see the thorough biography by F. Beaucamp, *Le Peintre lillois Jean-Baptiste Wicar, son oeuvre et son temps* (Lille: E. Raoust, 1939), 1:27 ff. On Drouais, the most up-to-date source is P. Ramade and R. Michel, *Jean-Germain Drouais, 1763–1788* (Rennes: Musée des Beaux Arts, 1985), 13–63. The most eloquent testimony to the intimacy between David and Drouais is the latter's surviving contributions to their correspondence, reproduced in J. L. J. David, *Le Peintre Louis David, 1748–1825. Souvenirs et documents inédits* (Paris, 1880), 34–51. For the later rivalry between Girodet and F. X. Fabre, see Ph. Bordes, "Girodet et Fabre, camarades d'atelier," *Revue du Louvre*, 24/6 (1974): 393–99.

2. See A. Péron's résumé of the recollections of David's pupil J. B. Debret, who accompanied his master to Rome: *Examen du Tableau du Serment des Horaces peint par David, suivi d'une Notice historique du tableau, lus à la Société des Beaux-Arts* (Paris, 1838), 33 ff.

3. See the exchange between then-director O. Wittman and R. Rosenblum, *Burlington Magazine* 107 (June 1965): 323–24; (September 1965): 473–75; (December 1965): 623; and 108 (February 1966): 90.

4. For a reproduction and discussion of this replica, see the author's "Une manière de travailler dans le studio de David," *Parachute* 56

(October–November 1989): 48–50. See also the illustration and entry on the Princeton canvas by Alan Wintermute in *1789: French Art during the Revolution* (New York: Colnaghi USA, 1989), 113–19. J. L. J. David (p. 59) refers to Girodet's painting some of the background figures in the original *Socrates*.

5. The contract between Coupin and Jules Renouard, the publisher of Girodet's *Oeuvres posthumes* (Paris, 1829), is preserved in the departmental archives of Yvelines, Versailles, dossier J2072: Coupin signed a receipt for the papers on 10 March 1826, stating that they belonged to Renouard, and the latter countersigned the same document on 12 October 1828, stating that the papers had been returned.

6. P. A. Coupin, *Essai sur J. -L. David* (Paris, 1827), 61–64 (copy in Bibliothèque nationale, Paris). The first mention of this list, to my knowledge, was made in Stephanie Brown, "Girodet: A Contradictory Career," unpublished Ph.D. diss. (University of London, 1980), 41.

7. Coupin, *David*, p. 61.

8. Ibid.; Coupin publicly objected on two occasions in *La Revue encyclopédique* to the owners of the copy, the Didot family printing firm, exhibiting it as a David (30:578; 33, s.v. "réclamations)".

9. Ibid., p. 62; there is a superb, highly finished drawing for this figure by David (Tours, Musée des beaux arts), the existence of which would be consistent with his guiding the work of a young pupil. In general, I would say that where such drawings exist from the 1780s, they suggest substantial student involvement in the motif involved.

10. Ibid.

11. Ibid., pp. 62–63. Girodet's superior command of "clair-oscur," mentioned by Coupin, would correspond to the treatment of the background at the left of the Princeton *Socrates,* which is more deeply shadowed than the original.

12. Coupin, *David,* 63.

13. The best discussion of this painting is in Brown, "Girodet," 55 ff.

14. See M. Pérignon, *Catalogue des tableaux, dessins et croquis de M. Girodet-Trioson* Paris (2 April 1825), 10.

15. The most comprehensive treatment of the painting, with relevant documents, is now to be found in the catalog of the exhibition at the Musée Calvet, Avignon: M. P. Foissy-Aufrère et al., *La mort de Bara: De l'événement au mythe. Autour du tableau de Jacques-Louis David* (Avignon: Musée Calvet, 1989); see esp. the challenging interpretation of its iconography, facture, and degree of "finish" by Régis Michel, "Bara: du martyre à l'éphèbe," 41–77.

16. For a representative discussion, see Joseph C. Sloane, "David, Robespierre, and the 'Death of Bara,'" *Gazette des Beaux-Arts*, 74 (September 1969): 153–55. The principal exceptions to this rule have been R. Michel, "Bara," and William Olander, "Pour transmettre à la postérité: French Painting and Revolution 1774–1795" (unpublished Ph.D. diss., New York University, 1983), 293–302, who writes (pp. 298, 302), "David's painting, though unfinished, is complete enough to suggest that its nudity, ambiguous sex and swooning, near eroticism were not merely aspects of a preparatory study but intended as the final image in order to convey the components of a universal *myth* and not reality. . . . Bara, as conceived by Robespierre and David, was the mystic [androgynous] Adam before the fall, recomposing itself throughout all civilizations, endowed with a single mind, and pursuing a single destiny throughout all history, to emerge in 1794 as this singularly frail boy-girl child. . . . For the men of Year 2, fanatical in their devotion and vision, Bara was a symbol of a universal mankind as created by the Revolution, of a paradise regained, of sublime virtue and beauty, before the fall."

17. As pointed out by Brown, "Girodet," p. 83, the specific iconography of Girodet's painting finds its closest antique source in Lucian's *Dialogues of the Gods,* in the passage of this satire on mythology in which Aphrodite chides Selene for her uncharacteristic infatuation with the mortal boy, describing her as a victim of Aphrodite's mischievous son Eros (Lucian, *Loeb Classical Library,* Cambridge, Mass., 7:328–31). The literature on the painting is not plentiful. Two extensive studies of sources and iconography exist: the pioneering work of George Levitine, *Girodet-Trioson: An Iconographical Study* (New York: Garland, 1978 [reprint of 1953 diss., 117–34]); and James Henry Rubin, "Endymion's Dream as a Myth of Romantic Inspiration," *Art Quarterly,* n.s., 1 (Spring 1978):47–84. See also Brown, "Girodet," pp. 73–91.

18. This view originates with Frederick Antal, "Reflections on Classicism and Romanticism II," *Burlington Magazine* 68 (April 1936): 132, and has been repeated by Albert Boime, *Art in the Age of Revolution* (Chicago: University of Chicago Press, 1987), 448–51. Because of its conspicuous departure from the manner and themes of David's more heroic subjects (and because Girodet was politically conformist later in his life), the painting is taken as sufficient evidence that he was unsympathetic to the Revolution and wished to keep himself apart from politics. The gaps in the research of both should be plain from what follows here. Olander's otherwise groundbreaking discussion of David's *Bara* ("Pour transmettre à la postérité," 299) accepts this view without comment.

19. There is in the collection of the Musée des Beaux-Arts in Lille a copy of the *Bara,* one that once belonged to Jules David, in which certain background details are more precisely described but the form of nudity of the figure is exactly preserved. See Michel, "Bara," 65–66, for a reproduction and for the argument that it is likely to be a studio copy of the period.

20. See "Règlements qui doivent être observés par les pensionnaires de l'Académie de France à Rome d'après les ordres de Monsieur le Directeur général," *Correspondance des directeurs de l'Académie de France à Rome 1663-1793* (Paris, 1904), 13:158.

21. On his petition to be exempted from the normal required copies and studies—and the angry response of the Director-General d'Angiviller—see *Correspondance des directeurs,* 15:100–106.

22. The title first appears in the *Procès-verbaux de l'Académie Royale de Peinture et de Sculpture, 1648-1792,* 10 vol. (Paris: J. Baur, 1875–92), 9:272. In a later print by Monsaldy (after Gautherot's drawing of the composition), it will be captioned "Le soldat blessé" (see Régis Michel, "Jean-Germain Drouais e Roma," in *David e Roma,* Académie de France à Rome [1981], 206, for a reproduction).

23. See, e.g., *L'Ami des Artistes au Salon par M. L'A.R.* (Paris, 1787), 14–15; [Louis de Carmontelle], *La Patte de Velours* (London, 1781), 36. For an excellent discussion of the cult of Winckelmann in France, see Edouard Pommier, "Winckelmann et la vision de l'antiquité dans la France des Lumières et de la Révolution," *Revue de l'Art* 83 (1989): 9–20.

24. See C. G. Heyne, "Eloge de M. Winckelmann," in *Lettres familières de M. Winckelmann,* trans. H. Jansen (Amsterdam, 1781), vii–xxi; also translator's introduction (i): "On verra dans ces lettres M. Winckelmann, combattant tous les obstacles qui s'opposent à son avancement, méditer Homère et Sophocle dans le silence de la nuit, après avoir passé toute la journée à remplir le rebutant emploi de Maître d'Ecole, ou à copier de vieux titres et de vieux chroniques; on le verra sans secours, sans enseignement, parvenir, dans un âge déjà avancé, à un point qui le met au-dessus de tous ses prédécesseurs, et qui peut-être fera le désespoir de tous ceux qui tâcheront de le suivre dans la même carrière." It is striking that Jansen's translation of the personal letters preceded that of Winckelmann's public writings.

25. See David's unfinished manuscript autobiography, written around 1800, where he recalls his requirement at the beginning of his teaching that all of his pupils at least know Latin and that Fabre, for one, had Greek (D. and G. Wildenstein, *Documents complémentaires au catalogue de l'oeuvre de Louis David* [Paris: Fondation Wildenstein,

1973], 158). Girodet was an amateur scholar of the classics during all of his adult life and produced translations of Greek poetry. Part of the legend of Drouais, who had less formal education than those two, was his feverish self-education in Latin. J. B. A. Suard, in an early biography (*Mélanges de littérature* [Paris, 1806], 3:281) writes, "On lui fit sentir la nécéssité d'étudier le latin; et quoiqu'il n'y pût donner que peu d'heures par semaine, en moins de trois ans il fut en état d'expliquer Tacite."

26. J. J. Winckelmann, *Geschichte der Kunst des Altertums,* ed. W. Senff (Weimar: Hermann Böhlaus, 1964), 192.

27. For a lucid summary of this aspect of ancient rhetorical theory to which I am much indebted, see Debora Shuger, *Sacred Rhetoric* (Princeton, N.J.: Princeton University Press, 1988), 21 ff.

28. See Torquato Tasso, *Jerusalem Delivered,* "The Allegory of the Poem," trans. R. Nash (Detroit: Wayne State University Press, 1987), 473; for a Platonic source for this understanding of the modalities of the hero, see Plato's insistence in the *Symposium* that Achilles was the "beloved" of the more mature Patroclus—beardless and excelling him in beauty—and not the other way around (Plato, *Loeb Classical Library,* 5:104–7).

29. See n. 21 above.

30. The magnificent and nearly complete *Philoctetes* (Chartres, Musée des Beaux-Arts) represents an extraordinary response to ancient and modern literary aesthetics of the mature male body and the heroic character; see Michel, in Ramade and Michel, *Jean-Germain Drouais,* 15–19.

31. See J. L. J. David, 53, for his famous lament: "J'ai perdu mon émulation." In April 1816, some four months after David had been forced into final exile in Brussels, a faithful student wrote conveying information about the disposal of the master's property. All the furnishings of the house in the rue l'Enfer were transported to the studio, he stated, adding that he had directed the remover to "le tombeau de Drouais" and other objects sealed in the walls (letter from Poisson to Navez, 1 April 1816, quoted in G. Wildenstein, "Les Davidiens à Paris sous la Restauration," *Gazette des Beaux-Arts,* 53 [1959]: 237). The tomb spoken of in this letter was not, of course, the actual one in Rome; it was David's substitute and the material repository he felt necessary for the physical remains he possessed of his revered pupil, his letters. The vessel was placed first in the garden of his residence in the Louvre, then sealed into his house in the rue l'Enfer. The extravagant posthumous mythology that surrounded Drouais's memory is briefly discussed

by P. Ramade in Ramade and Michel, *Jean-Germain Drovais*, 151-54. There is a great deal more to be said on this subject.

32. A number of the artist's letters collected in *Oeuvres posthumes*, 2, *Correspondance*, testify eloquently to Girodet's dissident attitudes; see particularly his letter to his guardian Trioson of 28 February 1792.

33. "Correspondance," letter to Gérard, 13 July 1791.

34. For example, Roland Barthes, *S/Z* (Paris: Editions du Seuil, 1970), 76-77.

35. See "Adresse des pensionnaires de l'Académie de France à la Convention," *Correspondance des directeurs* 16:251.

36. Dorat-Cubières [Michel Cubières-Palméyzeau], *La Mort de Bassville ou la conspiration de Pie VI dévoilée* (Paris, 1793).

37. The two existing accounts, one written from the French perspective, the other from the Vatican's, are F. Masson, *Les Diplomates de la révolution* (Paris 1882), 15-145; and L. Vicchi, *Les Français à Rome pendant la Convention (1792-1795)* (Fusignano, 1892), lxxxvii-cxxxvii, with extensive documents, pp. 8-91.

38. Cubières, 5.

39. See extract from the procès-verbaux of the Convention (25 November 1792), in *Correspondance des directeurs* 16:167; also letter of 24 December 1792 to Topino-Lebrun, in J. L. J. David, *Le Peintre*, 120-22.

40. Cubières, 14-15.

41. Ibid., 17-18.

42. "Correspondance," letter to Trioson, 19 January 1793.

43. Where and how Cubières came to have access to Girodet's testimony—from the artist's correspondents or secondhand from sources in Naples—still needs research.

44. In early 1794, *Aux armes et aux arts*, the journal of the Jacobin-oriented Société populaire et républicaine des arts, included (p. 158) a call by J. B. Wicar, David's devoted former pupil, for a reconquest of Italy so that the remains of the ancient Greek republicans would be in the hands of their modern counterparts, the French: Liberty "nous indique le lieu où jadis elle opéra tant de merveilles; elle nous commande d'y voler et de terrasser les monstres qui souillent aujourd'hui l'heureux climat qu'elle habitait autrefois; et de la même main, cette main triomphante, enlever les restes de sa splendeur. . . . Vénérable Antiquité! inspire-nous le vrai caractère, le seul digne de représenter la liberté et l'égalité." The Winckelmannian rationale for this appeal was explicitly confirmed in the next entry of the journal. Wicar was part of a delegation enjoined to visit the superior collection of first-generation antique casts owned by the sculptor J. B. Giraud to see whether they could be re-

produced for the benefit of the society's members. To accompany the
report on the negotiations, the journal's editor Detournelle inserts an
extended description (pp. 161–69) of some of the works. At the end of
it, he confesses—and this would have been obvious to an informed
reader—that his rhapsodic prose was all cribbed from Winckelmann.
And he goes on (pp. 169—70) to counsel young artists, fired by the
Revolutionary cause, to substitute this sort of contemplative erotics even
for the study of the model: "Je suis persuadé que plusieurs conviendront
avec moi qu'une leçon prise devant les belles figures que je viens de
décrire leur fera faire plus de progès, que s'ils copiaient servilement
pendant un hiver le modèle de l'école; car en dessinant on apprend à
la main à tracer, mais en restant dans la contemplation attachée sur les
contours, sur les formes, sur l'expression, on donne à son génie l'élan
sublime qui mène à l'immortalité." In the watchful atmosphere of this
period, there would be nothing printed in a journal such as this one
that was not deemed appropriate to a regime of violently enforced civic
virtue.

45. Cubières, 61.
46. *Moniteur Universel* (10 nivose An II), 403.
47. R. Michel (*Bara,* 67) has argued not only that the nudity represents David's considered final intention but that the handling of paint
represents an extension into a total pictorial vocabulary of the nervous
scumbling with which David surrounded his portrait subjects of 1793.
He sees the technique, first, in terms of popular oratory, on the Aristotelian model, which must imitate the painter of the sketch who avoids
superfluous, distracting details and fineness of effect. Further, it evokes
on its own the disorder of battle without falling into the inferior genre
of battle painting, and, finally, "le dynamisme de la touche sature la
toile d'une sorte d'immédiateté: elle rend l'Histoire vivante, où la fige
d'ordinaire la froideur du glacis. En d'autres termes, l'Histoire conjugue
au présent: elle devient visuelle et tactile, où la finition lisse l'empri-
sonne dans l'immobilité du passé révolu."
48. The unconscious response of the painter to this condensation of
erotic loci may be responsible for the unsettling trace of red paint along
the crease that marks the disappearance of the genitals, one that echoes
a similar trace across the lower lip.

*Joint Suicide in Eighteenth-Century French Literature and
Revolutionary Politics*

1. For a more complete discussion of Enlightenment and Revolutionary suicide in its various forms, the reader is referred to the forth-

coming *Death, Liberty, and the Pursuit of Happiness* by Margaret and Patrice Higonnet, to be published by Harvard University Press.

2. Rousseau, *La Nouvelle Héloïse*, translated as *Eloisa, or A Series of Original Letters*, by William Kenrick (London, 1803). The text is presented there as being in letter 114 (2:318). In the Pléiade edition (Paris, 1969), this appears as part 3, letter 21 (2:386).

3. Julie's own voice and desires on this matter are not described. See *Eloisa*, letter 136, Kenrick trans. (3:220–21). In the Pléiade edition, the incident is described in part 4, letter 17 (2:521).

4. See J. L. Bellenot, "Les Formes de l'amour dans *La Nouvelle Héloïse*," *Annales J. J. Rousseau* 33:194–95.

5. His collected works were reedited in Paris in the Year VII (1799–1800).

6. It may be relevant that Rousseau was the only *philosophe* (if he can be so called) who seriously considered taking his own life.

7. The glassmaker Ménétra recounts witnessing such a double suicide as a child. The case involved a married nail merchant and a counter girl in his shop on the Ile Saint-Louis who had taken poison together. Jacques-Louis Ménétra, *Journal of My Life,* trans. Arthur Goldhammer, with an introduction by Daniel Roche (New York: Columbia University Press, 1986), 175.

8. The bookseller S. P. Hardy, who was keenly interested in suicide, reported the case of one Raffenot who in 1780 stabbed himself and his wife in the Luxembourg garden. See Jeffrey Merrick, "Patterns and Prosecutions of Suicide," *Historical Reflexions/Réflexions historiques* 16 (Spring 1989): 24.

9. See Fernand Baldensperger, "'Les Deux amants de Lyon' dans la littérature," *Revue de Lyon* 1 (1), January 1902.

10. It seems best to leave these and other verses cited in this essay in the original. In these lines Rousseau reasons that the lovers committed no crime. Reason has nothing to say about this act that a piteous soul might blame but which sentiment admires. Rousseau's quatrain first appeared in Grimm's *Correspondance littéraire* and was reprinted first in Bauchaumont's *Mémoires secrets* and second in the *Almanach des Muses,* which framed Rousseau's verses with a long introduction describing the double suicide.

11. In a letter (no. 7907) dated 6 June 1770 to Vasselier, and in a letter (no. 7980) to Élie de Beaumont dated 30 July 1770. Voltaire, *Correspondance, Oeuvres Complètes,* ed. Beuchot (Paris: Garnier, 1882), 15:97, 159.

12. *Journal Encyclopédique* 2 (15 June 1770): 453–55.

13. Including yet another set of verses by Joseph Vasselier (1725–98), a poet, playwright, and postal employee at Lyon; as well as a play by Pascal de Lagouthe in 1776, entitled *Luzzila ou la force de l'Amour.*

14. In the essay entitled "De Caton et du Suicide."

15. A learned allusion perhaps to the abbé de Saint-Cyran, an often cited apologist of suicide. Voltaire described Saint-Cyran's views on chosen death at some length in his *Commentary* on Beccaria of 1766, and in his *Questions sur l'Encyclopédie* of 1770.

16. Alexandre Masson de Pezey (1741–77), *Les Tableaux* (Amsterdam, 1771), 52.

17. See the reedition of his *Essai* with an excellent introduction by Elisabeth Badinter (Paris: P.O.L., 1989), 58. Thomas also describes the stoic deaths of other Roman wives: Aria; Portia, the wife of Brutus; and Paulina, Seneca's companion.

18. Cited by Charly Guyot, *La Vie intellectuelle et religieuse en Suisse française à la fin du XVIIIe siècle. Henri David de Chaillet 1751–1823* (Neuchâtel: La Baconnière, 1946), 91, 96–97. I am grateful to Elizabeth Eisenstein for this reference.

19. Hapdé, the author of over a hundred plays, many of them on political subjects, was born in 1774 and died in 1839.

20. In the *Journal de l'Empire* of 23 June 1812. Geoffroy's career is described in Jeremy Popkin, *Revolutionary News. The Press in France 1789–1799* (Durham: Duke University Press, 1990).

21. The argument on female suicide and women's bodies presented here is derived from Margaret Higonnet's essays on the subject, which include "Delphine: d'une guerre civile à l'autre," in *Actes du Quatrième Colloque de Coppet* (Lausanne: Institut Benjamin Constant, 1988) and "Speaking Silences: Women's Suicide," in *The Female Body in Western Culture,* ed. Susan Rubin Suleiman (Cambridge: Harvard University Press, 1985).

22. Cited by Allessandro Galante Garrone, *Gilbert Romme, Storia di un Rivoluzionario* (Turin: Einaudi, 1959), 547.

23. See Alfred Börckel, *Adam Lux, ein Opfer der Schreckenzeit. Nach seinen Schriften und den Berichten seiner Zeitgenossen* (Mainz: Victor von Zabern, 1892), 6.

24. *La Mort du jeune Barra ou une journée de la Vendée. Drame historique en un acte par le citoyen Briois* (Paris: Barba, 1794), 9. The play was performed on 15 floreal, Year II.

25. Cited by E. Jauffret, *Le théâtre révolutionnaire 1788–1799* (Paris: Furne, 1869), 313.

26. Garrone, *Romme*, 211.

27. Stéphane-Pol (pseudonym of Paul Coutant), *Autour de Robes-pierre: Le Conventionnel Le Bas,* with a preface by Victorien Sardou (Paris: Flammarion, 1901), 136.

28. Cited by Dominique Godineau, *Citoyennes tricoteuses. Les femmes du peuple à Paris pendant la Révolution française* (Aix: Alinéa, 1988), 342. Richard Cobb gives a slightly different version of this event. For him, Denelle (and not Dunel) is described as "clearly a very stupid, very naïve, very violent man" who, after failing to gas his wife and children, hacked his companion and two of their three children to pieces. (See Richard Cobb, *The Police and the People* [Oxford: Oxford University Press, 1970], 158–59.) As Cobb goes on to add that Denelle was "a prototype of many poor sans-culottes both of his condition and of his Section," his overall interpretation is close to that of Godineau, who also writes: "Cas extrême, dira-t-on? Oui par l'émotion et l'horreur qu'il dégage. Non, car Dunel ne fut pas le seul à ne pas supporter l'échec de l'insurrection." In the context of joint suicide, however, the case of the Denelle is quite anomalous.

29. Godineau, *Citoyennes,* 343.

30. On Lux, see Börckel, *Adam Lux;* Henri Welschinger, *Adam Lux et Charlotte Corday* (Amiens: Delattre-Lenoël, 1888); and J. H. Lüse-brink, "Georg Forster et Adam Lux dans la France de 1793," *Revue de Littérature Comparée* 4 (October–December 1989): 463–78. The original documents are in the Archives Nationales, W 293, no. 213.

31. Börckel, *Adam Lux,* 6.

32. Archives Nationales, W 293.

33. Adam Lux, *Charlotte Corday* (Paris, July 1793), 3–4.

34. Cited by Annete Rosa, *Citoyennes, les Femmes et la Révolution française* (Paris: Messidor, 1988), 102. References to sentimental suicide are also to be found in Beaumarchais's play *La Mère coupable* of July 1792, but the theme is not politicized.

35. Dorinda Outram, *The Body and the French Revolution: Sex, Class and Political Culture* (New Haven: Yale University Press, 1989).

36. Manon Roland, *Mémoires,* 2:270.

37. Dominique Godineau, *Citoyennes tricoteuses,* 213.

38. Jean-Paul Marat, *Les Aventures du jeune comte Potowski* (Paris: Le Siècle, 1847).

39. Jules Massin, *Marat* (Paris: Club Français du livre, 1970), 29.

40. *Aventures,* letter 52, p. 57. Marat criticizes all enlightened despots in these pages. Of Frederick, he writes, e.g., that this mercantilist was even worse than Catherine: "[Il] a fait pis, il inquiette les riches marchands."

41. Ibid., letter 13, 140.

42. Ibid., letter 60, 169.

43. Ibid., letter 51, 156.

44. F. P. Tissot, *Souvenirs de la journée du 1er prairial an III* (Paris, an VIII), 86. See also Jules Claretie, *Les derniers Montagnards* (Paris, 1867).

45. "We must sacrifice our remaining days, and dedicate our sacrifice to our friends before the triumph of the wicked. Without equality, there is no fatherland. Liberty will reveal our innocence and explain why our sacrifice was necessary to save France."

46. John McManners, *Death and the Enlightenment* (Oxford: Clarendon, 1981); René Favre, *La Mort dans la littérature et la pensée françaises au siècle des lumières* (Lyon: Presses universitaires de Lyon, 1979); Richard Andrews, "Le Néostoïcisme et le législateur Montagnard, considérations sur le suicide de Gilbert Romme"; and Jean-Marie Goulemot, "Montesquieu: du suicide légitime à l'apologie du suicide héroïque," in *Gilbert Romme et son temps,* ed. Goulemot et al. (Clermont-Ferrand: Institut d'Etudes du Massif Central, Faculté des Lettres et des Sciences Humaines, 1966), 163–74.

47. Poison de Sivry, *Cato,* 4.5. In these lines, Cato explains that his death will be useful to the fatherland and that his name will forever be linked to the thought of liberty.

48. I am following here the argument of Margaret Higonnet's unpublished essay, "Suicide and Shadows: Examples and Effigies."

49. Quoted in P. Trahard, *La Sensibilité révolutionnaire* (Paris: Boivin, 1936), 122.

50. Cited by René Mauzi, "Les Maladies de l'ame au XVIIIe siècle," *Revue des Sciences Humaines* (1960): 480.

51. I. A. Richards, *Principles of Literary Criticism* (New York: Harcourt Brace, 1952), 345.

52. Angus Fletcher, *Allegory, the Theory of a Symbolic Mode* (Ithaca: Cornell University Press, 1967).

53. See her "Delphine: d'une guerre civile à l'autre."

54. Mme de Staël, *Delphine* (Paris: Edition des femmes, 1981), 2:370.

Marie-Antoinette in Her Fictions: The Staging of Hatred

1. Chantal Thomas, *La Reine scélérate, Marie-Antoinette dans les pamphlets* (Paris: Editions du Seuil, 1989). See also "L'héroïne du crime: Marie-Antoinette dans les pamphlets," by the same author, *La Carmagnole des Muses. L'homme de lettres et l'artiste dans la Révolution,* ed. J.-Cl. Bonnet (Paris: Armand Colin, 1988), 245–60.

NOTES TO PAGES 112–23

2. Lynn Hunt, "The Many Bodies of Marie-Antoinette: Political Pornography and the Problem of the Feminine in the French Revolution," *Eroticism and the Body Politic*, ed. Lynn Hunt (Baltimore: Johns Hopkins University Press, 1990), 108–30.

3. Sarah Maza, "The Diamond Necklace Affair Revisited (1785–1786): The Case of the Missing Queen," *Eroticism and the Body Politic*, 63–89.

4. See Arlette Farge and Jacques Revel, *Logiques de la foule. L'Affaire des enlèvements d'enfants. Paris, 1750* (Paris: Hachette, 1989); and Jacques Revel, "Marie-Antoinette," *Dictionnaire critique de la Révolution française*, ed. François Furet and Mona Ozouf (Paris: Flammarion, 1988).

5. A certain number of references can be found in the work of Robert Darnton. I also call to attention an unpublished study by Antoine de Baecque, "Les 'livres remplis d'horreurs.' La littérature pornographique et la politique au début de la Révolution française." I thank the author for letting me read this essay.

6. *Le Portefeuille d'un talon rouge contenant des anecdotes galantes et secrètes sur la Cour de France* [*The Portfolio of a Red-Heel Containing Galant and Secret Anecdotes About the Court of France*] (Paris: n.d. [1779?]), 2–3.

7. *Le Godemiché royal. Entretien entre Junon et Hébée* [*sic*] [The royal dildo. Conversation between Juno and Hebe] (Paris: n.d. [1789]).

8. Useful indications on this point can be found in the work by Antoine de Baecque cited above.

9. See, on the Bibliothèque bleue, Roger Chartier, *Lectures et lecteurs dans la France d'Ancien Régime* (Paris: Editions du Seuil, 1987); on the mazarinades, Christian Jouhaud, *Mazarinades. La Fronde des mots* (Paris: Aubier, 1986); on newspaper reading (the bibliography is enormous), the classic work by Richard Hoggart, *The Uses of Literacy* (London: Chatto & Windus, 1957).

10. *Marie-Antoinette dans l'embarras ou Correspondance de La Fayette avec le roi, la reine, La Tour du Pin et Saint-Priest* [Marie-Antoinette in Trouble, or La Fayette's Correspondence with the King, the Queen, La Tour du Pin and Saint-Priest] (Paris: n.d. [end of 1790?]), 11–12.

11. Let us note that the logic of spatial representations often serves to assure the ordering of libertine relationships: this is the case when Marie-Antoinette orders, in her private apartments, an even more private apartment to be made ready for her alleged mistress, Madame de Polignac.

12. Such testimonies are successively invoked in *La Vie privée, libertine et scandaleuse de Marie-Antoinette . . .* [The Private, Libertine

and Scandalous Life of Marie-Antoinette...], for example. Another frequent strategy is the confession read aloud and reported by a hidden witness; among other texts, this fiction can be found in *Les Adieux de la reine à ses mignons et à ses mignonnes* [The Queen's Farewell to her Favorites of Both Sexes] (Paris: n.d. [1792?]), where it is a national guard who reports and publishes these indiscreet avowals of the queen by "civic duty."

13. Among others, in *Les nouvelles du ménage royal* [News of the Royal Couple], in *Le ménage royal en déroute ou guerre ouverte entre Louis XVI et sa femme* [The Royal Couple in Disorder, or Open War Between Louis XVI and His Wife], or in *Nouvelle scène tragicomique et nullement héroïque entre M. Louis Bourbon, maître serrurier au Temple et Madame Marie-Antoinette, Archiduchesse d'Autriche, autrefois reine de France, et blanchisseuse de surplis*... [A New Tragi-Comic, Not-At-All-Heroic Scene Between Monsieur Louis Bourbon, Head Locksmith of the Temple and Madame Marie-Antoine, Archduchess of Austria, Onetime Queen of France, and Laundress of Surplices...], three plays in farcical form from the end of 1792 or 1793.

14. On these problems, see the twin works of Antoine de Baecque, *La caricature révolutionnaire,* and Claude Langlois, *La caricature contre-révolutionnaire* (Paris: CNRS, 1988).

15. *Les Embarass de Marie-Antoinette* [The difficulties of Marie-Antoinette] (n.d. [probably end of 1790]), 4–5.

16. Ibid., p.21.

17. *La Confession de Marie-Antoinette, ci-devant Reine de France, au Peuple Franc, sur les amours et ses intrigues avec M. de La Fayette, les principaux Membres de l'Assemblée Nationale, et sur ses projets de Contre-Révolution* [Confession of Marie-Antoinette, Onetime Queen of France, to the Frankish People, About Her Love and Intrigues with Monsieur de La Fayette, and the Prominent Members of the National Assembly, and About her Counter-Revolutionary Projects] (Paris: Imprimerie du Cabinet de la Reine, n.d. [end of 1792 or 1793]).

18. *Les Embarras de Marie-Antoinette,* 44. The italics are, of course, in the original text.

The Revolution That Will Not Finish: Mythologies of Method in Britain

1. Edmund Burke, *Reflections on the Revolution in France,* ed. Conor Cruise O'Brien (Harmondsworth: Penguin, 1976), 186.

2. Arthur Young, *The Example of France a Warning to Britain* (Dublin, 1793), 79.

3. Perry Anderson, "Components of the National Culture," *New Left Review* 50 (1968): 47.

4. M. Depont, *Answer to the Reflections of the Rt. Hon. Edmund Burke* (London, 1791), 15.

5. William Belsham, *Examination of an Appeal from the New to the Old Whigs; to which is prefixed an Introduction, containing Remarks on Mr. Burke's Letter to a Member of the National Assembly* (London, 1792), 7, 8.

6. George Rous, *A Letter to the Right Honourable Edmund Burke, in Reply to his Letter from the New to the Old Whigs* (London, n.d.), 124.

7. Joel Barlow, *Advice to the Privileged Orders, in the Several States of Europe, Resulting from the Necessity and Propriety of a General Revolution in the Principles of Government* (London, rpt. in New York, 1792), 1.

8. Thomas Cooper, *A Reply to Mr. Burke's Invective against Mr. Cooper and Mr. Watt, in the House of Commons, on the 30th of April, 1792,* 2d ed. (London, 1792), 66, 82.

9. *The Rights of Nature, against the Usurpations of Establishments,* 2 vols. (London, 1796), 1:13.

10. John Thelwall, *Sober Reflections on the Seditious and Inflammatory Letter of the Rt. Hon. Edmund Burke to a Noble Lord, addressed to the Serious Consideration of his Fellow Citizens* (London, 1796), 77.

11. Capel Lofft, *Remarks on the Letter of the Rt. Hon. Edmund Burke, Concerning the Revolution in France, and on the Proceedings of Certain Societies in London, relative to that Event* (London, 1790), 44.

12. *The Complete Writings of Thomas Paine,* ed. Philip S. Foner, 2 vols. (New York: Citadel Press, 1945), 1:315.

13. *The Logike of the Moste Excellent Philosopher P. Ramus Martyr,* trans. Roland MacIlmaine (1574), ed. Catherine M. Dunn (Northridge, Calif.: San Fernando Valley State College Renaissance Editions, no. 3, 1969), xviii.

14. *The Art of Logick . . . Published for the Instruction of the Unlearned,* by Antony Wotton (London, 1626), title page.

15. *Peter Ramus, of Vernandois, the King's Professor, His Dialectica, in two Bookes . . .* by R. F[age], Gent. (London, 1632), prefatory poem.

16. Abraham Fraunce, *The Lawyers Logike,* quoted in Wilbur Samuel Howell, *Logic and Rhetoric in England, 1500–1700* (Princeton, N.J.: Princeton University Press, 1956), 225.

17. See Christopher Hill, *Intellectual Origins of the English Revolution* (Oxford: Clarendon, 1965), 31–32, 292.

18. Walter J. Ong, S.J., "Peter Ramus and the Naming of Methodism: Mediaeval Science through Renaissance Homilectic," *Journal of the History of Ideas* 14 (1953): 235–48.

19. Francis Bacon, *The Great Instauration,* in *The Works of Francis Bacon,* collected and edited by James Spedding, Robert Leslie Ellis, Douglas Denon Heath, 14 vols. (London, 1857–74), 4:15. Christopher Hill has, however, suggested that Bacon was also an important icon for the parliamentarian cause, thus implying that the Puritans were able to find a place for both Ramus and Bacon; see *Intellectual Origins of the English Revolution,* 85–130.

20. Thomas Sprat, *History of the Royal Society,* ed. Jackson I. Cope and Harold Whitmore Jones (London and St. Louis: Routledge & Kegan Paul and Washington University Studies, 1959), 67.

21. Gerrard Winstanley, *"The Law of Freedom" and Other Writings,* ed. Christopher Hill (Cambridge: Cambridge University Press, 1983), 77, 251.

22. Newton's invocation as an ally of the establishment against Hobbes, Descartes, and the free thinkers has been well documented by Margaret C. Jacob, *The Newtonians and the English Revolution, 1689–1720* (Hassocks, Sussex: Harvester Press, 1976).

23. Etienne de Condillac, *La Logique: Logic,* trans. W. R. Albury (New York: Abaris Books, 1980), 41.

24. *Encyclopédie, ou dictionnaire universel des arts et des sciences . . .* (1765), "Discours préliminaire," xxiv, xxv.

25. Diderot, s.v. "Encyclopédie," 5:643A.

26. This is admittedly a reductive summary of a very complex debate. See Aram Vartanian, *Diderot and Descartes: A Study of Scientific Naturalism in the Enlightenment* (Princeton, N.J.: Princeton University Press, 1953); and Charles Coulston Gillispie, *The Edge of Objectivity: An Essay in the History of Scientific Ideas* (Princeton, N.J.: Princeton University Press, 1960).

27. *Sketch for a Historical Picture of the Human Mind* (1793), in *Condorcet: Selected Writings,* ed. Keith Michael Baker (Indianapolis: Bobbs-Merrill, 1976), 225.

28. *Lay Sermons,* ed. R. J. White (London and Princeton, N.J.: Routledge & Kegan Paul and Princeton University Press, 1970), 15–16.

29. *The Watchman,* ed. Lewis Patton (London and Princeton, N.J.: Routledge & Kegan Paul, 1970), 131.

30. John Thelwall, *The Natural and Constitutional Rights of Britons to Annual Parliaments, Universal Suffrage, and the Freedom of Popular Association . . .* (London, 1795), 95.

31. See, e.g., Paine, *Works*, 1:320; Mackintosh, *Vindiciae Gallicae*, 112 f., 123. The massive sales figures for the various editions of Burke's and Paine's texts must have seemed to reinforce the belief in the power of print; see James T. Boulton, *The Language of Politics in the Age of Wilkes and Burke* (London and Toronto: Routledge & Kegan Paul and University of Toronto Press, 1963), 80–88.

32. Anon. [Catherine Macaulay], *Observations on the Reflections of the Rt. Hon. Edmund Burke on the Revolution in France, in a Letter to the Rt. Hon. the Earl of Stanhope* (London, 1790), 5, 7.

33. Anon.[David Williams], *Lessons to a Young Prince, on the Present Disposition in Europe to a General Revolution* (London, 1790), 9.

34. For a detailed account of Wordsworth's political economy, see David Simpson, *Wordsworth and the Figurings of the Real* (London: Macmillan, 1982), esp. 122–69; and *Wordsworth's Historical Imagination: The Poetry of Displacement* (London and New York: Methuen, 1987), esp. 56–78.

35. *The Poetical Works of Erasmus Darwin*, 3 vols. (London, 1806), 1:iii.

36. Rev. Richard Polwhele, *The Unsex'd Females* (rpt. New York, by William Cobbett, 1800), 14–15.

37. William Blake, "Introduction" to *Songs of Innocence*, in *The Complete Poetry and Prose of William Blake*, rev. ed., ed. David V. Erdman (Berkeley and Los Angeles: University of California Press, 1982), 7.

38. On the mythology of the national character, see Seamus Deane, *The French Revolution and Enlightenment in England, 1789–1832* (London and Cambridge: Harvard University Press, 1988), esp. 21–42.

The Tyranny of Revolutionary Memory

1. With his "Conspiracy of the Equals" (1796) Gracchus Babeuf introduced for the first time the idea of communism in Revolutionary politics.

2. Louis de Bonald, *Théorie du pouvoir politique et religieux dans la société civile, démontrée par le raisonnement et par l'histoire* (1796), 3 vols.

3. Benjamin Constant wrote his first important political text on the French Revolution in 1797: "De la force du gouvernement actuel et de la nécéssité de s'y rallier." This brochure has been reprinted with a preface by Philippe Raynaud (Paris: Flammarion/Champs, 1989).

4. The "biens nationaux" are the holdings and estates of the Catholic Church and the nobility that were appropriated and sold by the National Assembly to help reduce the crippling public debt.

Staging Stanisława Przybyszewska's The Danton Case

1. Daniel Gerould, Introduction to *The Danton Case and Thermidor,* by Stanisława Przybyszewska (Evanston: Northwestern University Press, 1989), 294.

2. Stanisława Przybyszewska, *The Danton Case,* trans. Bolesław Taborski. Directed by Craig Kinzer. Scenic design by Jonathan Darling. Costume design by Frances Maggio. Lighting design by Shelley Strasser. Sound design by Michael Knoblauch. Premiered at Northwestern University, Ethel Barber Theater, 10 November 1989.

3. Polish director Andrzej Wajda staged the play at the Powszechny Theatre in Warsaw in 1975, and used the text as the basis of his 1982 film, *Danton.* Critical response to this cinematic version pointed to the parallels between the two central players in Poland's 1981 Solidarity crisis and the film's protagonists.

4. A version of Taborski's translation was performed at England's Royal Shakespeare Company in 1986. The adaptation, by playwright Pam Gems, considerably altered Przybyszewska's text and focused on the simple narrative line. Most significantly, Gems eliminated much of the crowd's action and diminished them as force in the drama. The complex interrelationship of characters and events was missing.

5. The opening segment of act i, scene iii, involving Danton's break with the English prime minister, was eliminated. This scene portrayed Danton as a paid agent of the enemies of France, an accusation still hotly debated, and placed him rather too strongly in the role of villain.

Contributors

PETER BROOKS is Tripp Professor of Humanities and director of the Whitney Humanities Center at Yale University. The author of *The Novel of Worldliness* (Princeton, 1969), *The Melodramatic Imagination* (Yale, 1976), *Reading for the Plot* (Knopf, 1984), and of numerous articles on eighteenth- and nineteenth-century French and English literature, he is currently working on a study of narrative and the body.

THOMAS CROW is professor of history of art at the University of Sussex, U.K. He is the author of *Painters and Public Life in Eighteenth-Century Paris* (Yale, 1985), "Modernism and Mass Culture in the Visual Arts," "Versions of Pastoral in Recent American Art," and other articles on eighteenth-century and contemporary art.

BERNADETTE FORT is associate professor of French at Northwestern University. She has published *Le Langage de l'ambiguïté dans l'oeuvre de Crébillon fils* (Paris, 1978) and articles on eighteenth-century French literature and art criticism. She was awarded the 1990 Clifford Prize by the American Society for Eighteenth-Century Studies. She is at work on a study of the rhetoric and politics of eighteenth-century French art criticism.

FRANÇOIS FURET is director of the Institut Raymond Aron in Paris, after many years as director of the Ecole des Hautes Etudes en Sciences Sociales. Among his many books on the French

Revolution, most of which have been translated into English, are *La Révolution française* (with Denis Richet; Hachette: 1965), *Penser la Révolution française* (Gallimard, 1978), *Marx et la Révolution française* (Flammarion, 1986), and *La Révolution française: de Turgot à Jules Ferry* (Hachette, 1988). He has also coauthored the *Dictionnaire critique de la Révolution française* with Mona Ozouf (Flammarion, 1988).

PATRICE HIGONNET is Goelet Professor of History at Harvard University. He has written extensively on the literature, history, and culture of the late eighteenth century. His publications include *Class, Ideology, and the Rights of Nobles during the French Revolution* (Oxford, 1981) and *Sister Republics: The Origins of French and American Republicanism* (Harvard, 1988).

CRAIG D. KINZER is assistant professor of theatre at Northwestern University and chair of the Master of Fine Arts Program in Directing. He has directed professionally in New York and Chicago. He was the artistic director of the Classic Stage Company, an off-Broadway repertory theatre, where he staged productions of Ibsen's *Brand*, Sternheim's *The Underpants*, *Frankenstein*, and Sophocles' *Ajax*, among others.

JACQUES REVEL is directeur d'études at the Centre de recherches historiques of the Ecole des Hautes Etudes en Sciences Sociales, Paris, and coeditor of the journal *Annales. Economies, Sociétés, Civilisations*. He is the author of numerous articles and books, including, with M. de Certeau and Dominique Julia, *Une Politique de la langue: la Révolution française et les patois. L'enquête de l'Abbé Grégoire* (Gallimard, 1975), with A. Farge, *Logiques de la foule: l'affaire des enlèvements d'enfants* (Hachette, 1989), and *Histoire de la France*, vol. 1, *L'Espace français* (Seuil, 1989). He has contributed the articles "Grande Peur" and "Marie-Antoinette" to the *Dictionnaire critique de la Révolution française*, ed. F. Furet and M. Ozouf (Flammarion, 1988).

DAVID SIMPSON is professor of English at the University of Colorado, Boulder. His numerous publications include *Irony and Authority in Romantic Poetry* (Macmillan, 1979), *Fetishism and*

Imagination: Dickens, Melville, Conrad (Johns Hopkins, 1982), *The Politics of American English, 1776-1850* (Oxford, 1986), and *Wordsworth's Historical Imagination: The Poetry of Displacement* (Methuen, 1987).